PERFORMANCE CYCLING

To our families for their continuing support.

PERFORMANCE CYCLING

THE SCIENCE OF SUCCESS

EDITED BY
JAMES HOPKER, PhD AND SIMON JOBSON, PhD

BLOOMSBURY
LONDON • BERLIN • NEW YORK • SYDNEY

Note

Whilst every effort has been made to ensure that the content of this book is as technically accurate and as sound as possible, neither the author nor the publishers can accept responsibility for any injury or loss sustained as a result of the use of this material.

Published by Bloomsbury Publishing Plc
50 Bedford Square
London WC1B 3DP
www.bloomsbury.com

First edition 2012

ISBN (print): 978-1-408146-51-4
ISBN (e-pdf): 978-1-408160-78-7

Acknowledgements
Cover photographs © Getty (front), © Shutterstock (back)
Inside photographs pp 20, 23 © Oli Beckinsale, 116, 121, 176, 217, 280 © Gerard Brown, 194, 200 courtesy of Aukje de Vrijer, 105, 112, 115, 117–119 courtesy of Ami Drory, 219, 222, 287 © Getty Images, 27 © Balint Hamvas, 111 (top) © Louise Garneau Sports Inc., 143, 245 © Shutterstock, 221 courtesy of David Stone
Illustrations by David Gardner (unless otherwise stated)
Cover designed by Nick Jakins, text designed by James Watson
Commissioned by Charlotte Croft
Edited by Kate Wanwimolruk

This book is produced using paper that is made from wood grown in managed, sustainable forests. It is natural, renewable and recyclable. The logging and manufacturing processes conform to the environmental regulations of the country of origin.

Typeset in 10pt Minion by seagulls.net

Printed and bound in India by Replika Press Pvt Ltd

CONTENTS

SECTION D
HOW DO I GET THE BEST OUT OF MY BIKE?
THE BIOMECHANICS OF CYCLING

SECTION E
HOW DO I GET IN THE RIGHT FRAME OF MIND?
THE PSYCHOLOGY OF CYCLING

SECTION F
WHAT DO I NEED TO EAT AND DRINK DURING TRAINING AND
COMPETITION? NUTRITION FOR CYCLING

SECTION G
HOW SHOULD I RACE?

SECTION H
ARE THERE ANY POPULATION-SPECIFIC CONSIDERATIONS FOR TRAINING AND RACING?

SECTION I
HOW DO I GET THE MOST OUT OF COACHING? THE COACH—ATHLETE RELATIONSHIP

SECTION J
WHAT ARE THE MEDICAL CONSIDERATIONS IN CYCLING?

FOREWORD

When my cycling career began in the mid-1990s, there was a limited pool of both coaching expertise in the UK and objective information about the sport of cycling. I decided (rightly or wrongly) that the pathway I would take to become a better cyclist would be to find out more about what the current world's best athletes and coaches from a wide array of sports (including cycling) were doing and why they were doing it. This information came from books, magazines and the internet and from speaking with athletes and coaches. Once I had gathered the information, I searched for common elements in the athletes' and coaches' regimens and tried to identify any potential causal relationships that were supported by credible research. It was very much a scattergun approach, but would serve as the foundation to my cycling protocols.

Fortunately, times have changed and I now rely on other people to guide me in my quest to become a better cyclist. Whether they are coaches, analysts, nutritionists, doctors, physiotherapists, aerodynamicists, psychologists or physiologists, nearly all the information they present is backed up by objective evidence that comes from their own experience or the ever increasing body of specific data that is now available on cycling.

You're probably thinking, 'Well, that's great for you, but what about the rest of us who don't have a group of experts on hand?' Fear not; help is at hand! This book brings together some of the world's leading cycling practitioners to give the reader an evidence-based view of the major components within the sport of cycling that have a positive effect on performance, including the highly controversial effects of illegal doping. The book has been written in a way that will appeal to anyone who has an inquisitive mind and wants to better understand the sport of cycling from an objective point of view.

Whoever you are and whatever your goals, I hope you find the book a useful guide in your quest to become a better cyclist.

Jason Queally MBE, Olympic, World and Commonwealth champion

PREFACE

In the past decade, cycling has changed enormously. Not only have we seen changes in bicycle design and technology, we have also seen the development of new training methods and training tools that have allowed greater scientific input into the way cyclists train and race. For example, power meters were rare 10 years ago but are now widely used at both professional and amateur levels.

A parallel development has taken place in the sport sciences. In particular, there has been a dramatic increase in the volume and quality of research in all aspects of cycling science. Cycling is a very gruelling sport, possibly one of the most physically challenging of all. Nevertheless, at all levels of the sport it is often the finest of margins that distinguishes the winner from the rest of the field. Therefore, a scientific approach involving the aggregation of marginal gains is critical to provide the optimal performance.

There now exists an enormous amount of cycling-specific scientific information. However, most of it is not accessible to athletes and coaches as it is located within specialist research journals. Indeed, even if this information were available, it is rarely presented in a way that is useful to a non-academic audience. Assessment of the quality of the work and the interpretation of the findings and their application to the real world is difficult.

The purpose of this book is to present usable guidelines for cyclists and their coaches based on up-to-date scientific information. To make this book as contemporary as possible, we have invited contributions from a number of world-renowned colleagues working at the cutting edge of scientific research and applied practice. Each chapter reviews the current research on a given cycling science topic and provides discussion on how to apply these concepts to enhance performance.

The book contains 10 distinct sections. Section A discusses the physiological determinants of cycling performance. In chapter 1, Damian Coleman discusses the determinants of road racing, describing the vital link between physiology and performance. In chapter 2, Louis Passfield, Mark Walker and Paul Barrett then discuss the differing performance determinants and physiological attributes required for success in mountain biking, cyclo-cross and bicycle motorcross (BMX).

Section B discusses the different methods of performance assessment. In chapter 3, we describe the tests used to assess the physiological attributes outlined in section A. The chapter considers both laboratory-based and field-based testing to provide a comprehensive review of the physiological tests currently available to assess rider performance.

Section C describes how the physiological determinants of performance and laboratory and field test results can be combined to produce an effective training programme.

In chapter 4, Iñigo Mujika and Paul Laursen discuss how the principles of training can be applied to cycling and describe the latest approaches to developing a training programme. Chapter 5 provides specific details on how to plan and monitor training using heart-rate monitors and power meters. Next comes the question of what to do with all the data that the heart-rate monitor or power meter provide? Rather than just downloading the data onto a computer and forgetting about them, chapter 6 describes some approaches to dealing with the data and provides insight into what they can tell you. Finally, in chapter 7, Bent Rønnestad addresses the much-debated area of whether cyclists should incorporate strength training into their schedule.

Section D discusses how to get the best out of your bike. In chapter 8, Ami Drory deals with different bike set-up methods and how body position might be optimised to enhance aerodynamics. Chapter 9 examines force transference from cyclist to bike at the pedal, with Thomas Korff, Paul Barrett and Scott Gardner describing the extent to which pedalling mechanics affect cycling performance.

Section E deals with the psychology of cycling. Chapters 10 and 11 discuss different approaches to getting in the right frame of mind for success in training and competition. First, Julie Emmerman considers the relationship between the mind and the body. Chris Beedie goes on to discuss simple but effective psychological strategies that can be used in planning, training and competition.

Section F considers the optimal strategies for nutritional intake in preparation for training and competition, during competition and in recovery. Chapter 12 examines the nutritional intake required for both short-term and prolonged cycling performance. This chapter also discusses fluid intake and hydration strategies. Then, in chapter 13, Kevin Currell deals with the confusing area of sports supplements, including what to take and when.

In section G, Florentina Hettinga considers pacing strategies both for individual and for team events (e.g. track sprinting, time trialling) and mass starts (e.g. stage racing). She considers what an optimal pacing strategy might look like and whether this can be trained for.

Section H discusses how training, nutrition, psychological intervention and equipment may be adapted for different cycling populations. In chapter 15, Tammie Ebert identifies specific considerations for female cyclists, while in chapter 16, Gary Brickley focuses on the Paralympic cyclist. Finally, in chapter 17, Richard Davison considers the ageing cyclist.

Section I provides an account of how to ensure a successful relationship between the athlete and the coach. From her experience as a high-level athlete, and now coach, Helen Carter provides an insight into how she works with cyclists from amateur to professional levels.

Finally, section J deals with medical and legal issues. In chapter 19, Roger Palfreeman discusses the typical cycling injuries, their treatment and, in the case of overuse conditions, their prevention. In chapter 20, Roger combines with Yorck Olaf Schumacher to discuss the explosive issue of doping in cycling. They consider the methods used in illegal doping, the biological passport and the pitfalls of using over-the-counter medicinal and herbal products for the unsuspecting cyclist.

James Hopker and Simon Jobson

ACKNOWLEDGEMENTS

We would like to thank all of the people who have in some way contributed to this book. First and foremost, thanks to our contributing authors, who have juggled their many professional commitments in academia or cycling performance to put pen to paper. Thanks also to those who have assisted in proof-reading the material and providing feedback on its content. Finally, we would like to thank the coaches and cyclists who we work with on a regular basis for providing us with the motivation to write this book.

Chapter 4

The authors extend their appreciation to Daniel Plews for assistance with figure designs and drawings.

Chapter 8

The authors would like to thank the athletes and coaches for their patience and trust. He would also like to thank and acknowledge David, Tim, Greg, Mike and others at the Department of Mechanical and Aerospace Engineering at Monash University's wind tunnel for their passion, expertise, humour and generally for putting up with him.

Chapter 17

This chapter is written in memory of Dr James Balmer (1966–2009).

SECTION A

WHAT IS CYCLING? THE PHYSIOLOGICAL DEMANDS OF CYCLE SPORT

The first stage of planning a training programme aimed at enhancing performance is to identify what the requirements of the event actually are. Therefore, in this section we ask, 'What is cycling?' The physiological determinants of an explosive 30-second bicycle motorcross (BMX) race may look radically different from those required by a five-hour Tour de France stage. However, at times both require similar physiological processes. The end of the five-hour Tour stage may require an explosive sprint finish or a maximal 30-second all-out effort to chase down a break. Therefore, being able to identify the physiological demands of a particular cycle sport event will inform the subsequent training process.

Chapter 1 discusses the main physiological determinants of successful endurance road racing. The events of mass-start road racing and time trialling are discussed using a physiological model of cycling performance. The relative influence of physiological variables such as maximal oxygen consumption (VO_{2max}), lactate threshold and gross efficiency are covered, with examples of how they are influenced by training. In chapter 2, the events of cross-country mountain biking, cyclo-cross and BMX are discussed. The authors consider the demands of the events and how a rider's physiological ability may influence performance outcome. The authors of chapter 2 also consider some discipline-specific approaches to training and competition.

Section A will provide you with knowledge of the physiology that determines performance in both short-duration 'sprint' and long-duration 'endurance' cycling events. Armed with this knowledge, you will be able to develop a deeper understanding of the 'how' and the 'why' of both performance assessment and training, which are covered in sections B and C, respectively.

CHAPTER 1

THE PHYSIOLOGICAL DEMANDS OF ROAD CYCLING

Damian Coleman

There is a reasonable case to be made that road race cycling is one of the most complex disciplines within the family of cycling events. The demands of road racing and the associated physiological capabilities are varied. These can change depending upon the course demands (parcours), the weather conditions and the demographics of the competition. The time trial is a less complex discipline but still requires specialist attention because, despite some commonalities, there are some unique physiological attributes that dictate success and clearly differentiate specialist riders at all levels of competition. Theoretically, the optimal chance of success comes when there is synergy between the physiological attributes of a rider and the race type/parcours. This is demonstrated in the professional arena, where a rider might peak for a specific one-day road race or time trial event where their physiological attributes are more likely to lead to success. To some extent this is similar for stage race riders; however, the synergy and race plan may be much more complex as the race as a whole is made up of both time trials and road races.

Fundamentally, there are significant 'unknowns' associated with road race cycling. This is quite different from many events where an estimation of the energy expenditure associated with the event is fairly stable and average power or work is a key determinant of success (e.g. time trial cycling). In terms of road cycling, there are published data demonstrating low average exercise intensities during Grand Tour stages, with skilled riders completing stages at work rates of 132 watts (which is equivalent to a non-drafting velocity of about 25 km·h^{-1}). It is likely that many thousands of riders worldwide could maintain double this power output for many hours, demonstrating that the average exercise intensity during road cycling is not necessarily a key determinant of success. Theoretically, the rate of work production in specific phases of races is very important. The ability to identify, respond to and recover during those phases needs to be considered when planning for the success of an individual rider.

The scientific literature provides some very good descriptive physiological data of both amateur and professional cyclists. These data are generally obtained within a laboratory setting, with the responses and capabilities recorded under well-rested conditions and in a relatively short timeframe. Thus, the applicability of these data to the real world of competitive cycling is, to some extent, limited. With physiological responses potentially dictating capabilities in the seventh hour of a one-day race or in a later time trial stage of a Grand Tour, the way in which these responses relate to the data generated in a fresh laboratory scenario is currently – and likely to remain – unknown. However, on an individual basis, knowledge of your physical condition and markers of specific physiological components that can be enhanced through preparation could theoretically improve your road performance, regardless of the level at which you compete.

A number of researchers have attempted to model cycling performance by describing the multiple physiological systems that they believe contribute to performance. Although these are not necessarily specific to one cycling discipline, they are useful in explaining some of the key physiological factors associated with cycling performance. These physiological factors might be weighted in a manner that is specific to a particular cycling discipline or event. Therefore, knowledge of these event-specific physiological components should be considered in conjunction with the individual strengths and weaknesses of a rider. This type of analysis could then inform preparation and training, which can substantially influence overall performance in a specific discipline.

One such model is that of Michael Joyner and Ed Coyle, who have provided some of the most invasive physiological data on good-quality cyclists that are available in the academic literature. Joyner and Coyle propose that performance oxygen consumption, anaerobic contribution and the efficiency of movement are the three key physiological factors that can describe and explain cycling performance.

However, there are significant complexities associated with a model such as this. When you physiologically, psychologically or biomechanically attempt to unpick a component of the model, there are numerous additional components that could be included in each area. Despite the limitations that all proposers of such models acknowledge, these types of model are very useful for describing the physiological factors that contribute to an individual rider's success or limitations.

Looking at the top line of the model (*see* figure 1.1) in its simplest form ([A + B] x C = performance power), two individuals could have the same performance power or

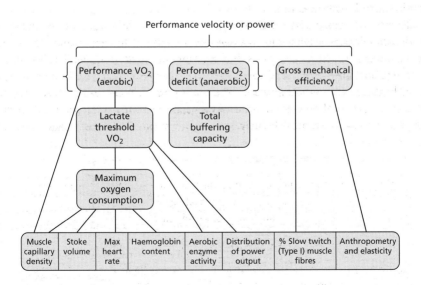

FIG.1.1 The Joyner and Coyle performance model. (Adapted with permission from Joyner, M.J., Coyle, E.F., 'Endurance exercise performance: the physiology of champions', *Journal of Applied Physiology*, 586 (2008), 35–44)

velocity without having the same physiological capabilities. A + B could be high and C low in one rider, and vice versa in another, but the output (power or velocity) could be identical. Such knowledge could help to determine specific training regimens for the two different riders in an attempt to enhance individual capacities. This then brings us to an obvious, but often overlooked, statement: because of the multifaceted nature of cycling highlighted by the model, it is very difficult to pinpoint an exact number or threshold value that might differentiate performance abilities for each physiological component. Even for maximal oxygen consumption (VO_{2max}), which incorporates many key physiological factors, this 'physiological descriptor' may not differentiate between abilities of riders. For example, values ranging from 60 ml·kg⁻¹·min⁻¹ to 85 ml·kg⁻¹·min⁻¹ have been reported in world-class riders, but even riders carrying second- or third-category British Cycling licences might achieve numbers at the lower end of this range for this parameter. In terms of a very basic analysis and application of this model, the conversion of energy to mechanical work (efficiency) is always going to be of primary importance during any cycling discipline. Whatever energy systems are engaged, if the cyclist is riding at his or her full capacity, or just at a low work rate, the highest amount of mechanical work generated from the energetic input is the aim.

The importance of the aerobic and anaerobic components of the model is cycling discipline specific. The components are not mutually exclusive in any cycling discipline, and it is relatively difficult to precisely weight the demands even in to these two broad divisions. This is because individual differences exist in the ability to use energy systems that contribute to work output. However, it is appropriate to discuss cycling events referring to 'predominant' energy systems (e.g. track sprinting using predominantly anaerobic sources of energy, and long-distance time trial cycling using predominantly aerobic sources).

Then, of course, there are cycling events where phases of competition may require both capabilities to be fairly equally weighted. Going a step further, events such as road and mountain bike races could be subdivided into hundreds of small phases, each one varying the contributions made by these two energy systems. This is further complicated by the scaling of these available rider abilities to the main resistive forces applied in cycling: gravity (body mass) and wind resistance (frontal surface area). Thus, the physiological capacity of a rider may be more or less suited to certain phases in a race.

Aerobic metabolism: Energy provision from chemical reactions that require oxygen to break down food. The use of oxygen is a relatively slow process. However, the provision of energy through aerobic processes enables sustained muscular contractions to occur.

Anaerobic metabolism: Energy provision from chemical reactions that do not require oxygen. These systems are rapid but have a very limited amount of energy provision in comparison with aerobic metabolism. Anaerobic systems also strongly influence fatigue.

This is clearly apparent in road race cycling, where the exact requirements in terms of aerobic and anaerobic contributions during the many different sections of a race may vary. Therefore, you should be aware of your own capabilities and how you can tactically manipulate your responses and those of others to ensure the highest potential finishing position in a race. Knowledge of your abilities will come from experience of racing and detailed knowledge of the race route and the opposition. This information can help you to establish a race plan. For example, if you can climb well in road races, identify the sections of the race where you can put pressure on the opposition. In this way you can align your attributes with the dominant demands of a specific phase or phases of a race. If being a climber means you are not particularly suited to riding fast on flat roads, ensure that you minimise the work that you do before and during the flat sections; otherwise, if you are working close to your limits and attacks occur, you may not be able to respond to them. If you have prior knowledge of the attributes of other riders, be very aware of the phases when they could potentially maximise their performance. Likewise, identify their potentially weaker phases such that you might be able to work on exposing them during the race.

TAKE-HOME MESSAGE

Knowledge of the physiological requirements associated with successful performance should be integrated with tactical awareness to suit your specific capabilities.

OXYGEN CONSUMPTION (AEROBIC PERFORMANCE)

One of the most discussed terms and researched aspects within all endurance athletic performance literature is oxygen consumption. If an individual can work aerobically and use aerobic processes to yield mechanical work, it is likely that fatigue will occur at a slower rate than when working anaerobically (i.e. without oxygen). There is a tendency for energy to be derived through anaerobic sources as an athlete gets closer to their upper limit of oxygen consumption (typically over 85 per cent VO_{2max}). The availability of energy through anaerobic mechanisms is not sustainable. Therefore, during endurance events, premature fatigue may occur in the scenario where an individual is exercising too close to their VO_{2max}. Maximal oxygen consumption is dramatically influenced by the cardiovascular capabilities of an individual, specifically cardiac output, which has historically been considered to be the major factor contributing to successful endurance athletic performance – endurance cycling being no exception. Despite similarities in maximal heart rates between all categories of cyclists, as a cohort, elite riders tend to have greater functional cardiac dimensions compared with lower-category riders (i.e. they have higher stroke volumes). This elevates the ability to deliver key nutrients, to remove byproducts of metabolism and to thermoregulate.

Cardiac output refers to the amount of blood pumped by the heart. Measured in litres per minute, cardiac output is calculated by multiplying the amount of blood ejected per beat of the heart (stroke volume) by the number of beats per minute (heart rate). Maximal heart rate multiplied by maximal stroke volume equates to the maximal cardiac output of an individual. High values for this parameter are associated with elite endurance performance.

During incremental exercise, it has been noted that the stroke volume of the heart initially increases and then plateaus at an average exercise intensity of approximately 50 per cent VO_{2max}. This is a relatively low exercise intensity that can be sustained for significant periods of time. Stimulating and overloading cardiac capacity is a key stimulus associated with adaptation and improved athletic performance.

The oxygen-carrying capacity of the blood (haemoglobin concentration) is another well-researched parameter that has been shown (through manipulation) to influence VO_{2max} and, anecdotally, to influence road race cycling performance. Ultimately, if the athlete can present more oxygen to the muscle cell, they are less likely to use anaerobic energy sources. The exception to this statement is where the muscle cell is working at full aerobic potential and is, therefore, unable to consume any further oxygen. It is likely that this will occur in muscle cells that have high anaerobic capabilities and low aerobic potential (e.g. fast-twitch type IIb muscle fibres).

In terms of presenting oxygen to the muscle cell, the muscle capillary network is an important determinant of the rate of oxygen delivery. Theoretically, greater capillary density will decrease the time required to deliver nutrients (oxygen, glucose, etc.) and reduce the time required to remove byproducts of metabolism (carbon dioxide, lactate, etc.) Researchers have investigated the muscle capillary structure of well-trained cyclists and have suggested that enhanced capillary density (i.e. more routes for blood to flow through active muscle) might be a differentiating factor in the ability to sustain higher fractions of maximal aerobic capacity for a longer period. This is likely to increase the sustainable power output of the rider owing to a greater aerobic contribution to the workload.

Interestingly, one major component associated with achieving high VO_{2max} *per se* is the ability to recruit a large amount of muscle mass. The performance model of Joyner and Coyle indicates that aerobic enzyme activity (proteins that are required

Capillary density refers to the ratio of very small blood vessels (capillaries) to muscle tissue. If the muscle tissue has a high capillary density, this enhances the ability to deliver nutrients and remove byproducts of metabolism – key factors associated with fatigue resistance.

to actually consume oxygen) is important in achieving a high VO_{2max}. However, if a greater muscle mass is engaged during exercise, more 'aerobic enzymes' are also engaged. If a greater muscle mass is engaged, the workload is shared between more muscle cells or fibres and, in turn, this reduces the stress per unit of muscle mass. Thus, the maximal ability of an individual's enzyme function is less likely to be reached. The provision of energy when the maximal capacity of enzyme function is reached simply leads to an increased contribution from anaerobic sources to cover the workload demands. Improving aerobic enzyme concentrations/function per unit of muscle mass, together with maximising muscle mass recruitment, should be considered key factors associated with improving endurance performance through training. From a practical standpoint, no studies have specifically ascertained the ideal exercise intensity to stimulate enzyme formation in athletes. However, the storage/operational sites for these enzymes are located within the muscle fibres in structures called mitochondria, which have been shown to increase in size and number at different exercise intensities. At low exercise intensities (approximately ~50 per cent VO_{2max}), increases in mitochondria have been observed in a relatively short time period (around six weeks) in slow-twitch muscle fibres. At higher exercise intensities (90–100 per cent VO_{2max}), mitochondrial development has also been observed in fast-twitch muscle fibres. A point to note here is that elevated levels of mitochondria require repeated training stimulation; therefore, extended time away from the bicycle will not be beneficial from this physiological perspective.

Slow-twitch muscle fibres are resistant to fatigue because they can use oxygen very effectively. However, these fibres have a minimal capacity to work without oxygen (anaerobically) and therefore they are recruited and used at low work rates. **Fast-twitch muscle fibres** cannot derive energy using oxygen as effectively as slow-twitch fibres. Instead, fast-twitch fibres have anaerobic capabilities and are therefore used at high work rates. The fast-twitch fibres tend to fatigue more rapidly than slow-twitch fibres.

LACTATE THRESHOLD

The provision of energy from aerobic sources is limited and, once maximal capacities are reached, further energy must be derived from anaerobic sources. There is some anaerobic contribution before achieving VO_{2max}. This anaerobic contribution presents (and is most easily monitored) as circulating lactate in the bloodstream. Lactate is derived from lactic acid and, although many athletes will have some basic knowledge of this area, research into the process and implications of lactic acid production is very controversial. Typically, and perhaps historically, these parameters have been seen as fatiguing agents that limit endurance performance. However, contemporary scientists actually question whether lactic acid exists, while viewing lactate as a key substrate that can be used as an energy source. The complete picture of the mechanistic role of lactic acid or lactate is currently unknown. However, as these parameters are derived from carbohydrate (muscle glycogen or glucose), lactate could simply be seen as a stress marker that is indicative of carbohydrate use during exercise. Lactate is then implicated in the prediction of performance because accelerated carbohydrate use (at a rate which does not correspond to exercise duration) is one cause of premature fatigue during endurance exercise. Indeed, the pattern of lactate accumulation changes with endurance training (figure 1.2 demonstrates three changes). Typically, aerobic exercise yields a rightward shift at the point at which lactate starts to accumulate above baseline values (see the power output values corresponding to arrows A and B in figure 1.2). This point is commonly referred to as the lactate threshold. The lactate threshold denotes a key exercise intensity above which the body is under significantly more stress, with accelerated use of carbohydrate stores. Therefore, pushing the lactate threshold rightwards and up to a higher power output before these responses occur is a major consideration when prescribing training. The horizontal line in figure 1.2 indicates the exercise intensity equivalent to a 4 mmol·l⁻¹ concentration of lactate. This intensity (or volume of accumulated lactate) is often reported as an intensity that can be maintained for a significant period of time (approximately one hour). Again, in the example in figure 1.2, the power output at a lactate concentration of 4 mmol·l⁻¹ has shifted to the right, thus elevating the work rate that can be sustained for the period of one hour (arrows C and D). The third response that has been seen in professional riders is the very low baseline level of circulating lactate (arrow E). This is indicative of very low rates of carbohydrate use compared with the pre-training condition or lower-ranked athletes.

Where high-intensity power values are required during road race cycling and these requirements cannot be wholly fulfilled by aerobic mechanisms, production of the required power output requires supplementation from anaerobic energy sources. Even though lactic acid and lactate are often discussed in the context of fatigue and negative consequences on rider performance, their production does yield a small amount of (useful) energy. This small amount of energy is extremely important in the

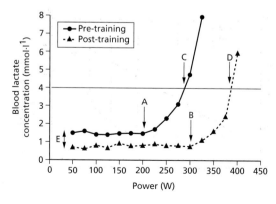

FIG.1.2 Lactate response to incremental exercise pre- and post-training

road race setting because it could make a difference in accelerating away from other riders, for example in a sprint finish, when escaping alone, when trying to join a small group or simply when making the 'selection' if the peloton splits. Thus, in terms of performance outcomes in road racing (e.g. attaining the highest finishing position), while the provision of these small amounts of energy may contribute only a few watts, those watts can have a quite dramatic influence.

Oxygen consumption and lactate responses during time trial cycling

At a basic level, time trial cycling is about maximising the work that an individual can achieve for a set distance or duration. Success is governed by the amount of mechanical work (power) delivered in relation to the resistances applied to the rider and bicycle. In cases where time trials are relatively flat, the resistive force is primarily wind resistance. Therefore, the key marker of success is power relative to the frontal surface area of the rider and bicycle. The ability to deliver mechanical work is dependent upon the physiology of the individual. In the time trial scenario, high and consistent work rates are important. With the majority of time trials having a significant duration component (over 2 minutes), the aerobic capacity of riders can yield vastly more energy than anaerobic systems. Thus, the aerobic systems predominate in the time trial event. However, despite contributing only a small amount to the overall energy used in a time trial, each time trial event does have an important anaerobic component. The anaerobic component may contribute a few watts to the overall average power output of the time trial race, with this value being dependent upon the size of the anaerobic 'capacity' of each individual rider. However, if the rider starts too fast in a time trial and utilises his anaerobic energy provision at a rate that will exceed his overall capacity before the end of the race, the rider will have to reduce his power output significantly below values that might be achievable with perfect 'pace' judgement. Bearing this in mind, it is important to judge and adjust the exercise intensity to achieve physiological responses that can be sustained for the duration of exercise

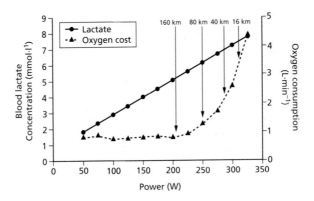

FIG.1.3 Lactate response and oxygen uptake in relation to time trial race distance

without premature fatigue and the associated time losses occurring. Figure 1.3 shows the oxygen consumption and lactate pattern (anaerobic contributions) of incremental exercise, with time trial capabilities plotted on the graph. Note that shorter races allow the individual to sustain a higher anaerobic contribution (lactate concentration) compared with longer races.

Riders often ask why they cannot sustain a power output for 40 km that they can sustain for 16 km time trials. The physiological responses underpinning this scenario are shown in figure 1.4. The workload at a lactate concentration of 4 mmol·l⁻¹ is an intensity that would theoretically be indicative of 40 km performance, which equates to 287 W in this individual. If the rider maintained an even pace (power output), he could sustain this work rate for the duration of the race. However, if the rider started harder (e.g. closer to a 16 km pace, i.e. 312 W), the oxygen cost of exercise would rise a little, but the concentration of lactate in the bloodstream would rise by almost 2 mmol·l⁻¹ (approximately 50 per cent). The rider must compensate and remove this lactate from the circulation. So, for every minute that the individual has spent accumulating the extra 2 mmol·l⁻¹ of lactate, he must return to the intensity that elicits a reduction of 2 mmol·l⁻¹ of lactate; because the relationship is not linear between lactate and work intensity (it is curvilinear), this equates to a power output of 235 W. So, if a cyclist spent 20 minutes at 312 W, 20 minutes at 287 W and 20 minutes at 235 W, his average power would be approximately 278 W, which would equate to about a 3 per cent reduction in performance power compared with riding at a sustained 287 W. The science of pacing is discussed further in chapter 14. Looking at figure 1.4, the performance oxygen uptake should also drop by about 3 per cent with the reduction in power output. However, owing to the involvement of oxidative (aerobic) processes in lactate disposal, the oxygen cost of exercise does not necessarily drop, in which case it appears that the rider is producing less power for a higher oxygen cost (in other words, he is less efficient).

Knowledge of heart rate data is useful for monitoring exercise intensity. Further accuracy can be gained by using power meters. However, the pre- (and even during) ride calibration procedures need to be followed strictly, as being a few watts out

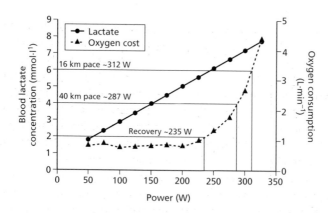

FIG.1.4 Lactate concentrations and pacing

TAKE-HOME MESSAGE

Calculating the upper rate of aerobic energy delivery is important. Underestimation would lead to a below-par performance based on capabilities not being used. Overestimation of the exercise intensity the individual can sustain for the duration of an event will lead to premature fatigue (with a reduction – often substantial – in power output), thereby reducing performance.

can again have performance-reducing consequences. This is further discussed in chapter 5.

Oxygen consumption and lactate responses during road race cycling

If the time trial cyclist has to be careful about pacing and cleverly monitoring exercise intensity in order to yield the highest mechanical work for his physiological capabilities, the road cyclist will be aware that, for substantial parts of the event, he will not be in control of exercise intensity. The knock-on impact is that there will certainly be periods of activity that yield very high lactate concentrations, with aerobic processes stretched not only to aid in energy provision but also to reconvert lactate or dispose of the byproducts of metabolism. At all times the road cyclist needs to consider how to minimise the energy cost of movement. The lower the exercise intensity, the lower the amount of lactate produced and the lower the impact of this fatigue-related metabolite.

Knowing that lactate is going to be produced leads to the conclusions that the road cyclist must be able to tolerate the accumulation of lactate (and associated metabolites) and be able to remove these metabolites to reduce the impact they have in terms of fatigue. Tolerance (or buffering of lactic acid) is discussed below in the oxygen deficit section (*see* page 13).

There is substantial variability in the removal rates of lactate from the bloodstream. Figure 1.5 demonstrates this variability in a group of 10 riders who have performed a maximal sprint and, for a 20-minute period following that sprint, actively recovered at 55 per cent of maximal capacity. At any time period on this graph, there is a wide spread of responses: the dashed line demonstrates that some individuals are halving their circulating lactate concentrations (50 per cent of peak lactate) within a 6- to 7-minute period, while others are taking almost twice as long. Aerobic processes are likely to be the key factor associated with the ability to remove lactate. Thus, lactate (and other metabolite) disposal will have an added oxygen cost; hence, those with faster disposal rates will engage the aerobic system in this manner for a shorter period. This whole picture is distorted when repeated successive demands are placed upon a rider during the phases where they are trying to clear these metabolites (e.g. covering repeated breaks from the peloton). Thus, the quicker the metabolites are removed,

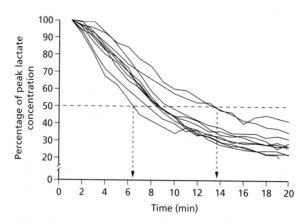

FIG.1.5 Individual blood lactate recovery curves; the dashed lines indicate the variability in time taken to reduce blood lactate to 50 per cent of peak value

the more likely the rider will be able to generate, tolerate and remove lactate from subsequent efforts.

Road race cycling is about the integration of physiological factors and tactics. Drafting is probably the most important tactic and is fundamental to success, because when drafting there is a reduction in the oxygen cost and lactate response for a fixed speed of the bicycle. However, on short, steep climbs where there is a reduction in or complete removal of the benefits of drafting, following riders will have to match – or more closely match – the work rate of the lead rider. Ultimately, if a rider is away in a small group sharing turns on the front and recovering with drafting, care is needed so that the recovery phase does not occur on the climb (because your recovery will be minimised). If you fall into this trap, there will be elevated lactate and oxygen uptake responses compared with the individual who has recovered on the flat and then led the climb: your physiological responses will be elevated as you will have effectively done a 'double turn' in terms of work. Experienced riders have an awareness of what will happen in this scenario so, if an experienced rider leads on the climb, he will judge his efforts to elevate the cost of this phase of the race in the other riders. If his co-escapees are still required for the break to succeed (e.g. if the climb is a long way from the finish), the experienced rider may still elevate the demands for the other riders, but not so dramatically that it causes the break to disintegrate.

TAKE-HOME MESSAGE

Take the opportunities to elevate the demands upon other competitors during the road race. Using this tactic subtly to tire other riders is important, especially in the scenario where the final kilometres or the finish might not specifically suit your capabilities.

OXYGEN DEFICIT

The distribution or variability of power output during any cycling event will fluctuate; this parameter transcends the aerobic and anaerobic component of the Joyner and Coyle model. The two extremes are time trial cycling (where there is a tendency for a power output distribution very close to the average value generally reported) and road race cycling (where significant proportions of time are spent at very low and very high power outputs, with dramatic fluctuations around a relatively low average value). Thus, for the road cyclist, the high variability is going to be reflected in an increased anaerobic contribution to performance to cover the intermittent demands. In this scenario, the cardiovascular (aerobic) system cannot instantly adapt to the variations in power output.

The use of the anaerobic energy systems in the context of road race cycling (and track cycling) is probably a little simplistic in the Joyner and Coyle model, because of the dramatic changes in work rate that occur in these divisions of the sport. Very short bursts are likely to be primarily fuelled by alactic energy systems – the splitting of adenosine triphosphate (ATP) and phosphocreatine (PCr) molecules to yield energy (*see* below) – while more sustained anaerobic efforts are fuelled by the provision of ATP through the formation of lactate. The extent to which this energy system can be used is probably dependent upon the ability to offset (buffer) the change in acidity that occurs through this process. The buffering capacity of an individual refers to the ability of the body to resist changes in acidity. The body has a number of natural buffer systems which reduce the impact that elevated acidity can have on the physiological function of the body and resultant fatigue.

Training can take a number of forms associated with the anaerobic energy systems. First, a rider may wish to minimise the amount of energy derived from these systems during normal low-intensity cycling, thereby increasing the amount of energy derived from the aerobic energy system. However, because almost all of the important moves that are made during road race cycling are anaerobic in nature, the rider must ensure that he can also derive a significant amount of energy from this system when required.

Adenosine triphosphate (ATP) is a substance that contains three phosphate molecules. The removal of one phosphate molecule from this substance (generally referred to as the splitting of ATP) releases energy, and this process is the only means by which we can derive energy for muscle contraction. We only store enough ATP in the body to fuel approximately two to three seconds of work; therefore, we must generate ATP from substrate (food sources and stored nutrients). Once ATP has been split, **adenosine diphosphate** (ADP) remains. **Phosphocreatine** (PCr), in the presence of the enzyme creatine kinase, can donate a phosphate molecule to 'rephosphorylate' ADP – in other words, to convert ADP back into ATP – which can then be split again to yield energy for muscle contraction.

Thus, minimising lactate and acidity, yet maximising tolerance to these components, should also be a consideration for the road race cyclist.

The rate at which individual athletes can consume oxygen in situations where pace is varied is another concept that has been investigated. From a theoretical standpoint, the rate at which an individual can respond to an increase in pace or power output using aerobic energy systems is clearly going to determine how much energy needs to be derived from anaerobic energy systems. The ideal physiological response would be for a rider to make transitions (consume oxygen) quickly and effectively, which would probably reduce carbohydrate usage and the production of lactate. Theoretically, a slow response could be a limitation to performance with a single transition from low to high intensity. However, the road rider will have to potentially deal with hundreds of such transitions in every race. In this scenario, a slow uptake response could have catastrophic consequences, leading to elevated anaerobic energy use and carbohydrate depletion, both of which could lead to premature fatigue. Power meter data from 67 professional riders on the Tour Down Under illustrate the variability of road cycling. These data suggest that in the short criterium stages, the cyclists were required to complete a sprint (at an intensity above maximum aerobic capacity) at a rate of one per minute for the duration of the stages. This reiterates the importance of power variation and the associated physiological processes and responses to cope with these demands as an important determinant of road competition success.

Figure 1.6 presents the responses from two riders. Both begin at a low power output of 100 W, before an instant load of 300 W is applied by the ergometry system. The application of the load is identical; however, the rate at which the two riders can use the aerobic energy systems is different. Rider 1 has faster kinetics, thus covering the energy demand by using aerobic sources more effectively than rider 2. Rider 2 still has an identical energy demand; he must therefore rely upon anaerobic energy sources more extensively than rider 1. This is a single transition from one low-power to another higher-power effort. In many of the cycling disciplines, this may occur many times across the event, in which case, if the same oxygen uptake response is presented for these two riders, it is likely that rider 2 will have to deal with substantially greater anaerobic metabolic costs in comparison with rider 1.

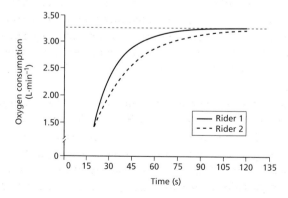

FIG.1.6 Oxygen uptake kinetic trendlines of two riders; rider 1 has faster oxygen uptake kinetics and thus, when intensity rises rapidly, rider 1 will derive less energy from anaerobic sources of energy supply

Oxygen deficit and time trial cycling

It is likely that the anaerobic contribution of work to a time trial will be fairly minimal (with the exception of very short-stage race prologue time trials or short hill climbs). The ideal scenario would be for the time trial rider competing on a flat and wind-free course to have fast oxygen kinetics (minimising the anaerobic contribution) at the start of exercise. Then, considering the lactate/oxygen responses to exercise, the rider would perform at the highest sustainable workload for the duration of exercise, with the accumulation of anaerobic waste products at a rate that will reach the maximal tolerable level at the finish line. In other words, selecting this intensity with knowledge of your physiological capabilities is essential, otherwise a reduction in work and performance will become apparent. However, time trials are rarely flat and wind free. Mathematical modelling suggests that the ability to increase work rates where resistances (grade or wind) are elevated, and backing off during descents and tail-wind sections, will yield the fastest times. There may also be sections that cannot be pedalled, technical corners and descents, in which case these are enforced recovery periods that might need to be factored in when considering the race strategy. The time triallist has to consider the course, conditions and his physiology to plan his race strategy. Typically, anaerobic work will not be considered a major component of success. However, where the demands become more intermittent or variable, a larger anaerobic capacity could theoretically have an impact on performance outcomes. This is further discussed in chapter 14.

Oxygen deficit and road race cycling

In terms of the distinct phases within a road race setting, there will be periods of relative inactivity and periods of some engagement in terms of effort on a continuum through to a maximal level. One of the key factors associated with road race cycling is that decisive actions usually involve significant anaerobic requirements. To attack, to ride hard up relatively short climbs and to adjust position in the peloton or group require anaerobic capabilities. If these capabilities are accompanied by fast oxygen uptake kinetics, aerobic metabolism will also support anaerobic demands (total work would equate to energy derived from anaerobic metabolism in addition to some energy supplied through aerobic work). As alluded to previously, any individual with sluggish oxygen kinetics will simply have to generate more energy through anaerobic processes during the thousands of elevations in exercise intensity that are seen during a road cycling event.

Peak explosive power may be a key requirement; some road-based categorisations of power values are available within the work of Hunter Allen and Andy Coggan (*see* Further reading, page 295). However, there are some fundamental considerations required when allocating high power outputs in the anaerobic domains to grade the ability of a cyclist. Figure 1.7 shows two veteran riders who are graded by the Allen and Coggan categorisation system as category 3 for their peak 5-second power output. Both of these riders performed an all-out 30-second cycle sprint in the laboratory. They had similar dimensions in terms of height and body mass. Rider B had

TAKE-HOME MESSAGE

If a rider can get up to speed faster than an opponent, the absolute power values have less importance. Very short periods of acceleration have to be matched by opponents, so training and developing split-second acceleration is vital for successful race finishes.

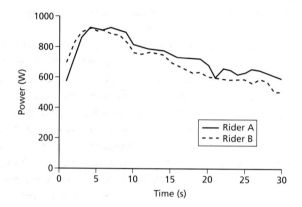

FIG.1.7 Similar laboratory sprint tests of two riders: a sprinter and a non-sprinter

a slightly higher 5-second peak power than rider A. However, rider A is a successful road sprint rider with national medals attained through using these capabilities. In the road setting, rider B is a poor sprinter. At first glance there appears not to be a huge difference in the capabilities of these two riders teased out by the laboratory-based sprint test. However, owing to rider A's more rapid ability to achieve high work rates (the first three data points in figure 1.7), very basic modelling of this data suggests that it would take rider B approximately 13 seconds to catch rider A in a sprint with no drafting. The majority of sprint finishes have been reported to be far shorter than this for the all-out phase (6–10 seconds), in which case the acceleration by rider A is the key factor in winning sprint finishes. Obviously, knowledge of your capabilities is important as this could help you to ascertain how far out it might be appropriate to initiate a sprint in order to maximise the likelihood of success in the finale.

GROSS MECHANICAL EFFICIENCY

Ultimately, VO_2, lactate or other physiological responses do not win bicycle races. However, the application of mechanical work or power output applied in the right context at the right time does win races. The final component of the Joyner and Coyle model, efficiency, describes the conversion of physical work into the mechanical work achieved on the bicycle. As mentioned previously, whichever energy system you are using, the ability to convert the available energy into mechanical work is an important consideration. Conceptually, you could be performing at the same level of physical stress as another cyclist, but if that individual can derive a higher power output for that identical energy cost, he is more likely to be successful. Typically, efficiency values from 16 per cent to 24 per cent are reported. To illustrate the impact of these extremes, if two riders with these values were compared, and both had an oxygen cost of 3 l·min^{-1} and fuel use of approximately 94 per cent carbohydrate and 6 per cent fat (carbon dioxide excretion of 2.94 l·min^{-1}), the rider who is 16 per cent efficient would produce 168 W compared with 252 W for the rider who is 24 per cent efficient. In other words, approximately 10 W are gained for each percentage point gained in efficiency in this example. Training data on improving cycling efficiency are very limited. Contentious data presented on Lance Armstrong from 1992 to 1999 have indicated that he improved efficiency by 1.87 per cent across this period. Over a much shorter period, our research group has presented data on a training protocol that improved efficiency by 1.6 per cent with just six weeks of specific intensified training.

Efficiency has been investigated by many researchers and has been considered from both physiological and biomechanical perspectives; however, there is still fairly minimal understanding of how this component might change with training. There is very limited information on the mechanisms that might lead to altered or reduced energy cost of movement. Some researchers have speculated that body size and muscle structure are the key components, although there may be many other contributing factors. Size could be linked to limb mass and the associated cost of moving a limb round in circles for hours. This would theoretically be different between a smaller rider and a larger rider. In terms of fatigue and heat retention/removal, the lower surface area to body mass ratio of a larger rider might also induce a higher physiological cost when competing in warm environments or in conditions of limited air movement.

Gross mechanical efficiency and time trial cycling

If the data in the example presented above are analysed via a speed power profile on an ergometer, the rider with a gross efficiency value of 16 per cent would be riding almost 6 km·h^{-1} slower than the rider with a gross efficiency of 24 per cent for an identical oxygen cost. Given this example, it is clear that low efficiency will lead to higher lactate values and oxygen cost at a fixed power output. All of these factors predict time trial performance. Therefore, this component of the model is critical from both a theoretical and an applied perspective. There are limited data on changes in efficiency over a period of exercise; however, it is likely that there is an elevated oxygen cost of exercise after sustained periods compared with the early stages of exercise.

Figure 1.8 demonstrates fairly consistent changes across a group of cyclists from 20 to 120 minutes of steady-state exercise. All riders demonstrated a reduction in efficiency and, as a general trend, it would appear that having a high efficiency value at 30 minutes is likely to lead to a higher value at 120 minutes (there is a strong correlation between the 30- and 120-minute measures). However, despite a strong correlation, which explains approximately 85 per cent of the finish score based on the starting

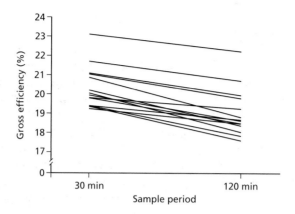

FIG.1.8 Gross efficiency in trained cyclists monitored over a two-hour period of ergometer cycling

score, there is some order change within the group, with the gradient of the lines being steeper in some riders (who deteriorated to a greater extent) than others. Greater reductions in efficiency have been associated with reductions in relative performance late in exercise. Thus, the time trial cyclist should consider this component of the model to maximise the value in the first instance and also to minimise reductions in this parameter, which are likely to be linked to local muscular endurance.

Gross mechanical efficiency and road race cycling

Fundamentally, in attempting to achieve the best result possible in a road race, peak performance as described by the model would be required at some juncture, be it a sprint finish, a lone attack or hanging on to a group. However, minimising physiological stress during the phases where the racing is not self-regulated is a key factor to consider (and is not considered by the model). Based on the Joyner and Coyle model, in periods where other individual riders are dictating the intensity of the race, it would be ideal if you did not have to secure a high proportion of either your maximal oxygen uptake or your lactate threshold. Ideally, you would be working with the lowest possible anaerobic contribution and the maximal efficiency (or power output) for that amount of energy. To achieve this, ensuring sound technical and tactical ability is one key consideration. Drafting, gearing, position in the peloton and so on are all strong considerations that can dramatically influence physiological response. In terms of preparation (training) before the event, ensuring that the ceilings for these factors are at their highest possible level will help to achieve a lower relative physiological cost during those periods of exercise that are not self-governed and to maximise mechanical work output when required.

TAKE-HOME MESSAGE

Efficiency appears to drop during exercise. Starting exercise with the highest possible efficiency will yield the highest amount of work for a given physiological cost. Incorporating aerobic intervals (approximately four minutes in duration) and sprint intervals (approximately 10–40 seconds in duration) into a weekly training programme have been shown to improve efficiency by 1.6 per cent over a period of six weeks (compared with a control condition). Split into two sessions per week, with all work intervals followed by 3- to 4-minute recoveries, the aerobic intervals began with three repetitions and progressed to a maximum of five repetitions per session. The intensive sprint intervals began with three repetitions for each duration of 40, 30, 20 and 10 seconds; this again progressed to five repetitions for the final two weeks.

KEY TAKE-HOME MESSAGES

- Knowledge of the physiology underpinning road cycling can be used to formulate tactics before and during competition.
- Be precise with pacing. Poor pacing will reduce work rate and elevate the physiological cost of cycling.
- Elevate the physiological cost for opponents if possible during competition. There are numerous potential physiological consequences if you are able to engage riders with this type of strategy.
- Bodyweight changes can influence the capabilities of a cyclist. Ensure that the force producing muscle mass is not compromised if weight loss is attempted.
- High efficiency is a major goal for all cyclists. Maximise mechanical work for the lowest possible physiological cost.

CHAPTER 2

THE PHYSIOLOGICAL DEMANDS OF OFF-ROAD CYCLING DISCIPLINES

Louis Passfield, Mark Walker, Paul Barrett

CROSS-COUNTRY MOUNTAIN BIKING

'To be a top mountain bike rider you need to possess a huge number of attributes. Physically a rider needs endurance, speed and power, whilst being as light as possible. The rider needs to be technically skilled in all conditions. Mentally they need to be determined and tough, but also able to adapt to changing conditions and courses. Basically it is one of the toughest sports out there.'
Oli Beckingsale (three times Great Britain Olympic mountain bike rider)

Race characteristics

The demands of cross-country mountain bike (MTB) racing differ quite markedly from those of many other competitive endurance cycling events. Typically, MTB races at senior level take about 1.5 to 2 hours for the winner to complete. The course for the race is normally almost entirely off-road and usually consists of five to seven laps. Each lap is 4–8 km in length, and the total amount of climbing can vary from less than 100 m to several hundred metres per lap. Average speeds for MTB race winners vary

Oli Beckingsale in action

but often range between 20 and 25 km·h⁻¹. Recently, there has been a move to change the nature of races at the highest level, that is, the Union Cycliste Internationale (UCI) World Cup, World Championship and Olympic events. These top events have become shorter races, with smaller laps and a correspondingly reduced overall race distance and duration. Thus, many major MTB races no longer involve traditional 'Alpine-style' courses that feature long, open, steady climbs. Instead, the majority are now 'park style', typically winding through woodlands and consisting of short, tight, technical climbs and descents. The descents can be fearsome and often feature a fast but particularly difficult racing line as well as an alternative, less challenging but longer and/or slower route. Much of the race course can be single track, making overtaking difficult or impossible. For this reason, riders are gridded at the start, with the highest-ranked riders allocated front grid positions. A relatively short, open start loop is normally included to allow riders the chance to compete for race position before the race funnels down into single file.

Physical demands of MTB racing

Physically, MTB racing is perhaps the most all-round demanding form of single-day cycle racing. The best MTB riders require outstanding aerobic and endurance fitness. Because of the repeated climbs and accelerations, they need to be very light too. In addition, MTB riders absorb a physical pounding as they race around the course. Therefore, they have to be physically tough and have good whole-body strength and conditioning.

The average race power output of the best MTB riders at first glance does not appear to be exceptionally high. This is not owing to a lower level of fitness among MTB riders; instead, it is because their power output has to vary enormously as they ride around the course. Thus, the power output may average a somewhat unimpressive 330–350 W for an elite rider during a race. However, throughout the race the rider will need to make repeated efforts over 1000 W on some of the short sharp climbs, when accelerating out of slow corners and when overtaking. It is not unusual to find an increase of more than 50 W when average power is recalculated as Normalized Power (*see* chapter 6).

The effort needed when climbing and accelerating is significantly reduced if bodyweight and equipment weight are reduced. Unsurprisingly, the best MTB riders have an exceedingly high power output when expressed relative to their bodyweight (power-to-weight ratio). The maximum power-to-weight ratio of top MTB riders is likely to be over 8 W·kg⁻¹ body mass, and their maximal oxygen consumption (VO_{2max}) around 85 ml·min⁻¹·kg⁻¹. I have worked with an Olympic MTB rider who I measured riding for 30 minutes up a climb at a power-to-weight ratio of 6.4 W·kg⁻¹. This is higher than the peak power output that many well-trained cyclists achieve for only one minute in a laboratory ramp test. Incidentally, the rider's time for this climb was better than that of Britain's best 4000 m track rider at the time. Indeed, several top-level MTB riders have transferred to successful careers in road racing and been noted for their climbing ability.

Finally, it is important to note that the physical challenge of MTB racing is not simply a function of the race terrain. Other aspects of the race environment can have just as large an impact. Because MTB race speeds are much lower than those on the track or road, high ambient temperatures and humidity can become much greater issues. The lower race speed means that the riders' relative air movement, and therefore cooling benefit, is reduced dramatically. Another major environmental challenge facing MTB riders can be the altitude of the race. Where an event is held in the high mountains, air pressure is lower and oxygen becomes correspondingly harder to conduct to the working muscles.

Technical demands of MTB racing

The technical skill and courage of top MTB riders is breathtaking. They are able to plunge headlong down descents that do not appear rideable. As they do this, they flick and hop their bikes over and around course obstacles. Most remarkably, they do all this while following within a few inches of the rider in front. One mistake and the consequences can be serious, not just for the blundering rider but for those following immediately behind too. The technical aspect of MTB races is provided by the nature of the course and the challenge of trying to hold a constant high speed, regardless of the terrain. Good off-road performances require the rider to hold and carry speed, particularly through descents and corners. The challenge of picking and holding the best racing line is further exacerbated by the changing riding surfaces, which normally include mud, rock, grass, gravel and tree roots in varying amounts. Moreover, a short rain shower can reduce a previously fast section of a course to a slippery, unrideable quagmire. A possible further effect of having to ride on these challenging and variable surfaces may be that MTB riders learn to pedal slightly differently from their road and track counterparts. This is not something that to my knowledge has been demonstrated scientifically; however, maintaining grip and traction is undoubtedly an important factor for fast off-road riding. Thus, some good riders have suggested to me that 'off-road' they adopt a more circular pedalling style. They do this to reduce the variation in pedal torque and maintain better traction. By contrast, there is some research that suggests the best road riders do the opposite of this; that is, they stamp on the pedal to generate a higher peak torque through the pedal's propulsive phase.

Each MTB course provides a distinctive blend of technical and physical challenges that change markedly from race to race. The effect of this can be to change the pecking order of the top riders according to their relative physical and technical abilities. Julien Absalon is a multiple champion rider who is notable for winning on any type of course, but the finishing order behind him is often markedly influenced by the nature of the course. Some riders will be better prepared for courses with a significant technical element, while others will prefer a more physically challenging course, perhaps, for example, with more climbing.

The extent to which the technical aspect of a course can make a difference to race performance was highlighted to me by data that I gathered at a demanding Alpine-style race that went straight up and down a mountain in Switzerland. Over the 10-lap race, the riders ascended and descended more than 1500 m. The reigning World and Olympic champion won the race, but the surprise for me was that it was his descending

A MTB rider on a technical descent

rather than his climbing speed that gained him his winning margin. Since that lesson I have *always* included technical training in the preparation of MTB riders.

Planning and organising MTB training

Although the demands of MTB racing feature some marked differences from other disciplines, the overall preparation strategy can be broadly similar to that of other endurance cyclists. As highlighted above, perhaps the main difference should be that MTB riders include a technical element within their training. The key to any successful training and preparation programme is having clearly identified objectives and a thoughtfully planned and executed training programme. In the 25 years that I have been studying, researching and working in sports science, I have seen many advances, but how best to write a training programme is not one of them. One thing I have noticed, however, is that those with a training programme tend to progress better than those without.

Planning an MTB training programme begins by considering the demands of the sport and identifying the resulting keystones. Keystones are the general but important aspects of your overall preparation that will underpin any improvement; and they are personal. It is important to write your keystones down. Typical examples of MTB keystones from riders I have worked with include mental skills, descending, off-road toughness, endurance, core fitness, climbing, good nutrition, a full night's sleep and low levels of stress. It is important to ensure that these keystones are maintained regularly (e.g. weekly). A simple tick list stuck on the fridge can serve as a means of monitoring and motivating yourself to do this. Once your keystones are complete, you can reward yourself with something from inside the fridge!

After MTB keystones, the major objectives for the year should be identified. Ideally, these should be no more than one or two important races in which peak performance is required. If several races are identified, unless they are grouped and continually stretching your abilities. So, flicking round a bend or sliding down a descent you're comfortable with does not constitute deliberate practice. Instead, find new and more demanding routes to master. Time yourself over them, then see if you can do it again, faster.

KEY TAKE-HOME MESSAGES

- Planning is a vital part of performing well, and even a weak plan is vastly better than no plan at all.
- Mix road and off-road riding in your programme for maximum training effect.
- Break down difficult MTB skills into simpler challenges, practise them slowly until you can do them reliably without mistake, and then perform them at speed.

CYCLO-CROSS

Despite its rich history, growing popularity and lucrative professional circuit, cyclo-cross has remained a largely unresearched cycling discipline. This section examines the unique demands that cyclo-cross places upon the athlete, using examples of field data collected from both amateur and professional races in the UK and mainland Europe.

What is cyclo-cross?

Cyclo-cross is a form of off-road cycle racing that pre-dates mountain bike racing and BMX by many decades. The first races started in France in the early 20th century, but it was not until 1950 that cyclo-cross was afforded the honour of a senior World Championship event, which was won by the 1947 Tour de France winner Jean Robic. Modern cyclo-cross racing has evolved enormously since the early days, when course designers were at liberty to force riders to negotiate all manner of obstacles (including waist-high hurdles and river crossings) into a sport whose character is now strictly regulated by the UCI.

Races are held during the winter months (September through to February in the northern hemisphere) and range in length from 30 minutes for juveniles through to 60 minutes for senior men. Competitors race in all weather conditions on a circuit that must have a minimum length of 2.5 km, although non-UCI-ratified events may vary. The circuits are designed to encourage changes of pace by incorporating a variety of surfaces, including road, meadowland and forest trails, as well as natural features of the land and manmade obstacles. This can create a very demanding race where competitors may encounter steep banks, manmade hurdles, sand dunes and artificial sandpits that, in many instances, will force them to dismount and run while carrying the bike. Consequently, physical capacity alone is not enough to be a good

TAKE-HOME MESSAGE

To be successful in cyclo-cross, your training should focus on improving both physical and technical ability. Think carefully about the skills you will need for racing and then structure your training in order to practise them regularly. Some riders will continue to do this through the off-season.

cyclo-cross competitor; you also need a high degree of technical ability to negotiate these obstacles, wasting as little time and energy as possible.

If cyclo-cross riders are specialised creatures, so too are their machines. Although cyclo-cross bikes share some similarities with their road-going cousins (drop handlebars and lack of suspension), they are specifically designed to cope with muddy conditions and to be carried easily. It is not within the scope of this section to discuss the intricacies of cyclo-cross bicycle design and set-up (the reader should refer to the work of Simon Burney for a full account; *see* page 295), but some of the key features of the bike include:

- wide (up to 33 mm), heavily treaded tyres run at low pressures to obtain grip on loose to muddy surfaces;
- lower gear ratios to suit the slower pace (usually no greater than about 46 x 12);
- deep wheel rims (often carbon fibre) to slice through thick mud;
- mountain bike clipless pedals; and
- a frameset that has wider clearance between the wheels to prevent clogging with mud.

Cyclocross-races require competitors to frequently dismount
and carry their bikes over different obstacles

In this example, the female professional rider's heart-rate response is effectively decoupled from changes in power to such an extent that it varies little, despite power fluctuating greatly. However, the data do demonstrate what every rider already knows: cyclo-cross is very hard work. Heart rate is typically very high during races, with average values in the region of 90 per cent of maximum. The intermittent work periods are rarely longer than 30 seconds and contain a high number of short (less than 10 seconds) anaerobic efforts above maximal aerobic power. In this respect, cyclo-cross can be regarded as a long session of mixed-intensity intervals.

Studies on intermittent exercise have shown that when the work interval is relatively short (30 seconds or less) and exercise intensity is relatively high (above maximal aerobic power), oxygen delivery to the active skeletal muscle is likely to be inadequate. However, skeletal muscle can reduce its reliance upon anaerobic metabolism by use of the muscle's own store of oxygen bound to the protein myoglobin (*see* chapter 1 for further discussion).

Heart rate is high throughout figure 2.2, ensuring the greatest possible delivery of oxygen to the working muscle during the work and recovery periods. Consequently, the rider has to perform a balancing act between brief high-intensity bursts of power and sufficiently long periods of recovery to enable the maintenance of high levels of aerobic metabolism.

The adoption of some high-intensity interval training is important in preparing both mentally and physically for the typical efforts experienced within cyclo-cross racing. Research has shown that high-intensity training can simultaneously develop both aerobic and anaerobic characteristics as well as improve muscle power. For example, both anaerobic capacity and maximal oxygen uptake have been shown to be developed with very short interval training of 8 x 20-second efforts at 170 per cent VO_{2max} with 10-second rest intervals (less than 5 minutes of total work).

TAKE-HOME MESSAGE

Your race-specific training should aim to improve your ability to make repeated strenuous efforts, even when levels of fatigue-causing metabolites are high. The prescription could include a combination of explosive strength training, plyometrics or high-intensity intervals of varying duration.

Measuring power output during cyclo-cross races: what can it tell us?

Compared with heart rate, power is a much more sensitive measure of external work (discussed further in chapter 5) that can provide much greater insight into the specific demands of cyclo-cross. This is illustrated in figure 2.3, which shows two representative 20-minute recordings of power data from a road race and a cyclo-cross race ridden by the same female professional rider. The power output is clearly much more variable in the cyclo-cross race than the road race. However, these sudden changes

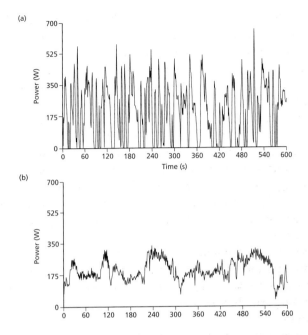

FIG.2.3 Two representative samples of power data from a female professional rider competing in a cyclo-cross race (a) and a road race (b)

in power can make the data difficult to interpret, and it is for this reason that some riders and coaches are sceptical of the benefits of measuring power in cyclo-cross. This concern is largely misplaced, and in the remainder of this section I show how the measurement of power has the potential to provide some useful insights into differences between races and the strategy employed.

Recording power output in races

There are a variety of off-the-shelf power meters available to cyclists, each system having its pros and cons for cyclo-cross use (*see* chapter 5 for a more general discussion of power meters). When choosing a power meter system, an important consideration is its compatibility with your equipment and preferred race set-up; the two main issues to deal with are tyre choice and bike changes.

Tyre selection in cyclo-cross, particularly at the top level of the sport, can be crucial. Many competitors, particularly elite amateurs and professionals, take several tyre/wheel options to races so that they can choose the best combination for the track conditions. For these riders, the best choice of power meter has to be one, such as SRM cranks or the Ergomo bottom bracket unit, that permits a free choice of wheels. If tyre choice is not an issue, a PowerTap wheel is a good option as it is less expensive than an SRM crank and can be easily swapped between bikes.

Some amateurs, and all professionals, take more than one bike to races to enable them to be swapped in the pits for cleaning. This poses the question of whether it is crucial to have data from the whole race or just a few representative laps.

> **TAKE-HOME MESSAGE**
>
> Although a power meter can withstand the harsh conditions encountered in cyclo-cross, you should treat it with care. Avoid spraying it directly with a pressure washer and ensure that the computer, cables and sensors are firmly secured with zip-ties and electrical tape.

Most amateurs will be obliged to choose the latter option as the cost of fitting power meters to both race bikes will be prohibitive. In this situation, the data analysis also becomes very complex, as telemetry from the two bikes has to be pieced together.

Ensure your power meter is calibrated according to the manufacturer's instructions and any automatic power-down function is turned off in order to avoid the computer stopping when the bike is carried or left in the pits; this makes post-race data analysis so much easier as these events will appear more obvious. Making post-race notes will also aid later analysis as you can record which sections of the course were run, on which laps pit stops occurred and when crashes might have happened.

Data can be analysed using any of the proprietary software packages, but if you are proficient in the use of spreadsheets it is possible to import the data directly into a spreadsheet package such as Microsoft Excel. This approach enables you to piece together data from two power meters (if using two bikes) or remove zero power values attributable to running (*see* chapter 6 for a discussion of how to analyse training and race data).

What can power data show?

The following examples are case studies taken from amateur and professional cyclo-cross races to illustrate some of the features to look for in cyclo-cross race data.

The fast start

Although races are generally not won off the start grid, a rider's progress can be significantly hampered by a poor start. Figure 2.4 illustrates the first 60 seconds of power output obtained from an elite amateur competing in a local league race using a PowerTap hub and from a male professional rider competing in a World Cup race using an SRM power meter.

In both examples, the riders produce extremely high instantaneous power outputs (over 800 W) from a standing start. These efforts amount to quite intense sprints and, although the amateur rider's absolute peak power is lower than that of the professional's, both cyclists maintain efforts above maximal aerobic power without pause for at least the first 10 seconds of their respective races.

The high muscle fibre tension produced from a standing start will favour recruitment of type II (fast-twitch) muscle fibres, which transfer energy into mechanical work using anaerobic energy supply pathways. The graphs show that heart-rate response lags well behind the increase in effort, and it takes some 18–20 seconds before something close to a steady state is reached. This delayed increase in oxygen delivery (oxygen

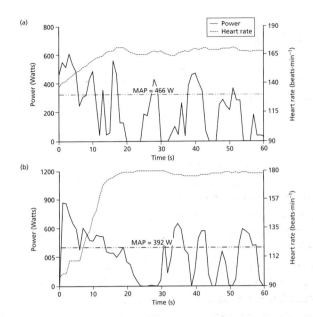

FIG.2.4 Relationship between heart rate and power output over the first 60 seconds of a race start for an amateur competing in a World Cup round (a) and an amateur competing in a local race (b). Note: MAP = maximal aerobic power.

kinetics) and reliance upon type II muscle fibres creates a tough situation for the riders. During this phase of the race, they accumulate an oxygen deficit that at some point has to be paid back. Unfortunately, their ability to recover this deficit is compromised as they still have approximately 60 minutes of high-intensity racing ahead of them.

Incorporating a warm-up into pre-race preparation may reduce the level of accumulated deficit. Studies suggest that a vigorous warm-up activity (over 100 per cent power output at VO_{2max}) which results in elevated muscle and blood lactate concentrations can reduce the oxygen deficit by increasing the VO_{2max} response at the onset of exercise. There is also evidence that a vigorous warm-up leads to increased motor unit recruitment, which possibly reduces strain on individual fibres, resulting in less phosphocreatine depletion and lower lactate accumulation. However, the characteristics of the most effective warm-up, that is the work rate, exercise duration and recovery period, are less well known. It is important for each rider to experiment with different warm-ups and find out what works best for them.

PRE-RACE WARM-UP

A vigorous warm-up will help you prepare for a fast race start. Experiment with different work durations and recovery periods to find out what works best for you, but do ensure that the warm-up involves some high-intensity efforts. These can be easily performed on a static trainer.

TAKE-HOME MESSAGE

It is important to undertake focused training in order to cope with very intense race starts. This training should include some technical work on the bike to learn the best gear choice and to practise clipping into the pedals quickly so that you don't get left behind. It is essential that you include some strength training and anaerobic intervals in order to develop the ability to produce the instantaneous power necessary at the start of a race.

Power distribution within the race

Owing to the highly variable power outputs encountered in cyclo-cross, using average power to identify differences between races can be a pretty blunt tool. Furthermore, data that have been filtered to remove zero power scores attributable to running will give a higher average power output than the same unfiltered data. Accordingly, a better way of analysing power data is to examine the power distribution; in other words, the time spent in different power bands. These power bands can be set from physiological markers determined in laboratory or field tests, or you can simply set the band limits to give you a distribution that is most sensitive to changes between races.

Understanding differences in riding style

A further, very useful analysis is to sub-divide the power bands into cadence bands. The data in figure 2.5 were collected from a male professional competing in a UK league race and a World Cup round on the infamous Koksijde sand dunes.

Within the league race, there is a broad distribution of power across the bands, with the most favoured being 300–500 W (approximately 28 per cent of race time) and a roughly even distribution of time within the 100–300 W and 500–700 W bands (approximately 20 per cent of race time each). During the World Cup race, a similar proportion of time (approximately 35 per cent) is spent in the 100–300 W band, but there is a relatively small period (approximately 7 per cent of total race time) in the higher 500–700 W band. The finding that the Koksijde World Cup race, which is regarded as being notoriously difficult, is ridden with less time in the higher power band seems contradictory.

An analysis of sprint efforts (above maximal aerobic power) sheds some light upon what might be happening. Figure 2.6 shows that during the course of the World Cup event the rider made 125 sprints, with the majority of them (120) under 6 seconds, whereas 134 sprints were performed in the league race, but a larger proportion of these were longer efforts of greater than 6 seconds.

Although we cannot be certain of the precise reasons for this distribution of efforts, the data do suggest that, compared with the league race, Koksijde required many more short, high-intensity bursts of effort, interspersed with longer durations at modest power outputs. This is consistent with the course design, which encourages riders to attack the numerous flat and uphill sand sections, riding for as long as possible before dismounting and running. Of course, running in sand is very difficult and this element of the workload is not reflected in the power data.

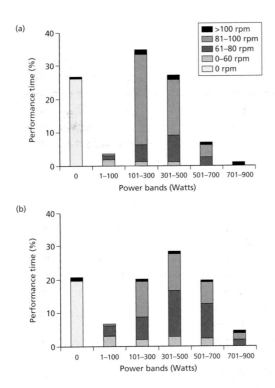

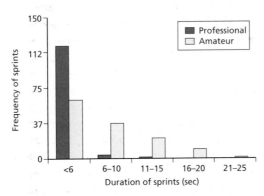

FIG.2.5 Percentage of total race time spent in different cadence–power bands for a male professional competing at the Koksijde World Cup (a) and during a league race (b)

FIG.2.6 Frequency and duration of sprints over maximal aerobic power for a professional competing on different circuits

Another interesting feature is the distribution of cadence; you will note that the higher 80–100 rev·min⁻¹ cadence band is favoured in Koksijde compared with the league race, where the 60–80 rev·min⁻¹ range is preferred. There are two possible reasons for this: first, the league race was ridden in very muddy conditions that necessitated the use of a lower cadence and higher gears to maintain traction. The conditions at Koksijde were less muddy and the course was regarded as faster, meaning that the non-sand sections were ridden at high speed and cadence. Second, the rider used this leg speed when hitting the sand sections at Koksijde in an attempt to maintain momentum and delay running for as long as possible.

This analysis is a good example of how power data from two races can potentially be used to understand the way in which differences in course design might affect the race. However, as stated earlier, some caution must be exercised as the relationship between course design and rider behaviour has not been fully researched and the data presented here are merely from single case studies.

POWER METER USE

Course design and changing track conditions necessitate different strategies that a power meter can help you to understand. Use it to study the cadence–power distribution and the frequency of high-intensity efforts so you can improve your race-specific preparation.

KEY TAKE-HOME MESSAGES

- Cyclo-cross is characterised by intermittent periods of work and recovery. A significant proportion of these efforts is at power outputs greater than maximal aerobic power, so it is important to undertake high-intensity interval training to enhance your ability to deal with these efforts.
- During races you need to consider how best to balance periods of work with recovery (i.e. a pacing strategy) to avoid developing a large oxygen deficit, which could lead to premature fatigue.
- Power distribution can vary considerably between races depending upon course design and track conditions on the day. Using a power meter can help you to understand these differences and to adjust your training and race strategy accordingly.
- The start in cyclo-cross has enormous tactical importance, but the high power output, in conjunction with a lag in oxygen delivery, potentially results in the accumulation of a large oxygen deficit. This deficit could be limited by engaging in an intensive warm-up that improves oxygen delivery at the onset of the race and reduces reliance upon anaerobic metabolism.

BICYCLE MOTORCROSS (BMX)

Bicycle motorcross (BMX) was introduced into the Olympic cycling programme at the 2008 Olympic Games in Beijing. There has been relatively little scientific interest in BMX in comparison with other cycling disciplines, although BMX is now attracting the attention of sports institutes and national governing bodies as they provide scientific support to coaches and athletes in the pursuit of Olympic medals.

Modern elite BMX competitions take the form of a time trial to qualify riders for the first round followed by several rounds of highly competitive racing to determine the gold, silver and bronze medallists. Each race begins with eight cyclists lined up in a gate at the top of a start ramp. The gate drops and the cyclists race over a track with large jumps and turns, taking approximately 30 seconds to complete the race.

Race analysis

A BMX race can be broken down into a series of short (less than 5 seconds), maximal all-out sprints. Although all the sprints within the race are relevant to the performance, the first sprint down the start ramp is tactically by far the most important aspect of the race. We know this because performance analysis data show that approximately 85 per cent of elite BMX races are won by cyclists who are in one of the top three positions by the end of the start ramp. Therefore, your race could easily be over by this point if you are not at the front of the field. Information collected from on-board data loggers further reveal how extreme this performance environment is: at the end of the start ramp, after just 3 seconds of racing, a world-class BMX cyclist has accelerated from a stationary position to over 50 km·h^{-1} and is pedalling at over 200 revolutions per minute.

Physical and physiological determinants

To maximise acceleration, the cyclist must maximise his mechanical power output and minimise any resistance to motion. Elite BMX cyclists produce extraordinarily high maximum power outputs to facilitate their fast accelerations: up to 2500 W of peak power. By comparison, amateur road cyclists will typically generate approximately 1000 W of peak power and Grand Tour road sprinters have been reported to generate approximately 1400 W. It is worth noting that this high maximum power output often translates very well to other sprint cycling disciplines, as can be seen from the number of BMX cyclists who have successfully transferred into world-class track sprint cycling (such as Sir Chris Hoy, Jamie Staff and Shanaze Reade). A BMX cyclist must also be able to produce power across a range of cadences, right through to cadences of over 200 revolutions per minute. This has implications for training programmes, as BMX cyclists need not only strength at low cadences but also the ability to produce power while pedalling at a rate of over three revolutions per second.

We can use the relationship between power and cadence to better understand the determinants of maximal cycling power. The physiology of muscle is such that, as cadences increase from zero, the amount of power that a cyclist can maximally exert also increases. This continues up to an optimal cadence of around 120–130 revolutions per minute, at which point the cyclist will produce his maximum power output. As cadences increase beyond this point, there is a reduction in the maximal power output that can be produced. It is interesting to observe that elite BMX cyclists will have higher optimal cadences than elite endurance cyclists. Laboratory-based cycling studies have shown that higher optimal cadences correlate with higher percentages of powerful fast-twitch fibres in the muscles of the leg. It is understood, therefore, that BMX cyclists are able to generate very large power outputs, partly as a result of a higher percentage of fast-twitch fibres in their muscles. We also know from laboratory studies that lean muscle mass correlates positively with maximum power in cycling. Therefore, the combination of a large musculature and a high proportion of fast-twitch fibres corresponds to a high maximum cycling power and optimised performance in BMX.

Other considerations

It is also worth highlighting the relevance of fatigue within a BMX race. At less than 5 seconds, the length of each sprint within a BMX race is understood to be too short to cause significant fatigue within the sprint itself. However, a BMX cyclist must be able to repeatedly sprint during the race and, therefore, the ability to maintain maximal power output during successive sprints is also an important quality for successful BMX performance. Some researchers have suggested a link between aerobic fitness and fatigue during multiple sprint work. In line with this, BMX cyclists will typically supplement strength and power training with road cycling or interval training to improve aerobic fitness and, therefore, resistance to fatigue during a race.

Future directions

With the inclusion of BMX in the Olympics Games, it is anticipated that there will be increased investment in BMX research. This, alongside the development of BMX-specific power measurement tools, will increase our understanding of the physical and physiological factors of BMX performance. In turn, this should aid the progression of the sport and enhance the performance of some of the world's most powerful athletes.

KEY TAKE-HOME MESSAGES

- BMX race performance is largely determined by the ability of the cyclist to accelerate rapidly from a standing start.
- Maximum cycling power is a key determinant of BMX performance. The combination of a large musculature and a high proportion of fast-twitch fibres corresponds to a high maximum cycling power and optimised performance in BMX.

SECTION B

HOW DO I COMPARE? PERFORMANCE ASSESSMENT

Before an individualised training programme can be developed, it is first necessary to identify the relative strengths and weaknesses of the cyclist. This is most precisely assessed in the carefully controlled environment of the laboratory. However, laboratory testing is often expensive and may lack ecological validity (i.e. testing in a 'false' environment, for example on a stationary cycle ergometer, may not entirely replicate your racing bike set-up). Field testing may therefore be preferable as often only a heart-rate monitor and/or power meter are required in addition to your normal bike set-up. However, obtaining reliable data from field testing is difficult owing to varying weather and road conditions. Therefore, the relative pros and cons of laboratory and field testing must always be considered. Section B discusses these issues along with how best to prepare yourself for performance assessments. A description is given of how to assess the different physiological determinants of performance outlined in section A and how to interpret test results.

After reading section B, you should have knowledge of what information performance assessment can provide in terms of identifying strengths and weaknesses. You should also understand the principle of test reliability and know what to do to ensure pre-test standardisation. Section B also provides you with some knowledge of the different laboratory tests and what they can tell you about your performance. Finally, the field testing section will allow you to select appropriate performance assessments to identify your functional threshold power, power profile and training status.

CHAPTER 3

LABORATORY AND FIELD ASSESSMENT OF CYCLING ABILITY

James Hopker and Simon Jobson

Chapters 1 and 2 have established the physiological requirements of different cycling disciplines. From this, you will have developed an understanding of what components of physiology require training to optimise performance. The starting point of this process is to identify your strengths and weaknesses relative to these demands. This can be facilitated through laboratory or field based fitness testing. This information can then be used in the design and modification of your training. These tests can then be re-administered at different time points across the year in order to assess the effectiveness of your training. You can also then use the results of these tests to modify and set goals for your subsequent training.

To achieve these aims, the tests you conduct must be reproducible. To produce meaningful data that you can compare across different time points of a season or seasons, the tests must also be reliable. Here, reliability refers to the precision of a test; that is, a test should have a high degree of accuracy and minimal variation owing to chance or random fluctuations. Excessive variability within a test or its administration can render the results meaningless. For example, if you were to compare your results across several repeated tests, they would be meaningless if the observed changes in performance were attributable simply to the inherent variability in the test rather than to changes in your fitness.

There are a number of factors that can affect the reliability of a test. For example, it is important that your power meter records power accurately. If possible, you should zero offset your power meter before each test. The purpose of this is to measure the base level of stress on the internal strain gauges of the power meter before any pressure is applied to the pedals. The forces measured during cycling will then be adjusted for this baseline. Factors such as temperature and pressure will also affect your power meter. This is normal; you just need to accommodate these factors to be sure that the power meter is providing you with accurate data.

You should always test on the same stretch of road with the same weather conditions or on an indoor turbo trainer and, where possible, at the same time of day. You should also try to minimise the influence of nutritional state (by eating and drinking similar things in the 24 hours before the test), stress levels and the amount of sleep you have the night before so that you can be confident when comparing the results from repeat tests.

PRE-TEST PREPARATION GUIDELINES FOR LABORATORY AND FIELD TESTING

To maximise the reliability of testing and the ability to make comparisons between testing sessions on a prolonged basis, it is important that a degree of pre-test standardisation occurs. Before testing, follow these criteria:

- Have an easy training day or complete rest day before each test. This is to ensure that you are in a fully rested state before the test. Additionally, list the training that you conducted in the days preceding the test.
- Do not eat in the 2 hours immediately before the test.
- Have a standardised nutritional intake in the 24 hours before the test (that is, eat and drink the same things each time). Ensure that you are fully hydrated and carbohydrate loaded before the test. Essentially, you should prepare for each test as if it were a race.
- Drink only water or use the same sport drink during every test.
- Avoid alcohol in the 24 hours before the test.
- Do not test if you have not been free of illness/infection during the preceding two weeks.
- If testing on the road, ensure that weather and road conditions are standardised as much as possible. There is no point testing in conditions of slippery roads or strong headwinds. Similarly, ensure the chosen road for testing has a low traffic volume and is free from tight bends, traffic controls and hazardous junctions.
- If testing on a turbo trainer, ensure that you follow the manufacturer's procedures for correct use. For example, particular attention should be paid to tyre pressure and rolling resistance between the tyre and trainer. These should be standardised on all repeat tests.

LABORATORY TESTING
Maximal oxygen consumption (VO_{2max}) test
What is it?

Sprinting is a key component of many cycling events. The energy to fuel these sprints is supplied anaerobically; that is, by metabolic processes that do not require oxygen. However, despite the importance of sprinting, most cycling requires energy to be supplied aerobically (i.e. by metabolic processes that require oxygen) most of the time. As discussed in chapter 1, the rate at which this oxygen is consumed (VO_2) has a significant impact on cycling performance. In an ideal world, it would be possible to increase the rate of this oxygen consumption indefinitely to meet the demands of increasing power output. Of course, we don't live in such a world. Instead, there is an individual limit to the amount of oxygen that can be consumed by each of us. This limit is known as VO_{2max}.

The rate of oxygen consumption during a bout of exercise will be at some percentage of VO_{2max}. For example, a typical mid-length time-trial (e.g. 40 km) will be completed at approximately 85 per cent VO_{2max}. Therefore, training to boost performance VO_2 may be targeted at either increasing the percentage of VO_{2max} that can be sustained or at increasing VO_{2max} itself. If VO_{2max} is increased and the percentage of VO_{2max} that can be sustained is maintained, performance VO_2 (and, therefore, performance) will necessarily be increased.

How is it measured?

VO_{2max} can be estimated using sub-maximal exercise tests such as the Astrand-Rhyming and YMCA tests. While the estimations provided by such tests are satisfactory when summarising the fitness of large population groups, they are not accurate enough to inform the training of individual athletes. Instead, VO_{2max} should be measured directly using a maximal test protocol.

A typical VO_{2max} test will administer an increase in work rate during incremental exercise. Conducted on a calibrated cycle ergometer, the test is started at a relatively low power output (e.g. 100 W). Power output is then increased incrementally until 'volitional exhaustion'; that is, until you can no longer continue. The rate at which power output is increased varies among laboratories. Researchers have shown that the duration of test stages and the rate of increase in required power output have a significant impact on test results. For this reason, it is important that your VO_{2max} testing be conducted using the same protocol each time you test.

The duration of test stages may vary from 60 seconds to 3 minutes, while power may be increased by anything from 10 W to 50 W per stage. The standard protocol used in the UK uses a 20 W increase in power output every 60 seconds. Many sport scientists will aim for a VO_{2max} test that lasts between 8 and 12 minutes (excluding warm-up and warm-down). However, the research evidence would appear to suggest that valid VO_{2max} values can be achieved for tests lasting anywhere between 7 and 26 minutes.

A typical VO_{2max} test will provide values for VO_{2max}, maximal aerobic power (MAP) and maximal heart rate. Your VO_{2max} value, expressed in litres per minute or in millilitres per kg of bodyweight per minute, describes your maximal ability to take in and consume oxygen. Your maximal aerobic power describes the highest power output that you can sustain with energy generated through aerobic metabolic pathways. Finally, your maximum heart rate is the fastest rate at which your heart can beat.

How often should I test?

Each of the laboratory tests described in this chapter should be performed three to four times per year. To inform the planning of training, a typical cyclist should look to test at the beginning of the training year, shortly before the beginning of the competition phase and mid-way through the competition phase. This schedule allows appropriate early season training targets to be set. Testing before and during the competition phase allows the impact of past training to be evaluated while also giving the opportunity for future training to be optimised towards the maximisation of performance VO_2.

How do I compare?

The highest VO_{2max} values are seen in top professional riders. Nevertheless, there are many successful professionals who do not have 'off the chart' VO_{2max} values. There is, therefore, a lot of overlap in the VO_{2max}-related values seen across the various levels of cycling (see table 3.1).

Category	Sedentary	Trained	Well trained	Elite	World class
MAP (W)		250–400	300–450	350–500	400–600
Power:weight ratio		4.0–5.0	5.0–6.0	6.0–7.0	6.5–8.0
VO_{2max} ($l \cdot min^{-1}$)	3.0–3.5	4.5–5.0	5.0–5.3	5.2–6.0	5.4–7.0
VO_{2max} ($ml \cdot kg^{-1} \cdot min^{-1}$)	40–45	64–70	70–75	72–80	75–90

Adapted from Jeukendrup, A.E., Craig, N.P., and Hawley, J.A., 'The bioenergetics of world class cycling', Journal of Science and Medicine in Sport, 3 (2000), pp. 414–433.

TABLE 3.1 Typical maximal values for cyclists

Lactate threshold

What is it?

As discussed in chapter 1, success in most cycling events is not necessarily related to your VO_{2max}. However, the percentage of this value that you can sustain for a period of time is indicative of your endurance performance ability and is very responsive to training. Lactate threshold is often used as an indicator of this point as it denotes the point above which the body is under significantly more stress, with accelerated use of carbohydrate stores. Some sport scientists also refer to this point as the anaerobic or ventilatory threshold. However, while there is considerable debate in the scientific literature about the differences between the lactate and ventilatory thresholds, for the cyclist they are synonymous.

In an applied setting, research has shown that 40 km time trial performance is highly related to the power output at lactate threshold. Also, a 10 per cent improvement in anaerobic threshold has been shown to improve a 26 km time trial time by 4 per cent. Performance on the track, for example in the 4000 m individual pursuit, has also been shown to be related to lactate threshold. The higher your threshold is as a percentage of your aerobic capacity, the faster you will race, especially in steady-state events such as time trials. Therefore, blood lactate is now commonly assessed during laboratory testing to prescribe training intensity and to monitor changes in cycling performance.

Lactate threshold represents the highest steady-state exercise intensity that an athlete can maintain for prolonged periods of time (over 30 minutes), commonly at about 80–85 per cent VO_{2max}. In fact, most trained cyclists can sustain this level of intensity for about an hour.

How often should I test?

Ideally, the lactate threshold test should be performed three to four times per season.

How is it measured?

Lactate threshold tests are typically performed by riding on a treadmill or cycle ergometer. After an adequate warm-up period, the test starts at an exercise intensity of approximately 100 W. Each stage lasts 4–5 minutes, with a small finger-prick blood sample taken during the last 30 seconds of each stage to determine blood lactate concentration. The test is continuous, with the required power output demand increasing in steps of between 25 and 50 W at the end of each fourth or fifth minute. The cyclist stops only when an obvious spike in lactate concentration occurs. Often, heart rate, power output and VO_2 are also recorded during the test so that these values can be considered at the point the threshold is reached. As lactate threshold occurs sooner than VO_{2max}, the threshold is often expressed as a percentage of VO_{2max}. The simultaneous measurement of power output during the threshold test also allows the assessment of power output (usually in $W \cdot kg^{-1}$) at the lactate threshold.

How do I compare?

Many cyclists are not that interested in what their actual lactate threshold is. What is important is how fast and long they can ride at a given power output. However, from evaluating a cyclist's power output at his lactate threshold, a sport scientist can determine the potential for success. To be competitive in a race like the Tour de France, a male professional should be able to maintain 5–6 $W \cdot kg^{-1}$ at lactate threshold. This means that if the cyclist weighs 68 kg, he must produce 350–400 W while riding up a key mountain section. Power output data from the Tour de France show that a rider at the front of the peloton produces an average power output of 6.1 $W \cdot kg^{-1}$ for over 20 minutes.

An untrained individual may reach lactate threshold at about 60 per cent VO_{2max}, moderately trained cyclists at 65–80 per cent VO_{2max} and elite endurance cyclists at 85–95 per cent VO_{2max}. These data can then be used to prescribe training. This is discussed in more detail in chapter 5.

Efficiency

What is it?

Efficiency is another sub-maximal variable that is measured routinely in the laboratory. Here, the sport scientist measures the effective work completed on the cycle ergometer (e.g. riding at a set power output) and relates it to the amount of energy required to perform that work. Therefore, as outlined in chapter 1, to become more efficient a cyclist has to use less energy to complete the same amount of work. A higher efficiency will decrease the percentage of VO_{2max} required to sustain a given mechanical work and would thus be advantageous to the endurance cyclist. Efficiency can be reliably calculated using one of two methods: gross body efficiency or delta efficiency, the latter of which is suggested to be more related to muscle efficiency.

How is it measured?

To measure efficiency, it is first necessary to measure oxygen consumed during exercise. For efficiency, this is usually achieved using Douglas bags (large sacks which are used to collect the air that a cyclist breathes out during exercise). Once collected, the relative concentrations of oxygen and carbon dioxide in the bag are measured, following which the volume of gas in the bag is determined. Following this, the concentrations of air in the bag are compared with the gas concentrations of atmospheric air and, subsequently, the amount of oxygen consumed and energy expended can be calculated. The gas collection occurs during the last minute of a 6-minute period of cycling at a constant power output. Often, three to four successive power outputs (e.g. 150 W, 180 W, 210 W and 240 W) are used, with a short rest between them. However, all outputs should ideally be below the lactate threshold. Either a preferred or fixed cadence can be used, but this should be kept constant throughout the test and in any subsequent tests that are completed.

Owing to the effect that changes in body position have on the efficiency measurement, it is important that cyclists use their own bike during the test or have their bike set-up replicated on a laboratory ergometer. These settings should then be used in subsequent tests.

Finally, as with any exercise testing, control of the cyclist's pre-test regimen is an important issue. For example, research has demonstrated that there is an acute reduction in gross efficiency following a period of 60 minutes' cycling at 60 per cent VO_{2max}. This reduction in efficiency was significantly correlated with a lower 5-minute time trial performance. Similarly, there is also some evidence to suggest that muscle damage from high-intensity training might decrease efficiency during subsequent exercise performance. Therefore, it is important for cyclists to have a complete rest on the day before the test and to monitor their training in the days before that. This will allow for complete replication of the pre-test regimen on subsequent test occasions.

How often should I test?

Ideally, this test should be completed three to four times per year.

How do I compare?

Efficiency values reported in the research literature range between 16–28 per cent, with the maximal theoretical efficiency being 30 per cent. As a general rule, untrained individuals tend to be at the lower end of the range, with some values reported for world-class cyclists being at the upper end. However, as suggested in chapter 1, efficiency interacts with performance VO_2 and VO_{2max} to determine performance power output. Some research has suggested that VO_{2max} and gross/delta efficiency are inversely related. This means that when VO_{2max} is low, efficiency is high, and vice versa. Therefore, it is possible that efficiency may compensate for a low VO_{2max} and thus still enable a high level of performance power output to be sustained.

Anaerobic power and capacity tests

What are they?

As suggested in chapter 1, the decisive moments in bike racing are often determined by maximal anaerobic efforts. Similarly, some track cycling is solely reliant on anaerobic energy systems. Sprint efforts require a maximal rate of energy expenditure that must be matched by the rate of energy re-synthesis. Traditionally, within a laboratory setting the 30-second all-out Wingate test has been extensively used to assess this performance ability. Within this test, the cyclist is required to sprint for 30 seconds against a resistance equivalent to a set percentage of their body mass (often 7.5 per cent). From this, the total amount of work produced over the period of time, defined as the anaerobic capacity, is calculated. Additionally, the highest 1-second power output is established and defined as peak power output.

However, track sprints, BMX events and decisive moments during road, cyclo-cross and mountain bike races are often much shorter in duration, lasting 10–15 seconds. Therefore, a laboratory or field test to assess these abilities should be of a similar duration. Consequently, 5- or 6-second sprint tests are often used as they are more reflective of the efforts encountered during cycling performance.

How are they measured?

Within a laboratory setting, sprint tests are often performed on a cycle ergometer with torque being measured at a very high frequency (often 200 Hz) and angular velocity once every pedal revolution. If this degree of sampling frequency is not possible, the minimum recommended is to measure power output once every second. This is now possible with many commercially available power meters, so sprint tests can also be completed on a turbo trainer or on the road.

To ensure repeatability of the test, it is important that factors impacting upon the generation of maximal power are considered. These factors include the gear ratio, the resistance used to sprint against and whether a rolling start is used to commence the test. Additional factors to consider if performing the test on the road include traffic, weather and road conditions.

A 10–20-minute warm-up at a moderate exercise intensity is required before commencing the test. The make-up of this warm-up should be kept constant on all repeated tests. The test should then be performed as an all-out effort with the cyclist remaining in the saddle throughout the test. The test can easily be performed on a turbo trainer, provided that the bike is secured such that the rider can sprint safely on it and that it is correctly calibrated.

If conducting this test on the road, it is best to find a short, steep hill of about 6–8 per cent gradient so that you can sprint up for 5–10 seconds. Start at the bottom of the hill and approach it at a set speed, for example 25 km·h^{-1}. Then sprint up the incline for at least 5–10 seconds. If possible, put a marker on the power meter file at the start and end of the effort.

Upon downloading the data from the power meter head unit, average the power output over the first 5 or 6 seconds of the sprint and look for the highest 1-second average (usually achieved within the first 3 seconds of the test). This can also be done with cadence data. From this, it is possible to calculate features such as peak and average power-to-weight ratio ($W \cdot kg^{-1}$), percentage drop-off in power and the time at which the peak power and cadence occurred.

How often should I test?
This test should be performed three to four times per year.

How do I compare?
There are various 'norm' values against which you can compare your performance. These values are often established from testing lots of cyclists of different abilities. Examples of norm values for a 5-second all-out sprint effort are presented in table 3.2.

Category of cyclist	Average power output ($W \cdot kg^{-1}$)	
	Men	Women
World class (e.g. international professional)	21.86–24.04	17.70–19.42
Exceptional (e.g. domestic professional)	20.23–22.41	16.40–18.13
Excellent (e.g. first category)	18.60–20.78	15.11–16.83
Very good (e.g. second category)	16.97–19.15	13.82–15.54
Good (e.g. third category)	15.07–17.24	12.31–14.03
Untrained (e.g. non-racer)	10.17–12.35	8.43–10.15

TABLE 3.2 Average 5-second sprint power output for different categories of cyclists. (Adapted from Allen H., Coggan A., *Training and Racing with a Power Meter* (Velo Press, 2006))

Critical power
What is it?
Each of the tests described above provides an accurate description of a specific aspect of physiology that is important for cycling performance. Thus, a VO_{2max} test can quantify the upper limit of your aerobic capabilities, a lactate threshold test can quantify the point at which you begin to accumulate lactate and a sprint test can quantify the upper limit of your anaerobic capabilities. However, to get a full picture of your current physiological condition, it is necessary to complete three separate time-consuming and possibly expensive tests. It is also necessary to interpret the results of each of these tests in a cycling context. Such interpretation may require advanced knowledge of both exercise physiology and cycling science.

Critical power testing provides data in a more readily useable form (i.e. power output) that is relevant across (almost) the full range of physiological systems. The critical power model describes power output as a function of time. It is based upon the common sense observation that the length of time for which you can ride is dependent upon how hard you are riding. By establishing for how long you can maintain just three separate power outputs, it is possible to model your power–time relationship. As can

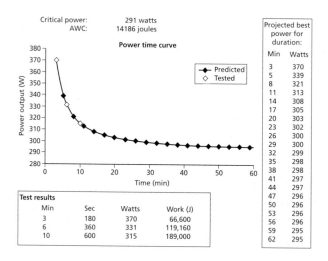

FIG.3.1 A typical power–time curve from which critical power and aerobic capacity can be derived

be seen in figure 3.1, this relationship is described by a curve. This curve can be used directly to establish at which exercise durations weaknesses are present. Subsequent training can then be targeted to increase power output over these specific durations.

The equation of the power–time curve can also be used to quantify both aerobic rate and anaerobic capacity. The linear inverse of time form of this equation is:

$$P = W^1/\, t + \mathrm{CP}$$

This shows that sustainable power output (P) is dependent upon anaerobic capacity (W^1) divided by time (t), added to critical power (CP). Critical power is, in theory, the maximum rate of work that can be sustained for a very long time without fatigue. Critical power is therefore a key characteristic of your aerobic energy supply system. The W^1 ('W prime') component of the model represents a fixed amount of energy that can be provided by anaerobic energy systems. Critical power testing therefore provides valuable information about both the aerobic and anaerobic aspects of physiology. Such testing also provides valuable information about performance capability over a large range of exercise times. Indeed, it is possible to use the power–time curve to predict the power that can be sustained for (almost) any given time period.

How is it measured?

The critical power concept is attractive because it generates valuable information across the range of physiological function using only a reliable cycle ergometer and a stopwatch. The drawback is that multiple maximal all-out efforts are required.

It is possible to derive accurate parameter estimates (i.e. CP and W^1) with just two predicting trials. However, the risk of one 'bad' test skewing results is high; as such, three to five trials are usually recommended. The recovery time between trials might be anything from 30 minutes to 48 hours. In a research setting, ensuring a minimum of 24 hours between trials is probably necessary. However, in a sport science support setting, a 30-minute recovery period is likely sufficient. This is desirable, as it would allow a full critical power test to be completed in a single laboratory visit.

Each of the trials is conducted on a calibrated cycle ergometer (e.g. SRM, Lode), with the participant completing a standard warm-up and warm-down. The duration of each all-out phase should be different in order to provide a good power–time range. Typically, the all-out phase will last between 1–10 minutes, although some researchers have used trials of up to 30 minutes. Data from longer tests will enhance the accuracy of the model, but, of course, such 'long' tests reduce the attractiveness of the critical power approach.

To derive the power–time curve and CP and W' values, the only data required are the mean power outputs for each trial duration. These data are then plotted, as in figure 3.1, and modelled using equation 1 (or an equivalent) (*see* page 48).

How often should I test?
This test should be performed three to four times per year.

How do I compare?
Critical power has been shown to correlate well with various 'threshold' measures, although it is usually a little higher. For example, critical power has been shown to be 28 per cent higher than lactate threshold and 13 per cent higher than anaerobic threshold. In general, values are similar to those described for functional threshold power below (*see* page 52). In trained cyclists, critical power has been reported to fall within the range 230–310 W, while W' has been reported to fall within the range 15–25 kJ.

FIELD TESTING
Lamberts sub-maximal cycle test (LSCT)
What is it?
To develop your fitness, you have to push your limits and then take time to recover to allow your body time to adapt. The problem that most people encounter is how to ascertain when full recovery has taken place. Leave the bike alone for too long and you may reduce the benefits of each training ride, but if you train too early, you will be tired.

The perception of how hard a training ride feels is a key factor that should not be ignored. If you use a heart-rate monitor regularly, you will know this. There may be days when you feel like you are flying, but heart rates can vary by many beats. Likewise, for the same heart rates on other days it can be a gruesome struggle to keep the heart rate close to target values. This is similar for many physiological variables, and it is only when you line these variables up with your perception of effort that you can make any significant judgements about your current training and health status. The Lamberts sub-maximal cycle test (LSCT) can be used to monitor training status and detect symptoms of overreaching.

How is it measured?

The test lasts for 17 minutes and can be completed as part of a training ride or at home on the turbo trainer. During the test, the cyclist is required to ride at different intensities based upon heart rate. The test has three stages requiring you to achieve a heart rate of 60 per cent, 80 per cent and 90 per cent of maximum. The rider's preferred cadence can be used and gears selected as required. The main target is to achieve target heart rate (within 1 beat·min⁻¹) for the duration of each stage. Immediately after stage three, stop cycling and continue to record heart rate for 90 seconds. Table 3.3 shows the LSCT protocol.

Stage	Duration (minutes)	Target heart rate (% maximum heart rate)
1	6	60%
2	6	80%
3	3	90%
4	1.5	Recovery

TABLE 3.3 The Lamberts sub-maximal cycle test protocol

During the last 30 seconds of each work stage, you need to rate how hard you find the exercise; that is, how hard, heavy and strenuous the exercise feels.

The perception of effort depends on how hard you are driving your legs, how heavy your breathing is and the overall sensation of how strenuous the exercise is. It does *not* depend on muscle pain (i.e. the aching and burning sensation in your leg or arm muscles). The rating of perceived exertion (RPE) scale is used because it recognises the non-linear response of many physiological variables (e.g. blood lactate) and therefore provides a good indicator of overall effort. Looking at the rating scale (*see* table 3.4), where 6 means 'no exertion at all' and 20 means 'maximal exertion':

- 9 corresponds to 'very light' exercise, for example turning a light gear slowly at your preferred cadence for some minutes;
- 13 on the scale is 'somewhat hard' exercise, but it still feels OK to continue;
- 17 is 'very hard' or 'very strenuous exercise' – you can still go on, but you really have to push yourself (it feels very heavy and you are very tired) and
- 19 on the scale is 'extremely hard' exercise.

You should try to appraise your feelings of exertion as honestly as possible without thinking about what the actual physical load is (heart rate, speed, power output or level of intensity). Care should be taken not to underestimate or overestimate perception of exertion. This scale aims to assess the individual's feeling of effort, not how it compares with others.

If you have a heart-rate monitor or power meter, this should be used to collect data throughout the test. Upon downloading the heart rate, speed, power and cadence

6	No exertion at all
7	
	Extremely light
8	
9	Very light
10	
11	Light
12	
13	Somewhat hard
14	
15	Hard (heavy)
16	
17	Very hard
18	
19	Extremely hard
20	Maximal exertion

TABLE 3.4 The Borg Scale for ratings of perceived exertion. From Borg, G., *Borg's Perceived Exertion and Pain Scales*, (Human Kinetics, 1998).

data, the first minute of data from each stage should be excluded. This is because it takes the heart time to respond to changes in power output and it will be hard to exactly hit the required heart rate straight away. Next, calculate your average heart rate over the remaining 5-minute period for each of the first two stages, 2 minutes for stage three and the 90-second heart rate recovery period. Also, your RPE score for each of the three stages should be recorded. These values should be stored so that, when the test is performed repeatedly over a period of a few months/years, a database of changes in power output, speed and/or RPE can be collated. These data can then be used to track changes in your fitness and level of training status. For example, as training status improves, heart rate decreases during exercise at a similar work rate. Therefore, from repeated LSCTs conducted over a period of training, the same percentage of maximum heart rate would elicit an increase in recorded power output or speed. Research studies that have investigated overtraining in athletic populations have shown decreased sub-maximal and maximal heart rates in a chronically fatigued state. Therefore, in the LSCT, this might manifest as an increased power output during stages two and three of the test as the pre-determined submaximal heart rates would be harder to achieve; RPE would also be much higher.

The average power output during stages two and three in the LSCT has been related to performance parameters such as 40 km time trial performance. Therefore, an increase in the mean power output from stages two and three of the test with no change, or a decrease in RPE, might be suggestive of changes in training status and an increased level of fitness.

One of the key areas to consider in the data is your heart-rate recovery. This has been used as a marker of bodily stress and training-induced chronic fatigue (it takes longer to recover when you are in this state) and of training status (it is quicker the fitter you are). So, within the LSCT, if heart rate is lower during exercise for a given power output but normal in the recovery stage, this might indicate that you have a bit of residual fatigue but that you will normally recover quickly. If your heart rate is lower in both the exercise and recovery components of the test, this might indicate longer-lasting fatigue or overreaching. You will have a natural variation in heart-rate recovery of roughly 5 beats·min[-1], but this is smaller than has been reported for changes as a result of improved training status.

Collectively, the combination of changes in power output, RPE and heart-rate recovery provided by the LSCT provide an effective tool to monitor the balance between your training load and recovery. It can therefore help you to achieve the optimal level of training status.

How often should I test?

Ideally, you should perform this test once a week, normally the day after a rest day.

Functional threshold power (FTP)
What is it?

As discussed above, there are many definitions of 'threshold'. In a laboratory setting, lactate threshold is the most widely used and perhaps the most biologically justifiable threshold. It is possible to conduct lactate threshold testing outside of the laboratory. Indeed, many coaches conduct such testing using turbo trainers and (relatively) inexpensive portable lactate analysers. However, individual cyclists are unlikely to be in a fit state to take their own blood during self-administered lactate threshold tests.

The work of Ed Coyle and colleagues in the late 1980s and early 1990s demonstrated that performance in a laboratory-based 1-hour time trial was highly correlated with a 'real' road-based 40 km time trial performance. Of course, this is unsurprising, given that the two performances are almost identical. Nevertheless, the maximal mean power output that can be maintained for 1 hour is also closely correlated with various (more 'scientific') thresholds. The highest power output that a cyclist can maintain in a quasi-steady state without fatiguing for approximately one hour is therefore a valid field-based measure of threshold. Andrew Coggan named this alternative as functional threshold power (FTP).

How is it measured?

Hunter Allen and Andrew Coggan have described several methods to estimate FTP from an analysis of training and racing data. However, the most accurate FTP values are determined during dedicated testing. From the definition of FTP given above, the best way to determine your FTP is to simply record your power output during a maximal 1-hour time-trial. This is the 'gold-standard' method and so, where possible, should be the method of choice. Of course, such a test is time consuming and both physically and mentally very demanding. For these reasons, Allen and Coggan have described an alternative threshold test.

The threshold test begins with a 30-minute moderate pace (i.e. 65 per cent maximum heart rate) warm-up that should include three 1-minute fast pedalling (i.e. 100 rev·min⁻¹) efforts between minutes 20 and 25. Next comes a 5-minute all-out effort to dispense of leg 'freshness'. This is followed by a further 10 minutes at moderate pace, which leads into the main part of the test, a maximal all-out 20-minute time trial. The goal during this phase is to produce the highest possible average power. Here, pacing is very important; it is not a sprint test. Finally, the test is completed with 15 minutes at a moderate pace and a further 15 minutes of easy warm-down.

Having downloaded your test data, determine your average power for the 20-minute time trial phase of the test. Then subtract 5 per cent from this number to give your FTP to a high degree of precision.

As with any type of fitness testing, it is important to be consistent when measuring your FTP. The difference between optimal training and overtraining is likely to be no more than a handful of watts. Therefore, it is important that your tests are as accurate and reliable as possible. To maximise this reliability, it is important to test under similar conditions each time. Try to stick with either the turbo trainer or the same stretch of flat road for every test. Try to have a similar training load (preferably zero) in the 24 hours before the test. Also, try to avoid repeat testing in very different weather conditions.

How often should I test?

The required frequency of testing will depend on your training status. The FTP of 'new' cyclists will increase rapidly, necessitating regular testing to ensure that training zones remain appropriate. The FTP of a more experienced cyclist will change to a lesser degree and so testing need not be quite so frequent. Nevertheless, the threshold test can be carried out far more frequently than the (usually) costly laboratory tests described above. For most, six FTP tests per year will be sufficient to ensure that training zones remain accurate, while not being so many as to induce 'test fatigue'.

How do I compare?

Within any racing category there will be a wide range of FTPs on display. This reflects the fact that performance is dependent on many factors other than threshold. Nevertheless, Allen and Coggan have provided FTP values for comparison across the range from the untrained cyclist through to the world-class professional. For example, FTP values (divided by kg bodyweight in order to minimise the impact of different body sizes) are below 2.58 W·kg⁻¹ in untrained cyclists, between 3.47 and 4.18 W·kg⁻¹ in category 3 racers and above 6.40 W·kg⁻¹ in world-class professionals (*see* figure 3.2).

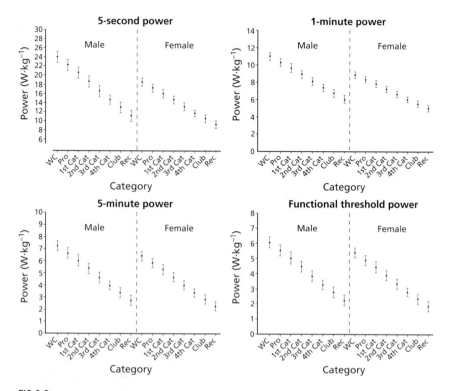

FIG.3.2 Power-to-weight ratio over set durations at all levels of road cycling. (Adapted from Allen, H., Coggan, A., *Training and Racing with a Power Meter* (Velo Press, 2006))

The power profile

What is it?

Cycle sport comprises a wide range of events, from short track sprints to ultra-endurance races. The physiology and psychology required to excel at these extremes are very different. As such, most cyclists tend to gravitate towards one type of riding based on their actual and/or perceived strengths. While a high 5-second sprint power is a prerequisite for sprint success and a high FTP is a prerequisite for time trial success, many cycling events require a good mix of physiological abilities. For example, road racing requires both sustained effort at threshold power (e.g. during breakaways) and frequent short sprint efforts (out of corners, etc.). While it is natural (easier and, therefore, more enjoyable) to focus on strengths, for many the greatest performance gains will be achieved by focusing on weaknesses. By establishing your peak performance over a range of durations, a 'performance profile' approach can provide vital information about where you should focus your training.

How is it measured?

A range of test durations has been used by researchers to develop performance profiles. Mark Quod and colleagues evaluated the power profile of professional cyclists using six test durations from 5 seconds to 600 seconds. Similarly, Allen and Coggan described a power profile test that evaluates maximal performance over durations of five seconds, 1 minute and 5 minutes. Following a 45-minute warm-up (including a 5-minute effort at FTP and three 1-minute fast pedalling efforts), the test begins with a 5-minute all-out (i.e. maximal) effort. This is followed by: 10 minutes of recovery at endurance pace, 1 minute all-out, 5 minutes of recovery, 1 minute all-out, 5 minutes of recovery, 15 seconds all-out, 2 minutes of recovery and 15 seconds all-out. Finally, the test is completed with an easy warm-down lasting at least 15 minutes.

Having completed the test, download your test data and find your highest power outputs for durations of 5 seconds, 1 minute and 5 minutes. Finally, combine these with the result of your FTP test to give your power profile.

How often should I test?

A power profile test should be completed three to five times per year.

How do I compare?

There is no physiological reason for selecting the specific test durations described by Allen and Coggan. Indeed, the alternative profile used by Quod and colleagues has been shown to be ecologically valid (i.e. to be an accurate measure of real-world performance). However, the only available power profile tables for the complete range of cycling abilities uses Allen and Coggan's 5–1–5–60 profile. Untrained cyclists might have the following profile (see figure 3.2): 5 seconds = 10.17 $W \cdot kg^{-1}$; 1 minute = 5.64 $W \cdot kg^{-1}$; 5 minutes = 2.33 $W \cdot kg^{-1}$; and 60 minutes = 1.86 $W \cdot kg^{-1}$. At the other end of the scale, a world-class professional cyclist might exhibit the following profile: 5 seconds = 24.04 $W \cdot kg^{-1}$; 1 minute = 11.50 $W \cdot kg^{-1}$; 5 minutes = 7.60 $W \cdot kg^{-1}$; and 60 minutes = 6.40 $W \cdot kg^{-1}$. Of course, any single cyclist is unlikely to exhibit such maximums across the full profile range.

SUMMARY

Laboratory or field-based physiological testing can be used to provide both athletes and their coaches with useful feedback about the relative strengths and weaknesses of the athlete and about the success of the training programme. The value of these physiological assessments to cyclists and their coaches, and the use that can be made of the data collected, depends on the reliability of the tests in question. If the tests are not reliable, the data they provide are more or less meaningless. Therefore, strict standardisation procedures should be followed both before and during the testing session.

Laboratory-based fitness assessments should be conducted between three and four times per year and should form the basis on which training programmes are developed. This is because of the need for specialised laboratory-based equipment and the precision that can be obtained in a carefully controlled, standardised environment. Direct comparisons can then be made between repeated testing sessions over significant periods of time.

DETRAINING

At the end of a targeted race, training cycle or complete season, cyclists often reduce their activity level or stop training altogether. According to the principle of training reversibility, insufficient training or training cessation results in a partial or complete loss of the adaptations and fitness that were gained over the season. Parameters such as VO_{2max} and blood volume can decrease 10–15 days after a cyclist stops training (*see* figure 4.4) and continue in a downward linear fashion for about six to eight weeks. They then typically stabilise at a level that is usually higher than that of people who don't exercise. Cyclists and their coaches should be aware that detraining implies increased heart rates at sub-maximal and maximal intensities and also during recovery. From a metabolic viewpoint, a cyclist's reliance on carbohydrate as a fuel source during exercise increases even after very short periods of no training (e.g. three days). It is then of paramount importance to implement nutritional strategies for non-training periods, even of quite short duration. Indeed, two weeks of training stoppage in endurance athletes brings about conditions that favour fat tissue storage.

Lactate metabolism is also affected by training cessation. After only a few days without training, highly trained athletes respond to sub-maximal exercise of the same absolute intensity with higher blood lactate concentrations (i.e. a drop in the lactate threshold). In addition, very short-term (five-day) periods of no training are enough to bring glycogen levels towards sedentary values.

Cyclists' muscles are also affected when training is insufficient or stopped. The number of muscle capillaries per muscle fibre can decrease after about two to three weeks of no training and, although muscle fibre distribution remains unchanged during the initial weeks of training cessation, there may be a decreased proportion of slow-twitch fibres in endurance athletes after eight weeks of training cessation. All this implies that your muscles will have a lower ability to produce the energy they need for high-intensity cycling. While this is part of the normal yearly training cycle, it is important to appreciate that you won't be right back to peak season levels when you re-commence your cycle training. Start back slow and steady using the principles

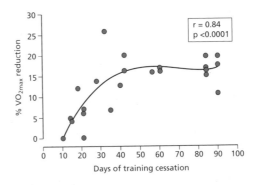

FIG.4.4 Relationship between the number of days of training cessation and the percentage loss in maximal oxygen uptake (VO_{2max}) in athletes. (Adapted from Mujika, I., Padilla, S. 'Physiological and performance consequences of training cessation in athletes: detraining'. In: Frontera, W.R. (ed.) *Rehabilitation of Sports Injuries: Scientific Basis*, (Wiley-Blackwell, 2003))

outlined in this chapter and it won't be long before you're back cranking out the high-power outputs we all love to push. If you want to limit the off-season loss of fitness, a cross-training programme (i.e. doing some non-bike training, such as swimming or hiking) could be of benefit.

SUMMARY

The goal of any cycle training programme is to progressively increase the training load by manipulating the intensity, duration and frequency of training as well as the recovery between training sessions. This training periodisation, or how such variables are organised, can be achieved using traditional or block periodisation methods. Overall, successful cycle training programmes tend to organise the training intensity in a polarised manner, where 80 per cent of training tends to be performed below the first ventilatory or lactate threshold and the remaining 20 per cent performed at or above this intensity marker.

The final ingredient in any successful training programme, performed just before a key event, is the taper, a marked reduction in the training load. Optimal performance gains during a cycling taper are maximised when training intensity is maintained but training volume is reduced. After the peak performance of the year, cyclists typically perform less training or stop training altogether, a process that may lead to detraining. Such practice is probably beneficial for the psychological health of the athlete, but a number of physiological markers are known to diminish. These will return slowly for the rider once the training programme cycle starts up again.

KEY TAKE-HOME MESSAGES

- A training programme for cycling should progressively increase the training load by manipulating the intensity, duration and frequency of training and recovery between cycle training sessions.
- Training periodisation, or how the intensity, duration and frequency of cycle training are organised in a programme, can be achieved using traditional or block periodisation methods.
- Successful cycle training programmes tend to organise the training intensity in a polarised model of training distribution, where 80 per cent of training is performed below ventilatory or lactate threshold and the remaining 20 per cent is performed at or above this intensity.
- The taper is a marked reduction in training load in a cyclist's programme and has been shown to be maximised when training intensity is maintained but training volume is reduced by 21–60 per cent.
- Periods of insufficient training have a negative impact on a cyclist's physiology and performance capabilities. These changes need to be kept in mind when cyclists return to full training.

CHAPTER 5

TRAINING WITH HEART RATE AND POWER

Dan Henchy and Helen Carter

'What gets measured, gets managed.' *Peter Drucker*

The growing popularity of high-tech bike computers and performance analysis software perfectly illustrates the growing influence of sport science on the cycling world. Arguably, this growth has not been matched by an understanding of the best use of these tools. It's important to remember that global positioning system (GPS) units, heart-rate monitors and power meters are just that – 'tools'. Benefit comes only from mastering their use; that is, having a clear idea of what the data means and, equally, does not mean.

A word of advice: all of these tools should complement, not replace, 'feel'. It is still important for an athlete to be attuned to the sensory feedback from his body and to be conscious of the signals in response to his efforts.

WHY MONITOR TRAINING?

Before examining how best to make use of the technology at your disposal, it's important to explain why the developments of the last 20 years have been beneficial. After all, cyclists were performing incredible feats long before the advent of even the most basic heart-rate monitor.

Training load

First, as explained in chapter 4, a successful training plan involves a careful manipulation of training load and subsequent recovery. Balancing training and recovery allows the highest possible level of performance to coincide with the most important competition or event. A big part of this is being able to accurately track training load: the key training principles of progression, specificity and overload are impossible to implement without this information. Training load comprises volume (session frequency x duration) and intensity. Training volume is simple to track: hours or miles per week are sound indicators of training volume. However, the same volume can be made up of very different types of riding. Take two athletes completing 200 miles per week of training: one could be riding 200 miles at a leisurely pace while the other rides at as fast a pace as possible. It is clear that the training effect of each athlete's programme would not be the same. We need a measure of the *relative* intensity of each programme to be able to discern between them.

While the concept of pace can be used (slow versus fast) in general, this is a poor measure of intensity for cyclists. Changes in conditions such as riding terrain, weather conditions (especially wind) and equipment make the link between riding speed and intensity a tenuous one. Remember that important concept of *feel*. A simple description of how hard an effort or ride was to complete is an improvement in monitoring intensity. Many successful athletes have used training plans based on descriptive phrases of effort such as easy, steady, hard and maximal. Indeed, this concept has been formalised using a rating of perceived exertion for each session (sRPE), where each training session is ranked on a scale of 1–10 based on the perception of effort required to complete the session. However, there are still limitations to this method, as follows:

- **subjective**: the judgement of how an effort feels is unique to the individual – one cyclist's 'steady' may be another cyclist's 'hard';
- **motivation**: sRPE and feel are based on perception and so are affected just as much by an athlete's mood and level of motivation as they are by the training intensity; and
- **comparison**: linked to the two previous points, using feel to rate training intensity allows little scope for comparison, either between two separate athletes, or more importantly, between multiple training sessions performed by the same individual.

Careful use of a heart-rate monitor and/or power meter addresses all of the above issues and makes it easy to quantify training intensity and, therefore, to accurately track an athlete's training load.

Individuality

Despite years of research into the optimal training methods for peak performance, it remains clear that the response to a training stimulus is highly individual. The same training session will affect each athlete in a different way, in part because of the variability in the gene sequences inherited from one's parents. Just as differences in our genetic code can influence characteristics such as height, eye colour, susceptibility to illness and so on, they can also determine how an athlete will respond to a given training load. Add in the confounding factors of training history, lifestyle stressors and nutrition, and it becomes clear that there can be no 'one size fits all' approach to cycling training. Collecting and monitoring training and performance data on an athlete can prove invaluable in establishing if the training plan is having the desired effect. Race (or event) results and performances can help in this regard, but judging your own personal performance against that of others can be fraught. For example, was your win attributable to poor performances by others, or did you set a slow time because of unfavourable weather conditions? Systematic analysis of historical data allows objective judgement on what works and what doesn't and on the possible increments in performance that can be expected for different training blocks.

The scientific method

A central tenet to analysing training data and the real scientific underpinning of training is the scientific method: treating cycling training as a scientific experiment. As discussed in chapters 1 and 2, exercise physiologists have studied the event demands of different cycling disciplines, rigorously analysing data on participants in the various cycling events and establishing the key performance indicators. This information gives us a clear picture of what it takes to succeed in a given event and provides the endpoint for where the training plan should aim.

To find the starting point, the cyclist's current fitness level needs to be assessed. This can take the form of a period of field testing or by undertaking a full physiological assessment with a sport scientist. Either option has its relative merits, but what is important is to choose a test battery that will encapsulate the key factors for success in the target event. For example, a cyclist training for a 100-mile bike ride will probably best be served by an assessment of his lactate threshold rather than his peak sprint power (*see* chapter 3 for more details on testing).

Following the above approach, you will develop a good idea of where you are now and where you need to be for success in your chosen event; the gap between these two is what the training plan aims to bridge. Along the way it is important to keep measuring progress towards the target level of fitness. A six-month build-up may consist of six 4-week blocks (or mesocycles) allowing a couple of weeks to freshen up, or taper, before the event. Each mesocycle should have a clear objective and this objective should be measurable (*see* chapter 4 for further discussion of how to plan your training programme). For these intermediate targets, it is perhaps unreasonable and unnecessary to schedule further laboratory testing or to disrupt the training process in favour of repeating your specific field-testing protocol. What is needed is a measurement tool that allows careful tracking of your progress during your training sessions. This is the real benefit of the popular availability of power meters: every session becomes a 'test', leading to fast identification of problems and changes required in the training plan.

Motivation

All athletes like to see the fruits of their labour manifested in improved performances. In the race season, results offer frequent opportunities to measure progress and check on form compared with the competition. In the off-season, it becomes easy to lose heart and motivation with a lack of evidence of progress. Laboratory testing and training data can help by providing clear and regular feedback. For those athletes training with a power meter, every training session becomes an opportunity to judge how well they are doing. Over time, the database of sessions will allow comparison of current form with previous weeks or even previous seasons, helping to make sure that progress is being made towards the main goals and events.

During the season, use of performance outcome alone to evaluate 'success' is risky. In timed events, weather and other environmental conditions such as road surface can make direct comparisons meaningless. Similarly, judging against the opposition can be equally fraught with dangers: it is impossible to know whether opponents are having a good/bad day, whether they are in a different phase of the training season or even how hard they are trying. Ultimately, success in a target event may depend on beating others, but giving too much credence to relative performance early in the season or during build-up events can prove detrimental.

Communication

The coach–athlete relationship is based on effective communication and nowhere is this more evident than in the management of the athlete's training plan. An objective measure of intensity allows the coach to set clear session outlines without the risk of the athlete misinterpreting what is meant by 'hard' or 'steady'. Equally, it provides a level of accountability and an opportunity for feedback on how the training session went. Also, it is not uncommon for coach and athlete to live far apart. Careful analysis of a training file from a heart-rate monitor, power meter or GPS unit allows the coach to closely relive the session. This is discussed in more detail in chapter 18.

HEART-RATE MONITORING

Heart-rate monitoring was first made possible over 200 years ago with the invention of the stethoscope. Next came the development of the somewhat 'bulky' electrocardiogram machines in the early 1900s, and the wrist-worn wireless heart-rate monitor by the 1980s. Fast-forward 30 years and heart-rate monitors are now capable of measuring and storing huge amounts of data.

The physiological basis of heart-rate monitoring

In the laboratory, a sport scientist would measure oxygen consumption as a means of assessing the energy requirements of a bout of exercise or the amount of stress that the body's systems are under. Such measurements require expensive laboratory-based equipment that is impractical for the real world – there's a good reason why you don't see many people racing or training with a mouthpiece to measure VO_2.

Oxygen is transported from our lungs to our muscles bound to haemoglobin in our bloodstream. Greater oxygen demands in the muscle require more blood to be pumped to the muscles, which is achieved by the heart beating more frequently. Therefore, by measuring heart rate we are indirectly estimating oxygen consumption.

Making this link between oxygen use and heart rate relies on a number of key assumptions, which are perfectly valid under most 'normal' circumstances. However, there are a number of factors that can cause this relationship to break down, as follows:

- **Fatigue**: fatigue in cyclists can result from a number of causes (e.g. glycogen depletion, muscular damage, altered nervous system function), each having a different impact on an athlete's heart-rate response. In general, as your individual muscle fibres fatigue, you are forced to recruit increasingly from your fast-twitch muscle fibre pool. These fibres are less adapted to aerobic exercise and so require a greater amount of oxygen to develop the same work rate. This is not necessarily a bad thing – the aerobic characteristics of these fibres can be improved through training (particularly the characteristics of the fast oxidative glycolytic fibres).

- **Heat:** just as blood carries oxygen, it also carries heat. Increasing blood flow to the skin allows (with the help of evaporating sweat) this heat to be removed from the body. This extra blood flow is additional to that required by the working muscles, so heart rate must increase to meet this demand.
- **Plasma volume:** the blood volume is made up of the blood cells and plasma. Under certain conditions, the plasma volume may shrink (when dehydrated) or expand (with improved training status), thus changing the relationship of heart rate and intensity.

These confounding factors have led to criticism of the use of heart-rate monitoring by a number of coaches and athletes. In many cases the heart-rate monitor has been abandoned as a training tool. Unfortunately, this approach ignores what can be a rich data source; with a little awareness, an unexpected heart-rate response can be the first sign that something is amiss.

Using a heart-rate monitor

In practice, successful use of a heart-rate monitor is based on a few key principles. The first of these is a need to 'anchor' readings against an individual's physiology; riding at

Domain	Lower boundary	Upper boundary	% VO_{2max}	Physiology
Moderate	Rest	Lactate threshold	Up to ~60%	VO_2 and HR stable and BLa close to resting values
Heavy	Lactate threshold	MLSS	60–80%	VO_2, HR and BLa elevated but still in steady state
Very heavy	MLSS	CP	75–90%	Presence of a progressive drift in VO_2, HR and BLa
Severe	CP	VO_{2max}	85–100%	Drift in VO_2, HR and BLa leading to maximum values
Supra-max	VO_{2max}	Peak power	100–200%	Unable to sustain exercise long enough to hit maximum values

BLa = blood lactate; CP = critical power; HR = heart rate; MLSS = maximal lactate steady state; VO_2 = oxygen consumption; VO_{2max} = maximal oxygen consumption

TABLE 5.1 The exercise intensity domains

Zone	Domain	Training session type	Approximate % of maximum heart rate
Recovery	Moderate	Short rides (non-training) for recovery	<60
Zone 1	Moderate	Long rides of up to 6 hours used in development of economy, efficiency and fat use	60–65
Zone 2	Moderate	Long rides of up to 4 hours; moderate stress work important in establishing a firm endurance base	65–75
Zone 3	Heavy	2–3 hours maximum used to develop aerobic capacity and endurance; important to stay in zone for maximum payback	75–82
Zone 4	Very heavy	Up to 1 hour; typical 'mean' intensity of most road races; useful for race preparation; sessions should be ended when the effort starts to tell	82–89
Zone 5	Severe	Sessions of up to 40 minutes will see improvement of lactate clearance and adaptation to race speed	89–94
Zone 6	Supra-max	Accumulating 20 minutes of work through high-intensity interval training; essential in increasing maximum power and improving lactate production or clearance	94–100

TABLE 5.2 The exercise training zones and their relation to the intensity domains. Note: There is also a seventh zone for neuromuscular-type training: we might think of it as sprint work. It is often excluded from tables like this because it cannot be prescribed using heart rate.

160 beats·min^{-1} may be a steady pace for one rider and a maximal effort for another. What is needed is a means of anchoring the heart rate to known landmarks unique to the individual athlete. The exercise intensity domains (*see* table 5.1) are the exercise physiologist's framework for dividing up the whole spectrum of intensities. Each domain possesses a unique physiological characteristic, based on standard laboratory measures of heart rate, oxygen uptake and blood lactate.

The exercise training zones are the conceptual equivalent but translated from the language of the laboratory into the real world of the athlete and coach. Table 5.2 shows how the exercise training zones are anchored around the intensity domains. Some coaches and training manuals work on systems based around fewer zones, but it is clear that, for a system based on actual physiological measures, all six are needed.

Given that these training zones are based around specific laboratory measures of various thresholds and physiological breakpoints, it becomes clear that undertaking a full physiological assessment is the best way of identifying these zones and ensuring that they truly are an accurate representation of an athlete's underlying physiology. Failing that, the training zones can be estimated from simple-to-perform field tests (discussed in chapter 3). A similar approach can be followed using maximum heart rate, but care must be taken to measure a true maximum: estimates based on age can significantly under- or overestimate the true value.

The second key to successful application of heart-rate monitoring is in pacing effort. With a thorough understanding of your training zones and a little experience of the kind of heart rates that you can maintain for efforts of different durations, it becomes fairly straightforward to ensure you hit the correct level of effort. This can be applied both to races and to training sessions, particularly for efforts in excess of 10 minutes. However, it is important to be aware of the delay in heart-rate response to a rise in intensity. It can take several minutes for the heart rate to react to a given increase in work rate. The danger is that the cyclist pushes too hard at the start of an effort to lift the heart rate to the required level, only to find that the early overexertion leads to a drop in work rate by the end of the session or interval. For this reason, it is often best to pace the early part of an effort based entirely on perception of effort and then use heart rate to fine-tune the level after things have settled down.

THE LONG RIDE

The long ride is a perfect session to guide effort with a heart-rate monitor. The cyclist is simply tasked by the coach to ride at an intensity that keeps his heart rate in a narrow band (perhaps 5–10 beats·min^{-1}) around the first lactate threshold heart rate (see chapter 3, page 43). If the heart rate rises above the target zone, the athlete simply eases off; if the heart rate is too low, the athlete must work harder to return to the target zone.

During such a ride, a number of the factors discussed in this chapter that cause the relationship between heart rate and intensity to break down may come into effect. Dehydration, increasing temperature or the fatigue of individual muscle fibres may cause the heart rate to rise; the athlete may need to back off to avoid his heart rate rising out of the zone. Alternatively, depleted muscle glycogen stores or fatigued motor units may lead to a drop in cadence and difficulty in elevating the heart rate; now the athlete needs to push harder to stay in the zone. Either way, the athlete may notice a change in speed or find that a gear that was easy at the start of the ride is suddenly a struggle. On varying terrain or in changeable wind, this might be difficult to discern, although you will likely be able to feel it. (Remember the warning at the start of the chapter: how a session feels should never be discounted. Every cyclist knows that feeling at the end of the ride when things are starting to get a little laboured and every little rise feels like a mountain.) What is really needed is an objective measure of work rate; thankfully, the power meter provides just that.

When training with a heart-rate monitor, it is vital to maintain good self-awareness. Because of the assumptions in using heart rate as a proxy for oxygen consumption, it is unwise to blindly accept that, if heart rate is in the correct zone, the session is going well. Changes in the sensations of the ride should be cross-checked with the heart-rate response and careful consideration of fatigue levels and environmental conditions should be made to ensure that the link between heart rate and intensity is still valid. For an example of how these principles might be applied in practice, *see* the example of the 'long ride' on page 72.

MONITORING POWER OUTPUT
The key concept

Power is defined as force divided by time and is measured in watts. To increase power, more force can be applied or developed over a shorter period of time (or both). It is important to stress that power is different from both strength and speed. Strength is a quality that does not involve movement – an iron girder supporting a bridge has tremendous strength but no movement (hopefully!), so it makes no sense to talk about a powerful girder. Similarly, a cyclist freewheeling downhill may be travelling at great speed but the only force in action is gravity, so again the notion of power is vacuous. However, a very powerful action is both forceful and fast.

Why is power important?

In the previous section we introduced power as an objective measure of work rate. This is the real key to understanding the benefits of a power meter (*see* table 5.3 for the pros and cons of measuring power output compared to heart rate). For a cyclist, riding at 200 W is riding at 200 W, regardless of terrain, weather, fatigue or any other factors affecting performance (provided the meter is correctly calibrated; *see* page 75). That 200 W may 'buy' 10 mph going uphill or 30 mph going downhill; it may feel incredibly easy for a fit cyclist without much fatigue, or it may require a maximal effort for a less fit individual at the end of a long ride. However, all else being equal, it is power that determines how fast an athlete propels his bicycle. Consideration of all the forces acting on a bicycle gives rise to the equation below. Essentially, the power you produce must overcome wind resistance (drag), inertia, the rolling resistance of the tyres, the force of gravity when moving uphill and any other resistive forces, such as drive-train friction.

$$Power = Velocity * [Drag + Inertial + Rolling]_{Force} + \frac{(Gravity)_{work} + (Misc)_{work}}{\Delta time}$$

How do we monitor power?

There are a number of different devices on the market for monitoring power. Without going into details on individual models, there are some broad differences to look at.

Once these are considered, the decision becomes that faced by a consumer in any market, determined by price, quality, availability and so on.

Measured versus derived power

One major difference among power meters is in the way in which the computer arrives at the power output that it displays on the screen. Most popular power meters make use of a careful array of strain gauges to measure an element of distortion in a component of the drive train caused by the cyclist applying force to the pedals. Careful calibration of the power meter allows this level of measured strain to be used to calculate the amount of torque produced. Remember that power is torque multiplied by velocity. So, by combining this torque with the speed at which the component is moving, it is possible to derive the power output being generated by the rider.

Alternatively, some systems do not directly measure the quantities involved, instead measuring other aspects of the bicycle's motion or mechanics and back-calculating the power output that would result in these measurements. In general, these systems have been shown to be less accurate and less reliable than direct measures of power output. However, these systems do tend to be slightly less expensive. Of course, there is little value in saving money but ending up with a power meter that may not give trustworthy readings and that may not offer any more benefit than training based on feel.

Crank-based versus hub-based (versus pedal-based) systems

Of those power meters that actually measure power, we can further sub-divide them into where on the bicycle the measurement actually takes place, namely crank-based or hub-based systems. Pedal-based systems are in the late stages of development and will soon add a third option (in practice, the pros and cons are unlikely to differ much from existing crank-based options, apart from maybe ease of movement between different bikes).

Pros	Cons
Completely objective measure of performance: unaffected by environmental factors	More expensive
Instant feedback: power is an instant measure of work rate as opposed to heart rate, which takes time to rise to indicate effort level	'Paralysis by analysis': some athletes can easily become too focused on the numbers at the expense of performance
Allows tracking of performance level	It is easy to become accepting of your current level and never take the risk to break through to a new level

TABLE 5.3 Pros and cons of monitoring power (compared with heart rate)

Crank-based options are ideal in that they allow the use of many different combinations of wheel, whereas hub-based systems are built into a specific wheel. This may not be a problem for many cyclists, but for some (racing cyclists in particular), choosing the correct wheels for the conditions is vitally important, and a crank-based system allows choice of wheels and valuable data to be collected. On the other hand, hub-based systems allow easy transfer between bikes, for example from training to racing bike. However, modern bottom bracket and chainset set-ups are relatively straightforward and swapping a crank-based power meter is not the hassle it once was. For infrequent moving between bikes, this is perhaps not a major factor in choosing between different types, but careful consideration is needed about your individual requirements before settling on the correct model.

Power meter basics
Calibration
The power meter is useful only as long as it is collecting accurate, reliable data. Regular and correct calibration is essential for this. A little more detail on how the power meter arrives at the figure on the display helps motivate the need for calibration and explains this procedure. Output from the strain gauges comes in the form of an electrical signal, the frequency of which varies according to the level of strain. The calibration process provides a conversion from the frequency output of the strain gauges to an equivalent level of torque. A number of known torque values are applied to the power meter (i.e. hanging a known mass from the crank arms) and the corresponding frequency signals noted. Plotting the range of values gives rise to a linear relationship, the slope of which provides the conversion from frequency to torque. In general, this relationship is fairly stable, so the calibration process need be performed only roughly once per season (the off-season break is perfect for this). The exact procedure varies according to the different meters available.

Any linear relationship is described by two parameters: a slope (or gradient) and an intercept. The relationship between frequency and torque in your power meter is no different. Zeroing the offset is a procedure common to all power meters and is essentially an insurance that the linear relationship between frequency and power is such that the power meter reads zero when there is no power applied to the pedals. Whereas the slope of the power meter tends to be fairly consistent over time, the offset does have a tendency to drift, so it is vital to ensure that this is adjusted before every ride. Factors such as large temperature variations can also affect this parameter, so it may even be worth re-checking mid-ride.

Anchoring
Just like when using a heart-rate monitor, it is important to anchor the power output to an athlete's physiological profile. Again, laboratory testing is preferable, but field tests can also be used. The heart rate training zones detailed previously (*see* table 5.2) are equally applicable to use with a power meter.

Variable/stochastic nature of power

It becomes clear on a cyclist's first ride with a power meter that power output is subject to fairly large variations on a second-by-second basis. This can make riding to a target power a little tricky. With practice, it usually becomes possible to even out this variation by careful use of gearshifts and an awareness of how to avoid spiking or dropping the power in changeable terrain and weather conditions. Other tips to help with this include the following:

- **Smoothing**: most power meters allow the display of a 5-second rolling average rather than the raw data. This hides much of the variation and can make sticking to a target power more straightforward.
- **Route selection**: if a training session calls for a long effort at a constant intensity, avoid routes with excessive changes in gradient. Also, take care where interval sessions are completed. For example, it makes no sense to begin a 5-minute interval at the base of a 3-minute climb as the following descent will make it impossible to complete the effort as planned.
- **Turbo training**: the home trainer can be ideal for controlling steady efforts at a specific target power. Remember, though, that if the aim is to compete on the road, the skill and ability to produce that effort on the open road must also be trained. The same session performed on the turbo trainer versus the road can have very different training effects, so be careful when choosing between the two.

Of course, for some sessions this variation may be incorporated as a training goal, particularly for events where frequent changes of power are necessary, such as mountain biking or criterium racing.

Using your power meter
High-intensity training

A common training strategy is to make use of high-intensity interval training sessions to accumulate an increased volume of work at a higher intensity than would be possible from a single extended bout of training. For example, cyclists can typically maintain maximal oxygen consumption (VO_{2max}) for between 4–8 minutes in a single exercise bout. However, by breaking the effort up into shorter intervals of work, it may be possible to perform a greater total amount of time at the target intensity (*see example 2 on page 77*).

These intervals, although short, still require a measurement of intensity. Some might argue that for such short durations it is simply a case of going as hard as you can. However, this strategy may not allow a complete quota of intervals or it may lead to a drop in intensity during subsequent intervals, perhaps to a point below the level needed to trigger the required adaptations. The use of heart-rate monitoring is not helpful in such sessions. It may take a cyclist's heart rate several minutes to rise to a level representative of the effort, leaving it too late to adjust effort levels to hit the correct intensity – the interval may even be finished. Indeed, such efforts are usually supra-maximal and so the heart rate could never 'represent' them. Similarly, guiding efforts on feel alone is also sub-optimal: what feels like a sustainable pace at the start of the interval and session can leave an athlete struggling towards the end (although it should be said that learning to pace an effort on feel is a very valuable skill that every cyclist should learn). In this situation, a power meter really comes into its own.

Example 1: Redline fartlek

The redline fartlek session (sometimes also known as over–unders) is a very effective means of improving sustainable race powers or the power that can be developed at the maximal lactate steady state (MLSS). The main piece of data you need to complete this session is your current power at MLSS, or your functional threshold power (FTP). Once this has been established (either by field or laboratory testing; *see* chapter 3 for details), the session simply involves working in alternating blocks of time slightly above and slightly below this level. For example, consider an athlete who can sustain 250 W for a 1-hour time trial. A typical training progression for this athlete using a redline fartlek session is shown in table 5.4.

Week 1	3 minutes at 240 W, 1 minute at 260 W, 3 minutes at 240 W; continue for 31 minutes in total
Week 2	3 minutes at 240 W, 2 minutes at 260 W, 3 minutes at 240 W; continue for 33 minutes in total
Week 3	2 minutes at 240 W, 2 minutes at 260 W, 2 minutes at 240 W; continue for 34 minutes in total
Week 4	2 minutes at 240 W, 3 minutes at 260 W, 2 minutes at 240 W; continue for 37 minutes in total

TABLE 5.4 Example progression for the redline fartlek session

Depending on your individual fitness profile and your cycling goals, the session can be adapted accordingly. Perhaps you need to progress at a slower rate to cope with the increasing demands, or you may choose to include a bigger difference between the 'unders' and the 'overs'. The key is to have a clear idea of what your goal is for the training block and set your progression accordingly.

Example 2: Six 3-minute intervals in zone 6 with equal easy recovery

A classic session for improving maximal aerobic power and VO_{2max} involves 3-minute intervals with equal recovery. An all-out time trial at the intensity required to elicit VO_{2max} (and stress oxygen delivery) might last 4–8 minutes. By breaking down the effort into bite-size chunks and not riding to exhaustion each time, an athlete may be able to build up to eight 3-minute intervals, or 24 minutes at VO_{2max} intensity. The key to this session is to go hard enough to hit VO_{2max} but not so hard that the intensity needed can no longer be sustained. The session instruction in this case may be to complete up to eight 3-minute intervals at a target of 320 W, ending the session if you can no longer average 300 W for an interval. In this way, a safeguard is in place to prevent the continuation of the session beyond the point where you are too fatigued to hit the desired training intensity. The target power could be chosen as the power that first elicits VO_{2max} in a ramp test (typically slightly lower than your maximum aerobic power owing to a plateau in oxygen consumption) or based on the lower end of zone 6.

For interval sessions like this, your power meter is generally sufficient to decide when enough is enough. For longer sessions at a lower intensity, this decision is perhaps not so clear cut. What we are searching for is the minimum effective dose: enough stress to trigger the required adaptation, but not so much that an extended recovery period is needed. To facilitate this, we need a more complete measure: stress and strain.

USING POWER AND HEART RATE TOGETHER

The preceding sections have shown that using a heart-rate monitor or a power meter can allow the collection of valuable data to guide and monitor a cyclist's training plan. The obvious question is: which is most useful? The invention of the power meter has certainly been the biggest development in cycling training in recent times. The merits discussed in the previous section have quite rightly seen it elevated to the ultimate training tool, often to the detriment of the heart-rate monitor and the athlete's self-awareness. However, there is no reason to abandon these other sources of information. Instead, the two can be viewed as complementary, helping to build a more complete picture of the training process.

Power and heart rate do measure different things, although we use both to describe 'exercise intensity'. One way to consider these ideas is to think of power being the *input* to the system and heart rate being the *output*. In other words, heart rate can be viewed as a measure of how much strain the body is under to meet the required level of stress. The heart rate response is very individual, so the relationship between heart rate and power (power:heart rate ratio) is of little value as a one-off measurement. However, when we begin to look at how this relationship changes over time (*see* case study on page 79), it offers a fantastic insight into how you are responding to the training plan.

SUMMARY

This chapter has highlighted some key issues in how to best approach the monitoring of endurance training. Recent trends to buck heart rate totally in favour of power, while understandable, are ill advised. The fundamental issue for the athlete and coach to consider is how to best use all the information at hand to optimise the training session. In asking, 'Which metric should I focus on in each session?' the athlete needs to know that the answer is, 'it depends!' This is not the most helpful of

CASE STUDY

Let's take a session already discussed in the previous sections on heart rate and power: the endurance 'base' or long ride. This provides a clear example of when a combined approach can offer much more than focusing on just one metric. Recall that in this session the athlete is asked to cycle at his first lactate threshold heart rate for 4 hours. For ease of explanation, let's assume that a recent laboratory test found this heart rate to be 140 beats·min^{-1} for a power output of 200 W. How can heart rate and power responses be used to monitor the training effect?

- **Within-session response:** over the course of this 4-hour ride, the athlete might observe a gradual increase in heart rate as the session progresses, despite no increase in power. Sometimes this might be cardiovascular drift caused by heat and/or dehydration. More often in rides of this length, this decoupling might be underpinned by changes such as muscle fibre recruitment and fuel status. The ability to maintain a stable power:heart rate ratio might indicate good endurance. In our example, a rider's power:heart rate ratio might drift by approximately 10 per cent over a ride in the early stages of training. Some 12 weeks later, this could become as low as 2 per cent.
- **Between-session response:** as the athlete continues to use this 4-hour session to boost his fitness, over the weeks we would expect training to bring about bradycardia, a training-induced reduction in heart rate at a given intensity. This means that, for the same heart rate, we will start to see power increasing. The key to remember is that the heart rate at the first lactate threshold will likely stay the same while the power at the lactate threshold will be increasing; that is, stress is the same for a higher strain placed on the body. In this example, we might see 220 W being held for the same 140 beats·min^{-1} heart rate.

answers from the coach, so another question needs to be posed: 'What is the aim of the session?' Every training session should have a clear purpose and role in moving towards the athlete's goal. Give some thought to what defines the success of the session and this will reveal one metric as preferable above others. For a race-specific session close to a goal event, a strict power target may be important to mimic the demands of the event. Four months out from the goal, the focus may be on more general endurance training, meaning that heart rate should used. Alternatively, there may be a session working on peak power output in a series of short sprints, with this being performed completely on feel – the aim is to go as hard as possible rather than to be constrained by a number. On the other hand, the same session might be monitored using a power meter, with the session terminated when you drop more than 20 per cent below the best effort. The deciding factor in each case is the aim of the training session.

KEY TAKE-HOME MESSAGES

- The use of heart-rate monitors and power meters is invaluable in quantifying a cyclist's training and racing efforts, allowing accurate tracking of training load and careful analysis of the success of this training load, in addition to providing instant feedback and a clear means of communication between athlete and coach.
- These tools should complement the ability to train on feel.
- The most useful metric at any time depends on the aim of the training session and which criteria are deemed most important for successful completion of the session.
- The combined use of feel, heart rate and power allows the athlete and coach to build a complete picture of the athlete's training. The relative strengths of each metric make up for the limitations of the others and ensure that any necessary alterations to the training plan are highlighted as soon as possible.

CHAPTER 6

HOW TO USE CYCLING TRAINING DATA

Simon Jobson and Louis Passfield

IT'S ALL ABOUT THE NUMBERS

As a cyclist, you are able to obtain a level of data on your performance that is exceeded only by motorsport, and that makes your friends in other sports envious. Athletes from many different sports visit their sport science laboratory to obtain data on their performance, but few are able to obtain much data on themselves during their training and competition. Given the widespread use of heart-rate monitors and, in particular, the growing popularity of global positioning systems (GPS) and mobile power meters, you could quantify every second of your cycle training and racing.

For some, such quantification is overly 'scientific'; it somehow diminishes the 'art' of cycling. It is certainly true that the data provided by heart rate monitors and power meters can be used to demystify aspects of cycling training and racing. Until relatively recently, an unexpectedly poor race performance could be deconstructed only with reference to reflections on how you 'felt' during the race. This type of subjective analysis can now be complemented by an objective analysis based upon your actual data. Did you train too much in the days leading up to the race? Did you ride too hard in the first hour of the race? Were you pushing it just 10 W too hard out of each corner? The answer may well be in your data.

It is, of course, easy to become overwhelmed by the amount of performance data that can be gathered. It is difficult enough to pick out the key points from a heart-rate file from a single session. How on earth do you go about picking out the key points from a full season of heart rate, power meter and, perhaps, even GPS data? For most people, the answer is that they don't. Clearly, this is a missed opportunity for any cyclist who is looking to improve his performance, whether the aim is to increase the speed of the Sunday café run, to improve time trial personal bests or to win the Tour de France. This chapter will help you start to mine your data in such a way that you can discover those nuggets of information that give you an edge over the competition.

What do we want from our data?

The more data you have, the more useful information you can pull out of it. However, to avoid drowning in numbers, you must carefully consider what information you want to extract from your data. Ultimately, it is possible to use your data in two ways: for retrospective analysis and for prospective analysis.

Most of your analysis will be retrospective. For example, you might be analysing single training sessions to see whether or not you completed all intervals at your target power output. Alternatively, you might be analysing data from a race to see what your average heart rate was or to see how many sprint efforts you completed over the course of the race.

Prospective analysis is, unsurprisingly, a bit more speculative. Here you use data from your past training and racing to give you some idea of what you will be able to do in the future. This might be in the short- or the long-term future. For example, in the short term, you might be able to use knowledge of your past data to give you an idea of how much longer you can maintain a solo breakaway effort before you have to back off to a more sustainable power output. In the longer term, it might be possible to use your past training and racing data to predict your peak performance level at some time in the future, for example on top-priority race days.

CAN'T SEE THE WOOD FOR THE TREES?

The first thing you notice when you open one of your heart rate or power meter files is that there are lots and lots of numbers. To extract some useful information, you must first corral those numbers into something a little more manageable.

Sport scientists have long known that training volume, intensity and frequency are the key factors that influence how an athlete adapts to training. For many years, endurance athletes have used training volume (kilometres per week and/or hours per week) as a measure of their training dose. However, this approach fails to accommodate the potentially important influence of training intensity. This is where your heart rate and power output data can become very useful.

Training zones

A single training session is often summarised as the average of all heart rate or power output values from that session; that is, average heart rate and/or average power (*see* page 85). Going one step further, training may be categorised into distinct training zones. There are many such training zone (or training level) systems in use, with most containing four to seven distinct zones, ranging from easy recovery to hard maximal intensities (see chapter 5 for more detail). The zones are defined as being at some fixed percentage of a maximum or threshold heart rate or power output value. In this way you can identify in which zone you spent most of a single training session (or a longer 'block' of training sessions). If the goal of your session was to develop your power output at threshold, training zone analysis can show you whether or not you actually spent sufficient time in your threshold training zone.

The training impulse

Heart-rate training zones provide a helpful guide to regulating effort while cycling. However, multiple zones are a little cumbersome when it comes to retrospective analysis. In a perfect world we would be able to summarise a single session with just one number. The training impulse, or TRIMP, is one way of producing such a number. The TRIMP method was first proposed by Eric Banister in the 1970s in an attempt to

THE PROBLEM WITH HEART RATE

Some caution should be exercised when analysing heart-rate data. This is because your heart-rate response may change in response to factors that are not related to how hard you are working or how fit you are. In particular, your heart rate is affected by changes in your body temperature, the air temperature and the amount of direct sunlight you are in, your hydration status and your body position on the bicycle. Despite all of this, heart rate is still a very useful tool that should not be dismissed. Indeed, the combination of heart rate and power output data is likely to be a very rich source of information about your performance, freshness and state of health. For more detail, *see* the section on the Lamberts sub-maximal cycle test in chapter 3 (page 49) and the section on training with heart rate in chapter 5 (page 69).

combine training volume and training intensity information. In its simplest form, the TRIMP score of a single session is calculated as the session duration multiplied by the average heart rate of the session.

The TRIMP method is attractive for two main reasons: it produces a single number that represents the training stimulus provided by the whole session; and it is relatively easy to calculate given access to an inexpensive heart-rate monitor. However, there are problems with Banister's original formulation. Consider the following examples:

- Session 1: 60 minutes at endurance pace, i.e. at an average heart rate of 140 beats·min^{-1} = 60 x 140 = 8400 TRIMP.
- Session 2: 48 minutes at threshold pace, i.e. an average heart rate of 175 beats·min^{-1} = 48 x 175 = 8400 TRIMP.

If you've ever used a heart-rate monitor, you will know that riding at 175 beats·min^{-1} is very much harder than riding at 140 beats·min^{-1}. The same TRIMP score for both of these sessions is, therefore, clearly not appropriate. Alternative methods have been suggested. For example, Hugh Morton, John Fitz-Clarke and Eric Banister modified the TRIMP equation to more heavily weight high-intensity training:

$$TRIMP = \text{exercise duration} \times \text{fraction of heart rate reserve} \times e^{(\text{fraction of heart-rate reserve} \times 1.92)}$$

Clearly, this equation isn't quite as user friendly as the original. Indeed, even with such modifications, you should still be somewhat careful in your implementation of TRIMP analysis. The big problem with TRIMP is that it is based on heart rate. This is fine up to a point, this point being your maximal heart rate. Maximal heart rate is achieved during a maximal oxygen consumption (VO_{2max}) test at somewhere between 200 W and 550 W (depending upon genetics and training status). However, a huge amount of cycle training and racing goes on above this level. During a criterium race, an elite rider will complete more than 60 out-of-the-corner sprints, each in excess of 600 W. A TRIMP value based on maximal heart rate clearly wouldn't reflect the true physiological strain of such an effort.

Post-exercise oxygen consumption

The impact of a training session can be measured directly in a laboratory by measuring variables such as oxygen consumption and blood lactate levels. However, these measures reflect only a momentary response to exercise. The measurement of oxygen uptake in the recovery period immediately post-exercise has been suggested to better reflect the cumulative response of the body to a whole training session. This excess post-exercise oxygen consumption (EPOC) reflects the body's attempt to return the body to a resting state.

Unfortunately, EPOC assessment is time consuming and requires expensive laboratory-based equipment, making it inaccessible to most athletes. Recognising this limitation, Heikki Rusko developed a heart-rate-based EPOC prediction method. Unfortunately, the calculation is relatively complex and so most users require proprietary software and hardware (e.g. the Suunto t6 heart-rate monitor). Furthermore, while the EPOC approach is attractive, users should retain a little caution in its implementation. The method has been validated in just one research study, in which only short-duration exercise (two 10-minute sessions) was investigated. Further research is required before we can be confident that this approach will work across the full range of training and racing sessions completed by cyclists.

Power output

Recognising the limitations of heart-rate data when analysing performance, in recent years many professional and recreational cyclists have invested in a power meter to provide an extra level of detail. As a result, many cyclists have found themselves in the position of having a shiny new power meter attached to their trusty steed only to find that they have no idea of where to start with the endless numbers that such systems can provide.

Power meter data from a training session or race often look something like those shown in figure 6.1. It is likely that the first thing you notice when looking at this graph is just how variable power output data can be. It is this variability that poses the biggest challenge when attempting to evaluate your training sessions.

As a result of the difficulties in interpretation of power output data, current practice for many athletes and coaches is to simply visually inspect individual training sessions. In this way, general features of the session may be identified, such as the point at which the highest power output was achieved, the number of intervals completed or the general level of power output variation. Clearly, such methods do not allow full analysis of the available data. An alternative approach is to evaluate the amount of time spent within given power 'bins' by using a histogram approach. One example of this approach was provided by Tammie Ebert and colleagues, who produced a graphical comparison of two types of women's World Cup cycle road races by evaluating the percentage of total race time spent within four power bins (0–100 W, 100–300 W,

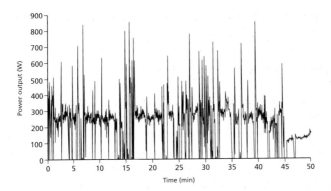

FIG.6.1 An example of training power output data measured with a PowerTap Hub system

300–500 W and over 500 W; see figure 15.1, page 207). Although simple, this method is excellent for the purpose of overall session comparisons. However, the histogram approach is limited by its inability to recognise separate efforts within any given power zone. For example, this method is unable to differentiate between a single 5-minute effort at 350 W and five 1-minute intervals at the same intensity, although the impact of these two bouts of exercise on your physiological adaptation may be very different.

Average power

Power output provides a direct mechanical measure of how hard you are working. This is in contrast to your psychological perception of effort or cardiovascular (e.g. heart rate) measures, which reflect your *response* to this work rate.

As discussed above, the variable nature of power output when cycling outdoors makes interpretation of the information from power meters challenging. A simple approach is to calculate mean or average power over the duration of your training and

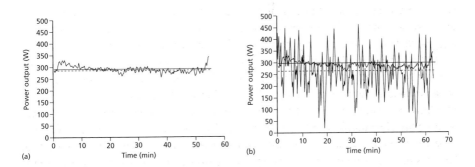

FIG.6.2 Thirty-second rolling average for power output during a flat time trial (a) and a criterium race (b) performed by the same cyclist; the average power (dashed line) varies widely between efforts, while the Normalized Power (solid line) is similar, indicating an equivalent physiological cost for both efforts

racing sessions. However, if the session is variable in nature, your average power may not truly reflect the psychological or physiological strain of that session. For example, a maximum effort in a 1-hour time trial over flat terrain may result in an average power output of 291 W and require little variation in power output over the course of the race (*see* figure 6.2a). By contrast, a maximum effort requiring marked changes of pace, such as a criterium or a hilly time trial, may result in the rider being able to produce a much lower average of only 261 W (*see* figure 6.2b).

Normalized Power™

Recognising the limitations of the average power approach, Andrew Coggan proposed a weighted averaging process. This process, which he calls Normalized Power™, attempts to take account of the disproportionate psychological and physiological strain you experience when your effort is not constant. Commercial software packages are available that automate the calculation of Normalized Power™ (e.g. TrainingPeaks WKO+). The calculation is relatively simple if you are familiar with standard spreadsheet software. Start by opening your power meter file in a spreadsheet software package. In a new column, create a 30-second moving average to smooth your data. Next, raise your smoothed data to the fourth power. Finally, average the transformed values and take the fourth root. You have now calculated your Normalized Power™ for the session in question.

Using Normalized Power™, it is possible to compare completely different types of training session. In the above example, for instance, the time trial Normalized Power™ remains at 291 W (see figure 6.2a), but the variable effort of 261 W when normalized becomes 291 W (see figure 6.2b). We can therefore see that both sessions required a similar (maximal) effort – that is, they imposed a similar mental and physiological strain – which was not reflected by the average power values.

WHAT IF I DON'T HAVE A POWER METER?

If you don't have a heart-rate monitor or a power meter, it is still possible to quantify your training and racing. The rating of perceived exertion (RPE) scale describes the intensity of discomfort or fatigue felt at a particular moment on a scale from 6 ('no exertion at all') to 20 ('maximal exertion'). Researchers have shown that this subjective measure correlates closely with actual physiological strain. Using the RPE scale to 'score' individual intervals within a session that you repeat on a fairly regular basis would, therefore, allow you to track improvements (or otherwise!).

It is also possible to provide a single number to summarise a session in a similar way to that described for average heart rate and Normalized Power™. Carl Foster and colleagues developed the 'session RPE' scale as an index of a whole training session. Rather than providing an RPE score for a specific aspect of an exercise session (e.g. an interval), session RPE aims to provide an RPE for the session as a whole. To determine your session RPE, 30 minutes post-workout simply ask yourself the question, 'How would I rate that entire workout?' (A scale from 0 = 'rest' to 10 = 'maximal' is usually used when determining session RPE.) The subjective nature of this measure means that it is a little less accurate than using heart rate or power meter data (see 'Training load' in chapter 5, page 66). Nevertheless, research has shown that the session RPE scale is a reliable and valid method of quantifying intensity during both endurance and resistance exercise.

I'VE SUMMARISED MY SESSION, NOW WHAT?

To optimise your performance, it is important that you understand the relationship between your training and performance. Summarising individual training and racing sessions using methods such as those described above provides the first step towards developing this understanding. Of course, the relationship between training and performance is highly individualised owing to variation in factors such as training background, genetics and psychology. Although this aspect of sport science is in its infancy, mathematical models have been developed that attempt to describe the relationship between training and performance. If you can identify how your past training impacted on your subsequent race performances, you may be better able to predict how you are going to perform in the future. Taking a more proactive approach, armed with such knowledge you may be able to structure your training in such a way as to achieve peak performance at your main target events.

A simple way to examine your training is by plotting it out as a graph. This visual picture of your training can help you easily spot gaps in your programme and trends in your fitness. Many downloadable training devices (such as power-measuring devices, GPS, cycle computers and heart-rate monitors) come with software that will help you. There are also several commercial programmes that provide a number of more advanced ways to visualise your training. Alternatively, it is relatively simple to plot your training using spreadsheet software such as Microsoft Excel. This approach has the added benefit of giving you much greater control over the examination of your data. While it may be interesting to look at your individual training sessions, it is typically more useful to analyse how your training has accumulated over a period of days or even weeks. This is because your training may combine different sessions to provide a variety of stimuli to develop your fitness. If you use training zones to denote how hard you were working, you can construct a simple bar graph or histogram of your training in each zone. Try combining a whole week's training and plotting this as the total time spent in each of your training zones. With this information, you can then quickly determine whether or not you have completed what you planned, if you are accumulating the time you expected in each zone and if there are obvious gaps in your training. Looking at individual sessions in this way is less informative as you won't work on all aspects of your fitness in a single ride.

Modelling the relationship between training and performance

A model may be based on detailed knowledge of all of the factors that underpin performance. Such knowledge would have to incorporate a wide range of complex

THE EFFECT OF STRENGTH TRAINING ON CYCLING PERFORMANCE

Time trials

Measurement of mean power output during 30–60 minutes of all-out cycling, or time taken to complete a 30–45 km time trial, represents the traditional approach to investigating the effects of simultaneous strength and endurance training on cycling performance. The majority of studies using this approach have found heavy strength training (4–10 repetitions maximum [RM]) to result in favourable adaptations. However, there are exceptions. For example, compared with heavy strength training, explosive strength training with low loads and many repetitions (e.g. low loads: 30 per cent of 1RM and 30 repetitions) are known to induce a lower strength gain and an apparent lack of performance improvement. In accordance with these findings, it is advisable to perform multiple heavy strength training exercises that target the most important muscle groups during the pedalling movement. In addition, it is important to remember that trained cyclists have a narrow margin for improvement after several years of training; therefore, you should give your strength training programme at least 12 weeks before you evaluate the effect. Indeed, it seems that well-trained cyclists may need longer than 12 weeks to fully transfer the increased strength to cycling performance improvement.

Improvement in time trials after heavy strength training may be attributable to postponed activation of the less economical type II muscle fibres, this being the result of increased strength in type I fibres. Furthermore, an increased rate of force development and/or increased maximal strength has been suggested to improve blood flow to the exercising muscles during endurance exercise. This is explained by the observations of momentary restriction of blood flow in contracting muscles during the pedal stroke and the assumption that a reduction of relative (pedal) force (owing to increased maximal strength) will induce less restriction of blood flow. The improved rate of force development may result in a shortened period of blood flow restriction during each pedal stroke owing to a reduction in the time required to reach the desired force. Indeed, elite cyclists are known to generate greater peak torque during the cycling downstroke than other well-trained cyclists. Increased rates of force development may contribute to increasing the peak torque during the downstroke or to shortening the duration of high relative force production in working muscles, thereby increasing the blood supply to the exercising muscles. Whether blood flow is enhanced after a period of simultaneous strength and endurance training has not been thoroughly investigated; however, in theory, increased oxygen and substrate delivery to the working muscles, as well as increased removal of waste products, can contribute to increased long-term endurance performance.

Prolonged cycling

The power output that a cyclist is capable of generating for a specific period is shown to have good reproducibility and has thus traditionally been used to measure performance in the laboratory to mimic time trials. However, many cycling road races include large periods of low-intensity exercise. In both the Tour de France and Vuelta a España, around 60–70 per cent of the race duration is spent at exercise intensities characterised as low intensity (below the lactate threshold). There has been minimal research investigating the effects of strength training on these types of prolonged efforts.

Returning to the discussion of cycling economy above, a study was mentioned in which cyclists rode at submaximal intensities for 3 hours. The cyclists also subsequently performed a 5-minute all-out trial. Twelve weeks of simultaneous strength and endurance training resulted in an approximately 7 per cent increase in mean power output (from around 372 W to around 400 W). It is likely that the improved performance in the 5-minute all-out trial by the strength-trained cyclists is at least partly a result of the superior improvement in cycling economy, heart rate and rate of perceived exertion during the last hour of the prolonged cycling trial. Figure 7.2 provides a summary of the theoretical effects of simultaneous strength and endurance training on important physiological determinants of cycling performance.

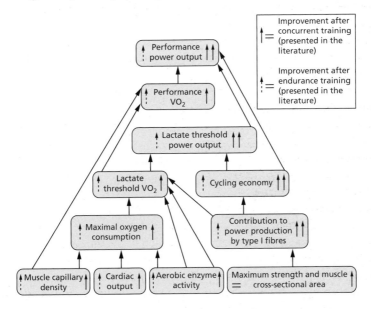

FIG.7.2 Model of the inter-relationships of the major physiological determinants of cycling endurance performance. Arrows symbolise theoretical effects of endurance training (dashed arrows) and simultaneous strength and endurance training (solid arrows). Two arrows indicate a larger effect than one arrow.

Short-term high-power output

The ability to generate high power output for a short period is an important factor in cycling performance. It determines the ability to close a gap, break away from the pack or perform well in a sprint, and thus may be crucial for the final result in a cycling race. The ability to generate high power outputs for a short period of time can be measured

TAKE-HOME MESSAGE

Supplementing endurance training with heavy strength training has a positive effect on short-term high-power performance and is also likely to have a positive influence on long-term endurance performance. There are no reports of a negative effect of strength training on cycling performance.

as mean and peak power output in a 6-second or 30-second all-out test (*see* chapter 3 for more details on power testing). Peak power output is mainly dependent on the size of the involved muscle mass and on maximal leg strength. Therefore, peak power output may be improved when cyclists start heavy strength training.

HEAVY STRENGTH TRAINING FOR IMPROVED CYCLING PERFORMANCE: PRACTICAL RECOMMENDATIONS
Specificity

To increase the probability of improved cycling performance after a period of strength training, the exercises should imitate the pedalling motion. This is based on the specificity training principle, meaning that a person achieves the largest strength increase in the trained movement. This is caused partly by adaptations in the neural system (e.g. via optimal activation of the involved muscles) as well as structural adaptations (e.g. increasing the number of active muscle cross-bridges [*see* box below]) in that particular range of motion. Therefore, cyclists are recommended to use strength training exercises that are coordinative and similar to the pedalling movement. Furthermore, it has been observed that the force developed during maximal contractions with both legs is generally smaller than the sum of the forces developed separately by the two legs. Since cyclists use each leg alternately when cycling, one-legged exercises should be chosen where practical. The major contribution to the power output during cycling is achieved from concentric muscle action during the pedalling downstroke. Peak force during pedalling occurs when the crank arm reaches an angle of approximately 90 degrees, which is usually equal to a knee angle of approximately 100 degrees. Therefore, a general rule is to focus on strength training exercises with a knee angle between 90 degrees and almost full knee extension.

MUSCLE CONTRACTION AND FORCE DEVELOPMENT

In muscle, proteins responsible for force production interact and create cross-bridges that ultimately make the muscle capable of contracting and exerting force. The number of active cross-bridges is important for the force-production ability of the muscle.

It seems that it is the intended, rather than the actual, velocity that determines the velocity-specific training response. This means that, even though the actual movement velocity is quite low, you may increase your rate of force development if you focus on performing the lift as quickly as possible. The cyclist should therefore focus on providing a maximal effort in the concentric, cycling-specific phase (pedal downstroke), performing the concentric phase as quickly as possible, while the eccentric, non-cycling specific phase should be performed more slowly (lasting around 2–3 seconds). The eccentric phase of an exercise is non-cycling-specific since cycling movements include almost no eccentric muscle actions. A slow muscle action during the eccentric phase also reduces the risk of injury and muscle damage.

TYPES OF MUSCLE ACTION

A concentric muscle action is characterised by muscle activity that involves shortening of the muscle length, while an eccentric muscle action is characterised by muscle activity that involves lengthening of the muscle, generally by an external load that exceeds muscle force.

TAKE-HOME MESSAGE

Strength training exercises should imitate pedalling movements. One-legged exercises should be chosen where practical. Focus on strength training exercises with a knee angle between 90 degrees and almost full knee extension and a maximal effort in the concentric phase of the lift.

HEAVY STRENGTH TRAINING PROGRAMMES

It is recommended that you build up your strength during the preparatory period leading up to the competition season. Two strength training sessions per week are sufficient to achieve an increase in strength during a 12-week period. We have seen an increase in maximum strength of 23–26 per cent by using a strength training programme designed as a 'daily undulating periodised programme', with progression in intensity (*see* table 7.1 for an example). This method varies the training load from session to session and progresses towards heavier loads and fewer repetitions. It is recommended to perform between 4RM and 10RM and two to three sets with approximately 2–3 minutes of rest between sets. Before starting with heavy loads, it is imperative that the correct lifting technique is established with lower loads.

	Preparatory period						Competition period
	Weeks 1–3		Weeks 4–6		Weeks 7–12		Weeks 13–25
	1st Bout	2nd Bout	1st Bout	2nd Bout	1st Bout	2nd Bout	1st Bout
Half-squat	3x10RM	3x6RM	3x8RM	3x5RM	3x6RM	3x4RM	2x5 reps @80–85% of 1RM
One-legged leg press	3x10RM	3x6RM	3x8RM	3x5RM	3x6RM	3x4RM	2x5 reps @80–85% of 1RM
One-legged hip flexion	3x10RM	3x6RM	3x8RM	3x5RM	3x6RM	3x4RM	1x6RM
Ankle plantar flexion	3x10RM	3x6RM	3x8RM	3x5RM	3x6RM	3x4RM	1x6RM

TABLE 7.1 Example of a strength training programme that has been shown to increase muscle strength and cycling performance during the preparatory period and to maintain the initial strength gain into the competition period. (Adapted from Rønnestad, B.R., Hansen, E.A., Raastad, T., 'In-season strength maintenance training increases well-trained cyclists' performance', *European Journal of Applied Physiology*, 110(2010), 1269–1282)

An easy way of controlling strength training intensity and progression is to use the 'repetition maximum' approach. This is a specific resistance that allows only a specific number of repetitions to be performed. For example, 10RM means that a weight is used that allows a maximum of 10 repetitions to be performed. When the strength level increases, the resistance is also increased to ensure a true RM target. Note that, in the beginning of a strength training period, it is common to get 'heavy' and 'sore' legs in the first few days after the strength training session. Therefore, it is important to take it easy with the endurance training during the first two to three weeks of a strength training programme. One approach to overcoming this initial strength training adaptation phase is to conduct it just after the end of a competition season, when endurance training has a lower priority.

Figure 7.3 provides examples of useful strength exercises that have successfully been used to increase cycling performance: half-squat, single-leg half-squat, step-up, leg press with one foot at a time, one-legged hip flexion (imitating the upward movement when pedalling) and toe raises (to ensure proper force transmission from the large thigh muscles into the pedal). You should perform 5–10 minutes of general warm-up before the strength training session begins. You should then focus

TAKE-HOME MESSAGE

During the preparatory phase of the season, when you want to focus on developing muscle strength, you are recommended to perform two strength sessions per week with multiple exercises for the lower body: perform two to three sets per exercise, with 2–3 minutes of rest between sets, with a load in the range of 4–10RM.

FIG.7.3 Strength training exercises proven to improve cycling performance: half-squat in a Smith-machine (A), leg press with one foot at a time (B), one-legged hip flexion (C), toe raises (D), single-leg half-squat (E) and step-up (F). (Photographs courtesy of Ronnestad, B.R., Hansen, E.A., Raastad, T., 'In season strength maintenance training increases well-trained cyclists' performance', *European Journal of Applied Physiology*, 110 (2010), pp. 1269–1282.)

on beginning with the exercise that involves the largest muscle mass, which is often the most coordinatively demanding exercise. Thereafter, complete two to three more exercises that focus on the important pedalling muscles in the lower body. Strength training sessions to increase cycling performance do not have to be time consuming: including the warm-up, they can be completed in 45 minutes.

STRENGTH MAINTENANCE TRAINING

During the competition phase of the season, the aim of strength training should be to maintain the strength gained during the preparatory period. It is well known that only a portion (0–45 per cent) of the strength gained during a previous strength training period remains after 8–12 weeks without sucg training. To counter the detraining effects, it is recommended that you perform a strength maintenance programme. This should include high-intensity muscle actions but at the same time reduce weekly strength training volume and frequency. It has been shown that one strength training session per week with some reduction in the number of sets is enough to maintain the initial increase in strength during the competition period. Table 7.1 provides an example of a strength maintenance programme that can be used to maintain the initial strength gain for 13 weeks into the competition period.

TAKE-HOME MESSAGE

During the competitive season or in training periods where you do not want to give priority to strength training, one strength session per week (low volume) at a high intensity is enough to maintain your trained strength level.

SUMMARY

Supplementing endurance training with heavy strength training seems to have a positive effect on maximal power output, lactate threshold and cycling economy. There are currently no studies that demonstrate a negative effect of strength training on cycling performance or VO_{2max}. As heavy strength training increases strength, it also improves short-term high-power-output cycling performance.

KEY TAKE-HOME MESSAGES

- Use strength exercises that imitate the pedalling action.
- Focus on the concentric phase in the lift.
- When focusing on developing muscle strength, perform two strength sessions per week with multiple exercises for the lower body, with two to three sets per exercise, 2–3 minutes of rest between sets and 4–10RM.
- To maintain the developed strength during the competition season, perform one strength session per week at high intensity.

SECTION D

HOW DO I GET THE BEST OUT OF MY BIKE? THE BIOMECHANICS OF CYCLING

When considering the main resistive forces that act on the cyclist, aerodynamic drag is probably the most significant. This force has been extensively researched over the past 20 years, with significant changes being made in bicycle design. However, more recently, advances in bicycle design have slowed owing to the stringent controls on bike shape and weight put in place by the Union Cycliste Internationale (UCI). Therefore, to seek further aerodynamic gains, scientific research has turned more towards the optimisation of rider position.

To effectively transfer power from the rider to the bicycle, the major concern is bicycle set-up and cyclist body position. Chapter 8 discusses how bicycle set-up might be adapted to ensure peak power production, to optimise aerodynamic position or to decrease the potential for injury. Chapter 9 then covers the efficiency of force transfer between cyclist and bicycle. The influences of pedalling mechanics are considered in detail, specifically in relation to numerous myths surrounding the interpretation of pedalling mechanics. In this context, three examples illustrating the applications and limitations of biomechanical analyses of cycling are discussed. These examples relate to: the relationship between the mechanical effectiveness of the pedal stroke and metabolic efficiency; the interpretation of joint powers and joint torques during maximal and submaximal cycling; and the usefulness of mechanical variables in the context of a cyclist's selection of preferred pedalling cadence.

By the end of section D, you should have developed an understanding of how you can modify your bike set-up and cycling position to get the most out of the power you put in to the bike. Section D also provides you with knowledge of the myths and realities with regard to pedalling technique and cycling cadence.

CHAPTER 8

BIKE FIT AND AERODYNAMICS
Ami Drory

Riding position is a key biomechanical factor influencing cycling performance and injury risk that has received significant attention from researchers and practitioners alike. However, despite considerable attention being paid to position, consistent findings and consensus are yet to be found. This is reflected by the abundance of methods available in popular coaching literature, on the internet and among commercial bike fit 'specialists' who claim to determine optimal cycling position.

Depending on the athlete, his experience in the sport and his access to bike fitting 'specialists', riding positions range from highly optimised positions to ones that increase the risk of injury and decrease performance potential. In particular, much has been written about 'aerodynamic' positions or use of aerodynamic equipment for optimising performance, without credible supporting research.

This chapter addresses some of the conflicting advice that currently exists in relation to bike fitting by reviewing the most commonly used methods and recent research findings. A brief overview of popular methods and considerations that affect bike fitting is provided, followed by a discussion of the relationship between aerodynamic drag and performance. Finally, we discuss methods used to measure and optimise rider position with the intention of minimising aerodynamic drag. A specific focus will be provided on the distinction between riding position for endurance events (e.g. time trial and track pursuit), for descents and ascents (e.g. during road racing) and for track sprint events.

POPULAR METHODS OF BIKE FITTING

Among the important bike fit parameters that have been examined, saddle height has received most attention. A number of methods for determining optimal saddle height for cyclists to maximise performance and minimise injury has been suggested in the scientific literature and popular cycling books. These methods include:

- saddle height, measured from the pedal axle to top of the seat, set at 109 per cent of inseam length (*see* figure 8.1);
- saddle height, measured from the centre of the bottom bracket to the top of the seat, set at 88.3 per cent inseam length;
- saddle height set by placing the heel of the foot on the pedal and locking the knee with the pedal at the bottom of the stroke, with the cyclist sitting on the seat; and
- saddle height set with the knee angle between 25 degrees and 35 degrees at the bottom of the pedal stroke (*see* figure 8.2).

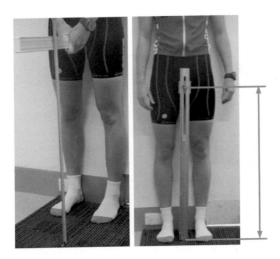

FIG.8.1 In seam measurement

FIG.8.2 Saddle height set with the knee angle between 25 and 35 degrees at the bottom of the pedal stroke

These four methods and others are routinely used. This degree of variability in the approach to bike set-up methods is not isolated to the saddle but replicated in many areas of the bike. The fact that no single method is universally adopted highlights the need for a better understanding of the relationship between bike fit and performance parameters through a standardised protocol.

The optimal bike fit for a particular athlete is a compromise between cycling performance, cycling economy, injury prevention and comfort. The interplay and precedence of these parameters depends on the cycling discipline and the individual circumstances. For example, a track pursuit rider, who spends 4 minutes on the bike at maximal effort, will have a much lower consideration for comfort than a 40 km time trial rider or a 200 km stage rider.

THE MYBIKESETUP PROJECT: TOWARDS A STANDARDISED BIKE SET-UP PROTOCOL

The Australian Institute of Sport (AIS) needed a system for ensuring that the approach for setting bikes for Australian national team cyclists was consistent, monitored and quality assured. Consequently, they developed an online database for monitoring bike set-up, athlete-specific anthropometric measures related to bike set-up, and bike components. The system is now freely available to the public for use at https://myequipment.ausport.gov.au.

The system allows athletes, team managers, coaches and support staff to record anthropometric data about cyclists and equipment set-ups relevant to a particular cycling discipline or athlete, generate theoretical set-ups based on athletes' anthropometric data and query historical records of athletes' anthropometric data and equipment set-up data.

Such a system allows conclusions to be drawn from the data over time about the ideal bike set-up for an athlete based on his anthropometric measurements. This will provide a critical data set required for longitudinal monitoring of bike set-up, as well as cross-sectional correlation of athlete anthropometrics with equipment set-up. In addition, it will provide a systematic quality assurance measure for consistent equipment set-up across all accredited testers. The data set created will allow biomechanists to optimise the algorithms used to estimate equipment set-up based on an athlete's body proportions.

THE IMPORTANCE OF BIKE FIT IN INJURY PREVENTION

Patellar tendonitis is a common overuse injury in cyclists and is usually associated with a low saddle height. A saddle that is too low can cause over-compression of the knee, resulting in anterior knee pain. As a result, it has been recommended that cyclists with patellar tendonitis move their saddle height to create a knee angle close to 25 degrees at the bottom of the pedal stroke.

Biceps femoris (hamstring) tendonitis is another common overuse injury in cyclists and can be caused by a saddle that is too high. If the saddle is too high, it can cause posterior knee pain by overextension in the dead spot at the bottom of the pedal stroke, which puts a heavy strain on the biceps femoris. As a result, it has been recommended that the saddle height be set for a 25–35-degree knee angle. However, while plausible, no evidence exists to suggest that the 25–35-degree knee angle position actually reduces the risk of injury.

THE DIFFICULTY OF RESEARCHING INJURY MECHANISMS

It is common for studies of injury mechanisms to struggle to demonstrate that a specific change reduces the risk of injury. An empirical study that can establish a cause and effect relationship between a position and injury risk reduction is hard to justify from an ethical point of view, as researchers would be aiming to cause injury among their participants. Hence, typically one of two approaches is used. The first is to estimate joint forces and torques or muscle activation patterns in a number of positions and make the assumption that reduced load is likely to reduce the risk of injury. Biomechanical modelling is also used to develop 'what if' theories for reducing injury risk. The second approach is an epidemiological one that looks at the correlation between rider position and incidence of pain or injury. However, it is important to acknowledge that finding a correlation does not prove a cause and effect relationship. There could be a good correlation (or relationship) between a particular saddle height and the incidence of patella tendonitis, but this does not necessarily mean that the saddle height caused the injury. Another factor could be equally, if not more, important in causing the injury.

COMFORT

Some attempts have been made to find a correlation between methods of determining saddle height and comfort. Iriberri and colleagues optimised the saddle height of 28 professional UCI male cyclists based on maximal power. They found that 21.42 per cent of the cyclists were not comfortable in this position. They differentiated the cyclists to three groups based on height to trochanteric height (leg length) ratio and adjusted the algorithm for calculation of saddle height accordingly. When saddle height was changed using the adjusted algorithm, the discomfort disappeared. Other researchers have found a weak correlation between methods of determining saddle height and comfort. Convincing evidence is yet to emerge for a position that allows both optimal performance and comfort.

BICYCLE SET-UP AND CYCLING PERFORMANCE
Power maximisation

In the context of cycling position, power maximisation refers to a position that allows the cyclist to produce maximal effective power. The force perpendicular to the crank arm (*see* figure 8.3) is considered the effective force. However, all of the forces and how they are applied to the pedal contribute to joint loading (e.g. at the knee) and allow insight into how individual athletes produce 'effective' pedal forces and powers (*see* figure 8.4).

In contrast with streamlined objects such as airfoils, where skin friction owing to wall shear stress dominates aerodynamic resistance, a cyclist has a complex three-dimensional geometry, often described as 'bluff body'. For such objects, flows are typically characterised by regions of separated airflow that may or may not reattach to the body's surface. Separated flow leads to a turbulent low-pressure region in the near wake of the object. This creates pressure differential between the low-pressure regions of trailing surfaces and the high pressure regions of leading surfaces, better described as 'pressure drag'.

AERODYNAMICS AND OLYMPIC GOLD

The team pursuit is widely regarded as the main event in every track championship. It is an indication of the depth of talent within a country's track endurance programme. At the 2008 Beijing Olympics, Great Britain won the men's team pursuit gold medal, setting a new world record time of 3 minutes 53.3 seconds and breaking the previous record held by Australia (2004 Athens Olympics gold medallists) by 4 seconds.

Analysis of the two world record races revealed that the average power produced by the two teams did not significantly differ. How then were the British cyclists able to lower the time by such a large margin? Most analysts believe that improvements in rider and team aerodynamics were the key to this result.

TAKE-HOME MESSAGES

- Know your event: prioritise bike set-up according to the demands of the event. There is no reason to adopt an aggressive aerodynamic position that may increase the risk of injury and reduce comfort when there is no direct performance benefit associated with it.
- Adopting a new and aggressive aerodynamic position is not trivial. You will have to invest significant time and effort in the gym to improve flexibility, muscular strength and endurance to hold the new position and still deliver power.

Aerodynamics and equipment

Over recent years there has been considerable hype in the media and on web forums about advances in the design and manufacture of cycling equipment. Mostly, these claims are concerned with significant reductions in aerodynamic drag. Understandably, this is predominantly driven by the manufacturing industry, as it is harder to market a new rider position than to market equipment that will make a cyclist go faster. However, it is important to understand that even a 5 per cent reduction in aerodynamic drag associated with a new bike frame will make only a 1–1.5 per cent difference to bike and rider total aerodynamic drag.

For bicycle frames, it is becoming increasingly unlikely that significant reductions in aerodynamic drag will be found. Like rowing shells, bicycles are highly evolved machines that have undergone more than a century of development. UCI regulations with regard to bicycle shape, dimensions and geometry impose further restrictions on the development of 'game-changing' technologies, with the justified intention of facilitating an even playing field for competition. It is more likely and increasingly apparent that greater gains in the reduction of aerodynamic drag can be found through research on the interaction between equipment and rider. For example, a helmet design with golfball-like dimples on the frontal surface (*see* figure 8.6) most likely assists airflow around the helmet, thereby reducing drag. Likewise, vortex generators at the sides and back of the helmet (*see* figure 8.6) reduce the possibility of, or delay, separation of the airflow, again reducing overall drag.

Wind tunnel tests of such designs will no doubt show reduced aerodynamic drag in some orientations, but it is critical to understand what the effect might be when combined with a cyclist who is moving about on the saddle, changing position or changing head direction. In the wrong orientation, such design can significantly adversely affect performance (*see* figure 8.7).

FIG.8.6 Garneau Vortice helmet. Note the golf ball-like dimples on the frontal surface and vortex generators in the mid-section.

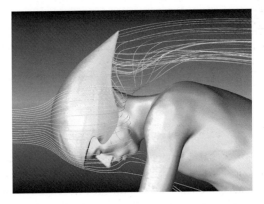

FIG.8.7 Computational fluid dynamics model of air flow around a cyclist's helmet. The visualisation of the turbulent flow between the back of the helmet and the cyclist's upper back demonstrates the adverse effect of less than optimal position in which a streamlined helmet design is detrimental to aerodynamic drag. (Source: Ensight.com and the Engineering Research Group at the University of Sheffield.)

FIG.8.8 Flow visualisation smoke technique used to achieve aerodynamic position for a time trial cyclist during wind tunnel testing

AERODYNAMICS AND WIND TUNNEL TESTING: WHAT DO THE NUMBERS MEAN?

A number of methods have been used to study airflow in cycling. These include flow visualisation techniques (*see* figure 8.7) including smoke (*see* figure 8.8) and oil spray of a cyclist in various positions, followed by visual identification of turbulent or laminar flow regions. Unfortunately, owing to their complex nature, a detailed description of these methods is outside the scope of this chapter. The CdA associated with a cyclist's riding position can be determined through wind tunnel testing. Typically, the bike and rider are placed in a tunnel where the air velocity and flow characteristics can be measured and controlled. The cyclist is positioned on a stationary force platform that measures the total drag in the propulsive direction.

Aerodynamic drag and projected surface area

Current approaches to finding the optimal aerodynamic position for a particular athlete and bike focus on trial and error manipulation of position to minimise CdA. It is important to appreciate that the treatment of data is tunnel specific and there is no consistent approach. This, in conjunction with the different flow characteristics and instrumentation, which are also unique to each tunnel, makes comparisons between various reported results dubious at best. For this reason, previously reported values for CdA vary greatly.

While reductions in CdA can be found for most cyclists through trial and error position manipulation, the mechanisms that lead to a reduction in CdA are poorly understood. Previous attempts to explain reduction in CdA focused on the manipulation of pFSA of the cyclist. Some suggest that pFSA is directly proportional to CdA; however, this is applicable only to constant drag coefficient conditions, which do not occur during cycling. The results of experimental work have been inconsistent, with some studies showing variations of up to 70 per cent in CdA with small changes in position and pFSA. However, the majority of research studies fail to report any differences in the airflow around cyclists as a consequence of position changes.

PROJECTED FRONTAL SURFACE AREA: HOW IS IT DETERMINED?

Two main techniques have been used to determine a cyclist's pFSA:

- Weighing a cut-out of a photograph of the cyclist's frontal image and comparing it with a cut-out image of a known area (e.g. a cut-out of a 1x1 metre square.
- Computing the area enclosed within the outline of a cyclist's frontal area using manual digitisation or computer vision techniques from photographs (see figures 8.9 and 8.10).

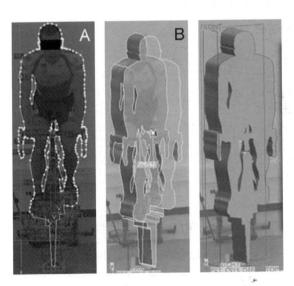

FIG.8.9 Computation of cyclist's pFSA using digitisation technique. (Source: Debraux, P., Bertucci, W., et al. 'New method to estimate the cycling frontal area', *International Journal of Sports Medicine*, 30(2009) 266–72.)

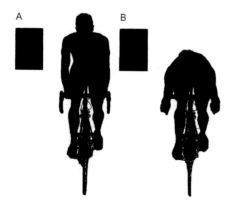

FIG.8.10 Computation of a cyclist's pFSA in upright and 'aero' positions and a square of known area. (Source: Debraux, P., Bertucci, W., et al. 'New method to estimate the cycling frontal area', *International Journal of Sports Medicine*, 30(2009) 266–72.)

'Brick' or 'blade'

Some coaches still hold the view that the dominant feature in determining the aerodynamic drag of a cyclist is their pFSA. They characterise athletes with large pFSA as 'bricks' and those with small pFSA as 'blades', in reference to streamlined objects.

To explore the relationship between pFSA and CdA, work at the AIS has attempted to extend the concept to other physical characteristics of the rider and to seek a relationship between CdA and anthropometric characteristics of each athlete. The CdA of elite national female road cyclists and elite international male track endurance cyclists was measured at test velocities of 14 m·s⁻¹ and 19 m·s⁻¹ for road and track cyclists, respectively, at a large open jet wind tunnel. Athletes were tested in their standard aerodynamic position as baseline, as well as in positions that included manipulated head direction, handlebar height and arm positions. Thirty-nine anthropometric measures of segment lengths, limb girths and skinfolds were taken from all athletes to characterise their body proportions. Results showed that anthropometric measures were not strongly correlated with CdA. CdA and Cd showed a weak correlation with pFSA. Low handlebar height was moderately correlated with CdA. Head direction showed weak correlation with CdA. A fully bent arms position showed moderate correlation with CdA.

To illustrate that the assertion that CdA and pFSA are directly related is an oversimplification, consider the two cyclists in figure 8.12. The solid line illustrates the two cyclists' pFSA in their baseline position. The double line shows the pFSA of each cyclist in a modified position. For the two cyclists, the pFSA was reduced in the modified position by 9.8 per cent and 7.1 per cent, respectively. However, the CdA was reduced for the cyclist on the left by 11.3 per cent and increased by 6.2 per cent for the cyclist on the right. Clearly, the reduction in pFSA fails to explain the changes in CdA. Hence, there are other parameters in play that explain changes in CdA with changes in position. The research study concluded that pFSA is a weak predictor of aerodynamic drag. Further research is required to adequately explain changes to CdA.

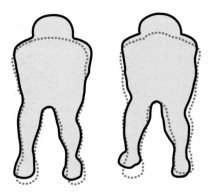

FIG.8.11 Relationship between reduction in projected frontal surface area (pFSA) and drag area (CdA). The baseline position of two athletes is marked with a solid line and a modified position by dotted lines. The modified position results in a reduction in pFSA of 9.8 per cent for the athlete on the left and 7.1 per cent for the athlete on the right. However, CdA is reduced by 11.3 per cent for the athlete on the left and increased by 6.2 per cent for the athlete on the right.

Aerodynamic rider position for endurance events (time trial and track pursuit)

The majority of past investigations into cycling aerodynamics revolved around position for endurance events, such as the time trial or track pursuit. As mentioned previously, early investigations focused on the relationship between CdA and pFSA. While some success in drag reduction was demonstrated for gross changes in pFSA through lowering the bike front end (i.e. lowering of handlebars), this failed to explain or predict changes in drag with more subtle changes. For example, in our laboratory we demonstrated that changing the riding position of two cyclists to reduce pFSA can cause a reduction in drag for one and an increase for the second (*see* figure 8.12). This demonstrates that the interaction between the two is more complex than at first it might seem.

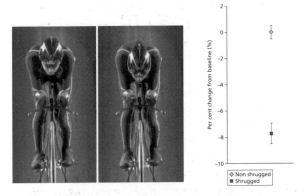

FIG.8.12 Percentage reduction in drag area (CdA) for a world champion endurance cyclist with non-shrugged (left) and shrugged shoulders (centre). The graph on the right shows the percentage reduction in CdA between the positions.

From our testing at the AIS, we observed that the helmet–trunk interaction is a dominant feature in the prediction of a cyclist's aerodynamic drag. Testing showed that if an endurance cyclist shrugged his shoulders, it elicited a large decrease in aerodynamic drag (by 5–15 per cent from the baseline position). In practical terms, this reduction in CdA corresponds to a significant increase in speed for the same power input, or substantial power savings at the same velocity. The reason why this reduction occurs is not yet clear.

KEY TAKE-HOME MESSAGES

- Shrugged shoulders significantly reduce your aerodynamic drag, which equates to savings of 5–15 per cent in your power input to achieve the same speed.
- To adopt shrugged shoulders, you will need to develop strength and flexibility around the upper back, shoulders and neck area.

The trunk–head interaction

Gaps between the helmet and trunk create turbulent airflow, which increases drag. This is well demonstrated through the flow visualisation techniques outlined above (*see* figure 8.9, page 113). The now banned rear back pad that featured in time trial races several years ago was an attempt to address the area of low pressure between the trunk and neck. The aim of the pad was to streamline airflow between the helmet and the back of the cyclist (*see* figure 8.13).

FIG.8.13 Back pad used under skin suit to streamline air flow from helmet to trunk

FIG.8.14 Changes in head–trunk interaction as the cyclist's direction of gaze changes: looking long distance (left), middle distance (centre) and near distance (right)

Head direction

An additional method of manipulating trunk–head interaction is via the head direction of the cyclist or, in practical terms, where the cyclist is looking when he rides. Looking at a point just in front of the wheel will lift the peak of the helmet, while looking a long way ahead will bring the peak down towards the trunk (*see* figure 8.14).

Interestingly, tests at the AIS have not shown a consistent trend with regard to which head direction is optimal for reducing aerodynamic drag. We found that the interaction is individual to each cyclist and his helmet of choice. Hence, individual-specific profiling is required.

TAKE-HOME MESSAGES

- The geometrical interaction between the head (helmet) and trunk has a significant effect on airflow and hence affects the overall aerodynamic drag of the cyclist.
- Choice of helmet, direction of gaze and trunk shape play large parts in this interaction. Streamlining is critical but is dependent on the athlete and his event.

Aerodynamic rider position for ascents and descents

In steep ascents, speed is low and the importance of an optimised cycling position to minimise aerodynamic drag is reduced. In descents, however, significant time can be gained and effort conserved through an optimised position. In road races where long descents are involved, cyclists aim to reach top speed as quickly as possible before then holding a static position (with their chest touching the top tube) without pedalling. By doing this they attempt to drastically reduce their projected frontal surface area.

A number of radical descending positions have been evaluated at the AIS to assess their effect on aerodynamic drag. We found that the position described above (*see* figure 8.15) resulted in a 20–25 per cent reduction in aerodynamic drag compared with the cyclist's normal descending position. Our analytical solution shows significant time-savings can be made on descents through reductions of CdA. For example, 3.97 seconds and 27.6 seconds can be saved in the cases of a 1 km and 5 km descent,

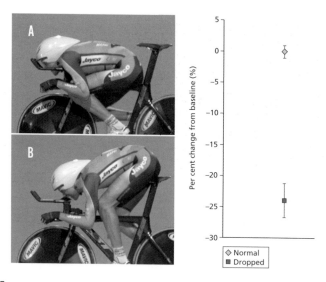

FIG.8.15 (a) aggressive 'dropped' descending position, (b) normal descending position. The graph on the right shows that for this athlete, a 17 per cent reduction in drag area can be achieved by using the descending position.

respectively, with a 10 per cent gradient and a 25 per cent reduction in CdA (though some assumptions have to be made about a cyclist's mass, the rolling friction and air density). Therefore, how well a rider descends can play a significant role in race strategy and tactics, for example, assessing the benefit of undertaking increased risk associated with a radical rider descending position, or the likelihood of a breakaway succeeding.

TAKE-HOME MESSAGES

- Significant time can be gained on long, steep descents by using an aggressive dropped position.
- This position limits your ability to control the bike and hence is dangerous. Use it wisely, and consider the consequences of a crash. Practice is paramount.

AERODYNAMIC RIDER POSITION FOR TRACK SPRINT EVENTS

Rider positions that minimise aerodynamic drag for track sprint events have, to date, received little attention in both the scientific and popular literature. Nevertheless, massive gains are to be had for sprint cyclists through position optimisation. This is particularly important in light of the high speeds that sprint cyclists achieve and, hence, the relative dominance of aerodynamic drag as a force acting against the cyclist.

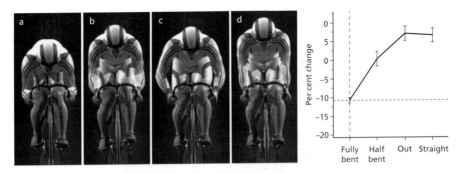

FIG.8.16 Example of change in drag area (CdA) for world champion sprinter with (a) fully bent arms, (b) half bent arms, (c) elbows out and (d) straight arms. The graph shows the percentage change in CdA between the positions, with a reduction of up to 17 per cent achieved for this athlete between the worst and best positions.

Investigating the riding position of track sprinters in a wind tunnel is no trivial task. Difficulties stem from a number of areas. For example, air vortices are randomly created and dissipated around the cyclist. This is further compounded by the movement of the cyclist. Sprinters, who spend most of their time accelerating and turning large gears at high cadence, use gross body movements. As a result, they find it difficult to hold a position for a sufficient length of time to allow for quality drag data acquisition. Consequently, criticism of the ecological validity of wind tunnel testing for track sprinters is well justified. Furthermore, a compromise needs to be found between a riding position that maximises the ability of the cyclist to produce power and a position that minimises aerodynamic drag. A characterisation of this trade-off is yet to be developed. Consequently, power production remains the prime focus of track sprinters and coaches.

Nevertheless, a few interesting observations can be made through wind tunnel testing of elite track sprinters. Arm position can have a significant effect on aerodynamic drag. In our testing we observed that fully bent arms (loosely, elbows at 90 degrees) is a position that reduces aerodynamic drag by up to 10 per cent compared with half-bent arms, and by up to 16 per cent compared with straight arms. For a male sprinter, who can produce around 2500 W, this corresponds to savings of greater than 400 W (*see* figure 8.16).

Curiously, arms that are bent out cost a sprinter up to 17 per cent in aerodynamic drag. However, this is a very common position held by sprinters as they jostle for a dominant line on the track or work the bike underneath them. It is unlikely that a sprinter will be able to perform at the highest level in a position that emulates that of an endurance cyclist. A more likely strategy is for a sprinter to assume a fully bent arms position as soon as practical, for example when jostling for position is complete. It is important to note that in these tests observations were not accompanied by comparable changes in the pFSA of the cyclist.

Where is it best to look? Under the arm or over the shoulder?

Track sprinters often peek at their opponents over their shoulder or under their arm. We did not find consistent results to demonstrate that one technique is more advantageous than the other. Furthermore, peeking at opponents typically occurs at low speeds, when reduction of aerodynamic drag is less important (*see* figure 8.17).

FIG.8.17 Frontal image of a world champion sprinter looking over her shoulder (right) and under the arm (left). There is no significant difference in either pFSA or drag area.

The aerodynamic effect of 'throwing' the bike over the finish line

It is interesting to observe sprinters 'throwing' their bikes forward over the finish line under the belief that it may help to sneak their wheel in front of that of their opponents. Newtonian mechanics, physicists and common sense will argue that this action does nothing to advance the bike over the line, and assists in the rotation of planet

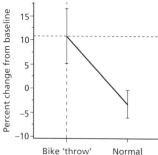

FIG.8.18 The graph on the right shows an 11 per cent increase in drag area (from baseline) of the 'throwing' position compared with an optimised (marked normal) position for a world champion sprinter

FIG.8.19 Sprinter 'throwing' the bike over the finish line in the final of the keirin at the 2011 World Championship

Earth only by a minuscule magnitude. Instead, the action in fact pushes the cyclist's body back, away from the finish line. We endeavoured to test the effect of this position on sprinters' aerodynamic drag. Our results show that 'throwing' the bike over the finish line may increase drag by up to 13 per cent (*see* figure 8.18). Furthermore, in this position cyclists are not turning the pedals and are therefore not producing any power. We haven't managed to convince any riders yet, though!

TAKE-HOME MESSAGES

- Keep your tucked elbows in and fully bent whenever possible. Having your elbows out will cost you dearly by increasing aerodynamic drag.
- You're not producing power when 'throwing' the bike over the finish line. In fact, you are decelerating. Keep pedalling past the line.

SUMMARY

Optimal bike fit for a particular athlete depends on the interplay between, and precedence of, cycling performance, cycling economy, injury prevention and comfort considerations. The compromise will be determined by the cycling discipline and individual circumstances. This means that it is not possible to provide a fixed rule for optimal bike set-up.

Nevertheless, irrespective of the discipline, aerodynamic drag is the dominant force acting on a cyclist at typical racing speeds. It therefore plays a significant role in affecting performance. Large performance gains can be made through minimising drag. While some general principles apply, more research is required to establish the mechanism by which this is achieved.

KEY TAKE-HOME MESSAGES

To achieve reduction in aerodynamic drag:

- shrug your shoulders;
- keep your elbows tucked in and fully bent;
- focus on maintaining a position that streamlines airflow around your head (helmet) and trunk;
- practise a dropped descending position if you want to consider gaining time on descents; and
- continue pedalling over the finish line rather than 'throwing' your bike.

CHAPTER 9

PEDALLING MECHANICS AND PERFORMANCE OPTIMISATION

Thomas Korff, Paul Barrett and Scott Gardner

Cycling performance is ultimately determined by the mechanical and physiological properties of the rider's muscles and the biomechanics of his cycling motion. Cycling obeys the laws of physics even if it is not always obvious to the rider. An internet search on 'pedalling mechanics' or 'cycling biomechanics' will generate hundreds of websites and articles with advice on how to improve your cycling with better pedalling mechanics. When relating cycling biomechanics to cycling performance, numerous assumptions exist within the cycling and coaching communities, many of which are misconceptions. The purpose of this chapter is to discuss the scientific evidence supporting and confuting some of these assumptions. This discussion is preceded by a description of the relevant biomechanical concepts.

RELEVANT MECHANICAL CONCEPTS: FORCE, TORQUE AND POWER

When we cycle, the forces that we produce to turn the crank are ultimately transferred from the foot to the pedal. If we know these pedal forces, we can calculate crank torque and crank power. Within the context of cycling, it makes sense to look at two components of pedal force separately: the force that is acting towards the crank centre (i.e. the 'radial' force component) and the force that is acting perpendicularly to the crank (i.e. the 'tangential' force component) (*see* figure 9.1). It is the tangential force component that causes the rotational movement of the crank. Crank torque is a measure of rotational force around the crank and can be calculated as the product of tangential force and crank length:

$$\text{Crank torque} = (\text{tangential crank force}) \times (\text{crank length})$$

Mechanical power can be defined as the product of crank torque and the crank angular velocity:

$$\text{Power} = (\text{crank torque}) \times (\text{crank angular velocity})$$

Crank angular velocity and the potentially more familiar terms 'pedalling rate' or 'cadence' describe the same physical quantity. Thus, conceptually, mechanical power can also be thought of as the mathematical product of crank torque (resistance) and pedalling rate.

When trying to ride efficiently, cyclists should not 'waste their energy' by pedalling in circles or pulling on the pedal. Furthermore, cyclists and coaches should not read too much into negative power measured during the upstroke of the pedal cycle. Negative power does not necessarily imply that the muscles are working inefficiently.

Thus, the understanding of the relationship between pedalling technique and efficiency might save coaches and athletes time, effort and money that might be better spent on more useful equipment (e.g. a heart-rate monitor, which would potentially allow the athlete to train in the appropriate training zones; *see* chapter 5, page 69, for further details).

If cyclists feel strongly about incorporating biomechanical principles into their training, the understanding of joint powers may be useful. For example, if cyclists wish to conduct resistance training to target specific muscle groups to increase submaximal cycling performance, they should focus on the main power producers: knee extensors (quads), plantarflexors (calf muscles) and the hip extensors (glutes). For maximal cycling, the flexor group may also be targeted.

Maximal cycling

Maximal cycling is characterised by a requirement to produce very large amounts of mechanical power in a short amount of time. World-class sprint cyclists train to produce the highest possible power output during competition. Although the demands (tactical and physiological) of each specific race vary slightly, overall performance in track sprint cycling is largely determined by the ability of the athlete to rapidly accelerate, achieve a high maximal speed and maintain speed by resisting fatigue for as long as possible. With recent advances in technology that can measure cycling power accurately, sport scientists and coaches have been able to collect data from competitions that have transformed our understanding of what it actually takes to accelerate the bicycle up to maximal speed. In this section we describe some of the scientific evidence and how it can be used for training prescription for athletes.

The torque–pedalling rate relationship

As we have seen, crank torque is the product of tangential crank force and crank length. The amount of torque that a rider is able to produce depends on his pedalling rate (or, more technically, the crank angular velocity). To illustrate this relationship, let us imagine a rider in a starting gate with the rear wheel of his bike locked and the pedals in a fixed position. The rider is then asked to stamp down on the pedals as hard as possible, but the bike is not released from the gate. Now, as long as the bicycle remains locked in position and there is no movement of the cranks, the rider will only be producing torque. In this situation, torque is very high but pedalling rate is zero. Imagine a different scenario, in which the rider is set up in the same way in the starting gate but this time is released from the starting gate. In this new scenario, torque is still very high (but lower than under static conditions), but this time the pedals move, which means that angular velocity is positive. In this second example, the torque exerted by the rider on the crank will be lower, as the crank is moving. In general, we know from experimental evidence that the higher the pedalling rate, the lower the

RESEARCH FOCUS:
FORCE VELOCITY AND TORQUE PEDALLING RATE RELATIONSHIPS

At present, little is known about why the torque–pedalling rate relationship is
linear. Some researchers have proposed that it is a consequence of the complex
multi-muscle, multi-joint nature of cycling. Furthermore, the intrinsic properties of
the muscles are likely to play a major role. From animal studies, Swoap and colleagues
have shown that muscles produce less force when they shorten at higher velocities.
This so-called force–velocity relationship of muscle is related to the muscle's inability
to be activated and relaxed at very high shortening velocities (excitation–relaxation
kinetics). Research from Jim Martin and colleagues suggests that these mechanisms
play a vital role during cycling. Therefore, it is likely that the intrinsic properties of
muscle (i.e. the interaction between both force–velocity properties and activation–
relaxation kinetics) are at least partially responsible for the relationship between
torque and pedalling rate being linear.

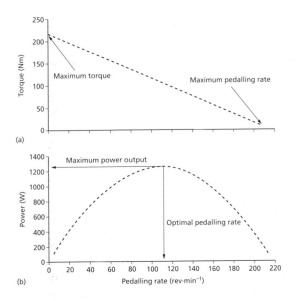

FIG.9.5 Illustration of (a) the linear force–velocity relationship and (b) the parabolic power output
velocity curve observed during maximal bicycle tests. Maximum power output is pedalling rate specific
and located at the apex of the power–pedalling rate curve. This figure is constructed from unpublished
mean data collected from five world-class female athletes during maximal cycling trials.

torque of the rider. For a given gear ratio, this so called 'torque–pedalling rate relationship' has been shown to be linear (*see* figure 9.5a). Given that track cycling rules
prescribe the use of fixed-gear bicycles, this means that as the rider accelerates, the
amount of force he can physically produce diminishes as the pedalling rate increases.

Power–pedalling rate relationship

As shown in the equation on page 123, power is the product of crank torque and crank angular velocity (or pedalling rate). Thus, the power that a cyclist can generate depends on the crank angular velocity. To illustrate this relationship, let us go back to our two examples. In the first example, when the bicycle was locked in the starting gate, there was no movement of the pedals (i.e. pedalling rate is zero). Referring to figure 9.5, this situation is represented at the point where the line representing the torque crosses the vertical axis. The corresponding torque value represents the maximum amount of force that a cyclist is capable of producing. This, by the way, is a good measure of cycle-specific strength. In this scenario, torque would be high and angular velocity would be zero. Therefore, power (being the mathematical product of the two) would be zero.

In the second example, the bicycle was released from the starting gate. A hypothetical scenario, in which the athlete is able to accelerate all the way to his maximum pedalling rate in the absence of fatigue, would bring us to the other end of the spectrum. This represents a situation where the pedals are spinning so fast that the neuromuscular system is no longer capable of producing any force or torque. In this scenario, pedalling rate would be high and torque would be zero. Once again, power would be zero (i.e. the rider would be freewheeling).

How does the relationship between power and angular velocity behave between these two extremes? If we take figure 9.5a and for each pedalling rate calculate the

RESEARCH FOCUS: POWER–PEDALLING RATE RELATIONSHIP

From a scientific point of view, optimal pedalling rate is an important variable that may be reflective of the distribution of fast- and slow-twitch fibres within our muscles. Scott Gardner and colleagues have found the optimal pedalling rate for elite sprint cyclists during standing starts to be 129±9 revolutions per minute.

The seemingly theoretical relationship between pedalling rate and power has concrete implications for competitive cyclists. Track sprint cyclists often train to produce higher optimal pedalling rates, which may serve to increase the percentage of fast-twitch muscle fibres. This could in turn result in higher maximum power outputs. Furthermore, sprint cyclists typically select gear ratios in competition that trade off between the increased ability to produce power closer to the optimal pedalling rate and the ability to produce enough power at slow speeds to accelerate.

Maximum power output is a useful measure because it reflects the optimal combination of force (or torque) and velocity. When comparing different studies, it is important to consider how exactly maximum power was defined. Maximum power output is usually reported as the maximum average recorded for one entire crank revolution (or stroke cycle). However, some testing methods also report maximum power output as an instantaneous value within a crank revolution or over a one-second duration. Jim Martin and colleagues have shown that this instantaneous power output is typically about 40 per cent higher than the average per-pedal revolution.

product of pedalling rate and the corresponding torque (i.e. calculate power at each pedalling rate), we see that the relationship between power and pedalling rate is represented by a parabolic curve (*see* figure 9.5b). This curve represents our neuromuscular ability to produce maximum power in relation to pedalling rate. The apex of the curve represents the highest power output that we can produce (maximum power output) and the corresponding pedalling rate represents the optimal pedalling rate for maximum power output production. It should be noted that, because of the parabolic relationship, the optimal pedalling rate is exactly half of the maximum pedalling rate. Maximum power output reflects an ideal combination of force production and muscle contraction velocity. Elite sprint cyclists are capable of reaching maximum power outputs in excess of 2000 W in accelerating to speeds above 70 km·h^{-1}.

Implications for training

The torque– and power–pedalling rate relationships provide useful tools for optimising an individual's performance during maximal cycling. By having a clear understanding of these relationships and how they change over time with different training activities, coaches and athletes can tailor their training plans to address an athlete's physiological and biomechanical strengths and weaknesses. Furthermore, when studied in training and competition, these relationships allow coaches and athletes to gain a deeper understanding of the fundamental elements of producing maximum power output for cycling.

Understanding the torque– and power–pedalling rate relationships makes it obvious that both strength and speed are important parameters that need to be targeted by coaches and athletes. To achieve training-induced increases in maximal cycling power, coaches and athletes need to build the ability to increase torque in combination with an appropriate pedalling rate range. Referring to figure 9.5b, the goal here would be to increase the area under the power–pedalling rate curve. In other words, by working maximally at both ends of the pedalling rate range, an athlete should be able to improve his maximal power output.

Strength training and the power–pedalling rate relationship

Strength training is commonly used by cyclists to improve their maximal power output. It can be performed on the bike using activities such as standing starts or short, big-gear hill repetitions, or in the gym using activities such as squats and leg presses. Strength training is considered to be base training for sprint cyclists. However, as we have already alluded, strength training is only one component of the equation; the speed (i.e. pedalling rate) at which the training is performed is equally important. This notion is supported by experimental evidence.

To study the effect of strength training on the torque– and power–pedalling rate relationships, a study was conducted at the Australian Institute of Sport (AIS) in the early 2000s. In this study, talented female athletes were trained in two phases. The first phase was primarily based on strength work in the gym, standing starts and seated accelerations on the bike. Results from this part of the experiment revealed that, when cyclists were predominantly given strength activities to complete over a three-week period, the maximum torque of the torque–pedalling rate relationship improved

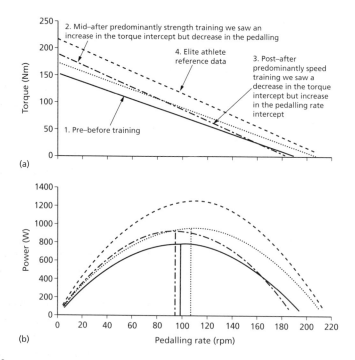

FIG.9.6 Average (a) torque– and (b) power–pedalling rate data from a study conducted at the AIS. Mean torque and power data are shown across 21 participants. Pre-, mid- and post-training are shown along with an elite athlete comparison (top dashed line) calculated from elite female 500TT data (n=5). Note that as a result of training, the area under the maximal power–pedalling rate curve in panel b continually increases even as the athletes' bicycle-specific strength decreases in panel a. The optimal pedalling rate can be observed by the corresponding vertical line in panel b.

greatly but the maximal pedalling rate decreased (*see* figure 9.6a). This means that the athlete's ability to produce force on the pedals at higher pedalling rates above approximately 130 rev·min⁻¹ actually decreased. As a result of strength training, the maximum power increased whereas optimal pedalling rate decreased (*see* figure 9.6b).

In quite a simple way, this study showed that strength training on its own may improve maximal power output, which could improve the initial acceleration of a sprint start. However, these results also imply that strength training on its own will likely reduce the optimal pedalling rate and hence limit the ability to achieve and sustain high maximum speeds in disciplines such as track sprinting and BMX where acceleration to high pedalling rates is required.

Owing to the velocity-specificity of the training response in the study, the athletes improved their torque production capabilities at slow, but not at high, speeds in response to *static* resistance training. Thus, caution should be taken if focusing solely on *static* strength training with the goal of increasing cycling performance. A possible unwanted consequence could be that a strong athlete with potentially rapid acceleration at low pedalling rates would decrease his ability to reach and sustain high maximum speeds.

Speed training and the power–pedalling rate relationship

The AIS study also tested the effect of speed training on maximum power production. Again, results indicated that training-induced adaptations were velocity specific. The speed training consisted of dynamic activities such as flying 100 m and 200 m efforts in a velodrome, where the athletes regularly reached pedalling rates in excess of 145 rev·min[-1]. In the gym, the athletes performed dynamic, ballistic power exercises such as lightly weighted jumps. The results revealed that, when the primary focus of training switched from strength to high-speed sprints, the athletes' maximum torque decreased but their maximum pedalling rate showed a large increase. In other words, they got weaker on the bike. However, owing to the increase in the maximum pedalling rate, the area under their maximum power curve showed an overall increase. Together, these findings suggest that training at high speeds can improve an athlete's ability to produce power at high pedalling rates. This can be beneficial for those disciplines in which relatively high power outputs need to be sustained for an extended amount of time. However, this comes at the cost of decreased maximum torque, which could impair the athlete's ability to accelerate explosively at the start of a race.

It becomes clear that there is a trade-off between maximising power production at slow speeds (beneficial for initial acceleration) and increasing maximum or optimal pedalling rates (beneficial for sustaining a high power output over an extended period of time). Any training programme should take this trade-off and the underlying mechanical principles into consideration and tailor them to the specific requirements of the cycling discipline in question.

Effect of crank length

Crank length does not affect maximum power production. The relevant research is summarised below. Similar to the recommendation that we made for sub-maximal cycling, athletes can choose their crank length based on personal preference and/or the minimisation of aerodynamic drag.

RESEARCH FOCUS: CRANK LENGTH AND MAXIMUM POWER CYCLING

Martin and Spirduso have demonstrated that, for a given pedalling rate, maximum power changes as a function of crank length. However, maximum power is unaffected once pedalling rate is adjusted appropriately. Paul Barratt and colleagues expanded on these findings and demonstrated that joint powers are also unaffected during maximum cycling, once the effect of pedalling rate is accounted for. Together, these findings indicate that crank length is not an important determinant of maximum power production during maximal cycling.

and during a race, optimal performance in a variety of competitive situations. In addition, the sport psychologist is optimally trained to help the rider constructively use and regulate his emotions insofar as they impact performance and key relationships, develop strategies for stress and conflict management, redirect self-sabotaging behaviors, utilise sound communication skills, provide support during times of injury, and help the rider plan and adjust to life after competitive sport.

KEY TAKE-HOME MESSAGES

- Process goals help a rider to build skills and confidence while simultaneously promoting improved results.
- Psychological skills such as imagery, relaxation exercises and self-talk are more effective when tailored to the individual cyclist, and taught by a trained sport psychologist familiar with applied research in these areas.
- Consistent optimal performance does not require a state of flow, but does require a cyclist have a strong, resilient and honest relationship with himself and his key support system.
- Feelings of identity, self-worth, social connection, freedom and meaning are likely to be impacted throughout one's athletic career.
- Sport psychology helps a cyclist to learn how to eliminate self-defeating thoughts and behaviours while simultaneously strengthening all that supports optimal performance.

CHAPTER 11

THE PSYCHOLOGY OF CYCLE TRAINING AND COMPETITION: A BRIEF INTRODUCTION

Chris Beedie

In chapter 10, Julie Emmerman presented an eloquent and insightful chapter on the psychology and philosophy of cycling. I, on the other hand, will present a rather inelegant and perhaps largely self-evident chapter, albeit one that I hope will enable the cyclist, whether novice or experienced veteran, to better prepare for training and competition. I doubt many readers will be surprised by the content, and I imagine that many will already be using some of the strategies I propose. In my experience, however, only the best bike riders use a number of these strategies and use them well. That in itself should tell you something: if the average rider uses some of the strategies adequately, while the best riders use most or all of them well, the benefits of refining those you are already using, or of adding one or two more to your mental preparation routine, might be substantial. While this chapter is simplistic, I make no apology for this; psychological skills do not need to be complex to be effective and, in fact, some of the simplest strategies are the most powerful. If you reach the end of the chapter and think, 'Well that was a waste of time, I'm already doing all that!', at least you can rest assured that, as long as you are using the strategies well, you are probably mentally well prepared for competition. That knowledge will in itself provide you with a psychological advantage over many riders.

As an endurance sport, cycling is unique. Compared with sports such as marathon running, race walking and long-distance swimming and rowing, racing bikes presents competitors with a number of serious challenges. These include: increased risk of harm to the rider presented by strong winds, unpredictable surfaces, complex high-speed descents and extremely fast and often unpredictable sprint finishes; mechanical factors such as punctures and breakdowns; strategic factors such as drafting, gear ratio selection, feeding and communication with teammates; and physiological factors such as dramatic changes in temperature, very high energy costs over extended periods and large variations in biological load, ranging from turning the pedals over at an almost guilt-provokingly easy tempo through to periods of physically painful and psychologically stressful maximal effort, the latter often with little warning as the pack 'decides' to chase down a break.

In short, there is a lot going on in a bike race. In fact, it could be said that cycling requires the physical endurance of a marathon runner, the strength of a mountaineer and the information-processing and decision-making skills of a Formula 1 driver. The latter determines that in a bike race, the brain has a lot of work to do. Like the body, the brain needs to be prepared for this workload and, in a similar manner to how we prepare the body for competition, preparing the brain is best achieved through systematic and measured training.

In relation to physical training, only the most naturally gifted athlete could say, 'I've got a race next weekend, I'd better start thinking about doing some training now'. It is likely a better strategy to think, 'OK, I've got a big race in a few months' time, I need to start doing some serious training now'. The same is true of mental training: a long-term approach works best. You will not read a chapter on sport psychology today and be a better athlete tomorrow.

While the strategies presented below seem simple, as is the case with physical performance, simply knowing what to do does not mean you can do it. The knowledge that you need to produce 550 W for 12 minutes to get away from the pack on a climb does not mean that you can produce that power for that period of time – you need to train in order to do it. The same is true of mental performance; you may know after reading this chapter that you need to think a certain way before, during and after competition, or that certain emotions help you ride harder, but that does not mean you will automatically be able to control your thoughts or your feelings during a race. The brain is a complex and at times quite unpredictable organ; powerful emotions, unconscious thoughts, mental fatigue, interrupting doubts and confusion can all stop the brain from doing what you would like it to do. That is what this chapter is about: knowing how to think about the problems you face as a competitive cyclist.

This chapter addresses competitive thinking in three contexts: planning, training and competition. It is aimed at the club- or regional-level cyclist who is looking to improve his performance. In writing it, I am assuming that the majority of interested readers will be riding for themselves pretty much unaided; that is, they will not have strict team strategies or orders, will not have radios and probably will not have dedicated team-specific support vehicles. That is not to say that this chapter is not relevant if you are racing professionally or in an organised amateur team, simply that some of the assumptions I make below will not apply to the same degree.

BEFORE WE START: THE IMPORTANCE OF BUILDING YOUR PERSONAL PERFORMANCE DATABASE

One of the most powerful resources that you have in a bike race is information. While information as to what your opponents are capable of doing or are going to do is useful, your most valuable form of information as an athlete relates to what yourself are capable of doing. Throughout this chapter, I will highlight information that you should be seeking to acquire about your own physical and mental capabilities, as these data are among your chief assets as a competitive cyclist. You might ask why information about yourself is more valuable than information about your competition; simply put, you cannot control the actions of others, but you can control your own. If you know you can ride for 25 minutes at 350 W and 180 beats·min^{-1}, you can factor that information in to your race strategy. Likewise, information as varied as what type of pre-race strategy works best for you, which emotions do and do not

TAKE-HOME MESSAGE

Keep a personal database of information that you perceive to be important. This information can relate to anything: from daily waking heart rate to recovery time from 180 beats·min^{-1} to 120 beats·min^{-1} during an interval session or race; or what makes you angry, to how anger affects your performance; or what does and doesn't help you get into the ideal physical and mental state before a race.

facilitate performance and how quickly you can recover from an all-out attack are all important factors in the psychology of performance.

PLANNING
Setting goals

Since my first encounter with sport psychology, the phrase 'it won't all go according to plan unless there's a plan' has been one of my guiding principles. The plan in question could be for a training session, a race, a season, an Olympic cycle or even a whole career. Whichever it is, developing the plan requires three processes: setting goals, acquiring feedback and making decisions. Or, in other words, knowing what you want to achieve, the degree to which you achieved it and what you are going to do about it.

Everything you do in sport is effectively a goal. Deciding to do a long race next week for training purposes is a short-term process goal, while setting your sights on the Olympic road race title in eight years' time is a long-term outcome goal. Of course, most sports goals relate to both processes and outcomes; winning the regional championships next month is a short-term outcome goal, but it is also part of the long-term process of Olympic selection; the decision to launch a speculative attack on a climb in a road race to test your opponents' legs and see who comes with you is a short-term process goal, while gaining 30 seconds over the bunch in doing so, and holding that advantage to the finish, will lead to the short-term outcome goal of winning the race.

The SMART principle for setting goals (*see* table 11.1) has been an effective method by which to motivate people in domains as varied as education, the military and health. It certainly works in sport. Essentially, if you use the SMART criteria (and bear in mind the three extra criteria in table 11.2), you cannot go far wrong.

Each explicit goal you set should conform to the SMART criteria: 'I will attack hard on one of the climbs' does not, while 'I will attack at around 170 beats·min^{-1} (which is measureable and achievable) for 60 seconds (which is timed and achievable) on the third climb of the day (which is specific), having seen who the other strong climbers are on the first two climbs' is. When a goal is SMART, the same criteria that determine exactly how you go about achieving the goal also determine that you know whether or not you have in fact achieved it. It's hard to know whether you achieved the goal of 'going hard on the first hill to see how it feels'; could you have gone harder for longer? What has this plan achieved? Does the knowledge gained help you develop a database of your potential? No. However, you can state categorically that you either were or were not able to ride at 170 beats·min^{-1} for the 12-minute long third climb and to recover back to 150 beats·min^{-1} within 2 minutes of going over the top, information that might be vital to you later in the race or at a later date. Making a goal SMART not only defines what you have to do but helps you know whether or not you have achieved it.

	Description	Bad example	Good example
Specific	Goal must be a specific state that you know that you have achieved	I will do well in every race	I will place in the top 3 at the divisional championships, and in the top 10 at the national championships
Measurable	Goal must be a specific amount	I will do a good time at the national 25 championships	I will ride between 51.30 and 52.00 minutes at the national 25 championships
Achievable yet challenging	Goal must be sufficiently challenging to motivate you but not so challenging as to de-motivate you	I'll do my best in each race/I'll win every race	I'll aim to win four of 20 of my road races this season
Regularly reviewed	Progress towards the goal must be regularly checked and, if too slow or too fast, the goal changed	I will do a 25 mile time trial two weeks before the national 25 championships to assess my fitness	I will do a 25 mile time trial six months and again three months before the national 25 championships to assess my fitness and to give myself time to change my training if I'm not happy with my performance
Timed	A timeline for goals allows you to establish the process by which to achieve them	I'm going to increase my power output gradually throughout the season	I'm going to be able to produce 300 W for an hour in January, 315 W for an hour in March and 330 W for an hour in June, and maintain that for the rest of the racing season

TABLE 11.1 Goal setting using the SMART system

	Outcome goal	Process
Outcome versus process	I will win the regional championships	If I can produce 330 W for an hour, and if I get into the right break, with my ability to sprint, I can win the regional championships
Short, medium and long term	I will ride the 2020 Olympic road race	I will need to be in the regional team by 2014 and the national team by 2016, and to be ranked in the top three in the UK by 2018
Controllable	I will be the strongest rider in the field	If I am able to produce 400 W per hour by the time of the race, I am likely to be one of, if not the, strongest in the field

TABLE 11.2 Incorporating process, multiple timescales and controllability into goal setting

Have one or more explicit goals for every training session, every race and every season

There has to be a goal for every session, and even those goals should be SMART. Everything from an easy recovery ride to an all-out hill interval session can conform to this rule. An example for the former would be: 'Ride at less than 130 beats·min⁻¹ (S, M, A) for no more than 90 minutes (T). Monitor heart rate every 5 minutes (R)'. An example for the latter would be: 'Ride 10 hill repeats (S, M) at no more than 170 beats·min⁻¹ (M) and higher than 80 rev·min⁻¹ (M) of 2 minutes each (T) with 3 minutes' recovery (T). If heart rate is increasing above 170 beats·min⁻¹ at 80 rev·min⁻¹ (R), reduce gear ratio or increase duration of rest periods'. In both cases, achieving or not achieving the goal is data to add to your personal performance database and to inform future decisions. These goals also prevent situations such as overtraining or regression to the mean (i.e. all of your training sessions ending up at the same moderate intensity).

Above, I suggested a race goal of attacking at around 170 beats·min⁻¹ for 60 seconds on the third climb of the day, having seen who the other strong climbers are on the first two climbs. An obvious question in this scenario would be: 'How do I know whether I can do that and still have the legs to go again if I have a gap over the bunch?' Easy: because you have done exactly that in training many times, and by doing so, you have developed a personal database of what you can and cannot do in that situation (that database is what enables you to set SMART goals for performance).

TAKE-HOME MESSAGE

Don't just think about goals in the long term; you should have SMART goals for every training session, every race and every season.

If...	Then...
If I arrive too early for the race	I will wait in the car and will not break my pre-performance routine
If I arrive late for the race	I will use my modified (shortened) pre-performance routine
If I don't get a good warm-up and the race goes out slowly	I will ride of the front at about 80% maximum effort early on to get myself mentally and physically ready to race
If I don't get a good warm-up and the race goes out fast	I will do a few turns at the front to get myself mentally and physically prepared and then sit back in the bunch until the race starts to unfold; if I can't get to the front, I'll drop off the back a couple of times and ride back hard
If there's an early crash and I'm caught behind it	I will pause and look around to see who's come down, who's behind us and how many have got away; I won't panic; I'll find other good riders to work with to get back to the bunch
If my break blocks are rubbing (or similar technical problem)	I will stop and adjust this early in the race; if I don't, it might cause me problems later on; even if it doesn't cause me problems, it will distract and annoy me if I don't sort it; I will ride back to the bunch efficiently
If it is raining	I will make or get away in an early break to avoid crashes and to get a decent view of the course
If it is windy	I will stay sheltered in the bunch for the early part of the race and wait for a strong break to develop before making a move
If it is cold	I will warm up a little longer than usual and overdress but ensure I can remove clothing as the temperature increases
If I puncture in the first part of the race	I will get a new wheel and ride to get back into the race
If I puncture in the second part of the race	I will repair the puncture and ride back to HQ
If a break goes early	I will stay in the bunch and see how it develops; if it's still away at half distance, I will look for a move to get across

TABLE 11.6 Sample if–then plans for a cyclist in a moderately important road race

If...	Then...
If a break is away and no-one is making a move across	I will sit slightly to the open (centre of road) side of the bunch and keep a good eye out for a drop in pace or a winding stretch of road with poor visibility, at which point I will launch an all-out attack and will not look behind me for the first 90 seconds, giving the bunch the impression that I'm strong and mean business
If I've chased a break and am caught between the break and the bunch	I will ride as if I am in a hard training session and set a goal of keeping ahead of the bunch as long as possible; once I'm caught, I'll sit in until the end of the race keeping effort and heart rate as low as possible
If I've caught the break	Irrespective of how I feel, I will sit in and pretend to be too tired to pull through until I've had long enough to size up the riders
If the break starts to slow	I will launch a solo attack
If a lone rider has jumped away from the break close to the end of the race	I will wait for someone else to chase; if no-one does, I will launch an all-out attack in an attempt to get across if we pass under the '5 km to go' banner; I would rather try to win with tired legs in a two-man sprint than wait for the race to come back together and sprint with fresh legs against the whole bunch
If the break stays away and rides towards the finish intact	I will attack with everything I have with 3 km to go; if another rider comes with me, I will ride on the front at 90% effort to maintain and control the speed but leave myself enough gas to resist the other rider trying to come past me in the final 200 m
If there's a strong headwind in the final straight	I will not lead out unless I have no choice; if I do, I will ride at 75% effort, ensuring that I can respond
If there's a strong tailwind in the home straight	I will lead out and wind it up with 400 m to go
If the sprint gets physical	I will maintain my line but not respond physically
If I win	I will thank the other competitors for a great race
If I don't win	I will congratulate the guy who won

Like the pedal stroke of a world champion cyclist to the casual observer, the mental training strategies suggested above seem simple. However, if you read the above chapter and thought 'I do all that already' or 'I was expecting something more complex', but you also suspect that you may not be at your full potential mentally, you might want to pause for thought. That is, like the pedal stroke, mental strategies, no matter how simple, require learning, refinement and repetition if they are to become effective. A strategy that is simple to use on the turbo trainer – for example, using imagery to dissociate from pain or boredom – can be quite difficult to 'switch on' in the heat of competition. This is why you have to train these processes at every opportunity, but most especially when you are on the bike, when you are training and even when you are racing.

When you ride a bike race, the legs do a lot of work, so you need to train them. However, if you want to win bike races, your brain is going to have to do a lot of work as well. The more you want to win, and the higher the level of competition, the more the brain is required to know what is going on in the pack, make critical strategic decisions, control emotions, suppress negative thoughts, give other riders the impression that you are tired when you are strong or that you are strong when you are tired, and a host of other things as well. To do all of this well, you are going to have to train the brain just as you train your legs.

KEY TAKE-HOME MESSAGES

- If you want to win a bike race, your brain will need to work as hard as your body. You need to train your brain for this in much the same way as you train your legs; that is, systematically and progressively.
- The brain responds to systematic training in the same way as the body. Like the body, the brain will become good at doing what it does a lot of; that is, habits will form. Therefore, make sure that your brain is doing during training what you want it to do during competition.
- Make sure all of your goals conform to the SMART principle. A goal that is specific, measureable, achievable yet challenging, regularly reviewed and timed is more likely to be achieved than one that is not.
- Know what you're going to do if things go wrong. Not having to make a snap decision about what to do reduces a lot of the stress and anxiety associated with coping and makes it more likely that your decision and action will have a positive effect on performance. There should be no such things as 'unforeseen circumstances'.

SECTION F

WHAT DO I NEED TO EAT AND DRINK DURING TRAINING AND COMPETITION? NUTRITION FOR CYCLING

The nutritional requirements of the training and competition programmes of endurance cyclists are challenging. Cyclists can expend a large amount of energy owing to the hours they spend on their bikes at moderate to high power outputs. Research suggests that male cyclists involved in an intensive period of training may consume in excess of 8 g per kilogram of their body mass per day to replenish this exercise expenditure. The challenge is how to do this, especially if the cyclist spends a long time in the saddle during stage races or cyclosportives, where consuming substantial amounts of fluid and carbohydrate while cycling can be difficult. Additionally, following racing or training, suppression of appetite owing to exhaustion might limit nutritional intake. Some cyclists take nutritional supplements to aid their preparation for competition and their post-session recovery. However, the claims associated with some supplements may not always be based on scientific findings.

Chapter 12 discusses food and fluid intake during training in preparation for competition, during competition and in recovery. Next, in chapter 13, the effects of different food supplements that could be used as ergogenic aids for training and performance are discussed. In both chapters some basic guidelines and recommendations are provided to enable you to make informed decisions about your nutritional strategy.

Having read section F, you should have an understanding of the optimal strategy for food and fluid intake during training, in preparation for competition and during competition. Additionally, you should be in an informed position that will allow you to make decisions about the necessity of using food supplements as part of your diet.

CHAPTER 12

NUTRITIONAL CONSIDERATIONS FOR OPTIMAL CYCLING PERFORMANCE

Mathew Cole and Nigel Mitchell

Competitive cycling comprises a number of events ranging in both duration and intensity, from short track events (<30 seconds to approximately 1 hour), to time trials over set distances (10–100 miles) to multistage tour events lasting several weeks. Differences in the desired outcomes associated with these events will place varying physiological demands on the cyclist. For example, during a short time trial of around 1 hour, the cyclist will aim to complete a set distance in as quick a time as possible; this will require predominant use of the cyclist's carbohydrate stores (muscle glycogen). On the other hand, during a long, flat tour stage (around 4–5 hours), the cyclist will aim to be the first over the line, regardless of time taken; therefore, during this event the main source of energy will be provided by the cyclist's fat reserves. It is thus essential that each cyclist aim to adopt an individual nutritional strategy according to the demands of the event he is preparing for. In this respect, it is key that a cyclist look at obtaining these nutritional needs from their diet. This chapter discusses the key nutritional issues that cyclists face and provides appropriate recommendations on how to best overcome these.

Owing to the large variability in the body mass of individual cyclists, it would be impractical to provide nutritional recommendations that did not take this into account. For example, if a recommendation of carbohydrate intake was 455 g·day^{-1} for all cyclists, this may be suitable for a cyclist with a body mass of 65 kg but not for a cyclist with a body mass of 82 kg. Therefore, it is common for nutritional recommendations to be provided as g·kg^{-1}·day^{-1}. The advantage of this is that the recommendation is adaptable for each individual cyclist. These units should be read as grams per kilogram of body mass per day. Applying this to the above example:

- Recommended daily carbohydrate intake for trained cyclist = 6–8 g·kg^{-1}·day^{-1}.
- Body mass of cyclist A is 65 kg: 65 x 6–8 g·kg^{-1}·day^{-1} = 390–520 g·day^{-1}.
- Body mass of cyclist B is 82 kg: 82 x 6–8 g·kg^{-1}·day^{-1} = 492–656 g·day^{-1}.

Therefore, based on the recommendation, cyclist B should aim to consume markedly more carbohydrate per day than cyclist A (assuming they are both undertaking the same training).

TRAINING NUTRITION

Any athlete will have increased nutritional requirements in comparison with the general population. Cyclists in particular will require higher energy intake to meet the demands of their training. This increased demand will depend on three aspects of their training: volume (the amount of training), frequency (how often training is undertaken) and intensity (how hard the training is). Generally, the higher these three variables are, the higher the cyclist's energy requirements will be.

Owing to a cyclist's high training load, there is potential for a high energy deficit. In other words, more energy will be used up as a result of regular training, creating a shortfall in energy that needs to be replaced. Therefore, the cyclist has to ensure that he eats enough food to achieve three main goals, which are to:

- overcome the energy deficit;
- maximise the adaptation to training; and
- refuel for the next session.

How do I ensure that I take in enough energy to replace what I am burning?

Ensuring that sufficient energy is replaced can be achieved by alteration of one key nutrient in the diet: carbohydrate. Carbohydrate is the body's predominant source of fuel during exercise. During training, carbohydrate will be used at a high rate to provide the vast proportion of energy required to push the pedals and propel the bicycle forwards. If this carbohydrate is not available, the relative contribution of fat sources to produce energy will increase. This will cause the cyclist to slow down, because fat cannot be metabolised as quickly as carbohydrate to meet the demands of high-intensity exercise. In addition, fat requires carbohydrate in order to be broken down and used as a fuel during exercise. Therefore, it is essential that before training you have enough carbohydrate within your system to meet the demands of the session and that you endeavour to replace what has been used after the session. Carbohydrate recommendations for cyclists vary depending on the amount of training undertaken. These recommendations are shown in table 12.1.

Training load	Carbohydrate ($g \cdot kg^{-1} \cdot day^{-1}$)
3–5 hours/week	4–5
1–2 hours/day	5–7
2–4 hours/day	8–10
4–6 hours/day	>10

TABLE 12.1 Recommended carbohydrate intake based on training duration

Food	Serving size	Amount of carbohydrate (g)
White rice (boiled)	180 g	56
Spaghetti (boiled)	220 g (cooked weight)	50
Malt loaf	2 slices	46
White bread	2 slices	35
Rice pudding	200 g	32
Baked/jacket potato	150 g	32
Shredded Wheat	35 g	32
Lucozade Sport	500 ml	32
Wholemeal bread	2 slices	30
Cornflakes	30 g	27
Banana	1 medium	23
Porridge	250 ml	22

TABLE 12.2 Foods that contain high amounts of carbohydrate

In the majority of cases, carbohydrate intake should contribute around 55–65 per cent of the total energy intake. Table 12.2 contains examples of foods that contain high amounts of carbohydrate to help achieve this requirement. During periods of high training loads, cyclists may wish to increase this intake to 8–10 $g·kg^{-1}·day^{-1}$ and, during a 'carbo-loading' phase in preparation for competition, intakes of over 10 $g·kg^{-1}·day^{-1}$ may be necessary. In addition, during these times, carbohydrate should contribute 65–70 per cent of your overall energy intake to ensure that you are meeting your energy requirements.

Monitoring bodyweight regularly can provide a simple and reasonably reliable method of determining whether energy intake is sufficient to meet energy demands. If a cyclist's bodyweight is relatively consistent, he is said to be in 'energy balance', whereby energy intake is matching energy expenditure. If over a given period his body mass increases, he is in 'positive energy balance'; that is, he is consuming more energy via his diet than he is burning through daily activities. If positive energy balance is sustained for a significant period of time, the cyclist will gain weight, which could be detrimental to his performance as the power-to-weight ratio will decrease. By contrast, if the cyclist's body mass decreases over a given period of time, he is in 'negative energy balance'; that is, he is not eating enough energy to meet the demands of training. If negative energy balance continues over a long period of time, the cyclist will enter chronic energy deficit, which could have detrimental effects on both health and performance. Nonetheless, it is important to note that on occasion negative energy balance may be desirable for some cyclists, for example if they wish to lose body mass in the lead up to the competitive season. In such situations, cyclists should monitor energy intake and expenditure carefully to maximise the weight loss strategy and minimise the likelihood of entering chronic energy deficit.

How do I ensure that I recover and adapt to training?

Linked to the above, it is also important to recognise that, if you are in energy deficit, this may inhibit your adaptation to training. While insufficient energy will hinder recovery, it is also essential that training is balanced with sufficient rest to allow adaptation to occur. Indeed, it is often stated that 'you don't get fit by training; you get fit by resting and recovering'. In other words, training causes breakdown of the body's tissues and, without adequate rest and recovery, these tissues will not repair and the body will not get any fitter. A key component of the recovery process is nutrition. The main nutrient that will aid recovery is protein. Proteins are often referred to as the 'building blocks of life', as they are primarily involved in the growth and repair of cells. For example, exercise places stress on fibres within the muscle, causing some to tear and break down. The symptom of this damage is the muscle stiffness or soreness that can occasionally be felt in the days following an intense training session. When rested and provided with adequate protein, the muscle will repair itself and become bigger, stronger or more efficient than before.

To provide a sufficient amount of protein to aid optimal recovery and adaptation to training, it is recommended that endurance-trained cyclists aim to consume 1.2–1.8 $g \cdot kg^{-1} \cdot day^{-1}$ of protein. For the vast majority of cyclists, this can be achieved without the need for supplementation as long as they follow a balanced diet that ensures their energy intake is sufficient to overcome the energy deficit. Sprint cyclists, or those undertaking specific strength training, require increased amounts of protein as more muscle damage is caused as a result of intense training. For these cyclists, the recommended intake is 1.7–1.8 $g \cdot kg^{-1} \cdot day^{-1}$ and, as before, there is good evidence to suggest that the majority of athletes can achieve this without the need for supplementation. Table 12.3 indicates how a 70 kg rider would comfortably achieve his daily protein requirements.

Meal	Food consumed	Amount of protein (g)
Breakfast	2 cups cereal	4
	300 ml milk	12
	2 slices toast	4
Lunch	2 bread rolls each with 50 g chicken	30
	250 ml flavoured low-fat milk	10
Dinner	Stir-fry with 2 cups pasta + 100 g stir-fried	
	beef steak strips	40
Snacks	1 carton yoghurt	10
	1 cereal bar	2
	64g REGO rapid	17
Analysis		**129 g**
		1.9 g/kg

TABLE 12.3 Amount of food that will provide adequate protein for 70 kg rider

Glycogen, the body's main source of carbohydrate, is stored in the liver and skeletal muscle. Liver glycogen stores help to maintain blood sugar levels and a supply of energy to the brain. During endurance exercise, muscle glycogen will provide the majority of energy and it is essential that these stores are replaced post-exercise. This replacement process is known as 'glycogen resynthesis'.

How do I refuel for my next training session?

Consuming a diet that is high in carbohydrate will help to restore the intramuscular stores of glycogen so that there is adequate energy for the subsequent training session. However, there are other factors that can aid the recovery process and help to ensure that replenishment is optimal.

First, it is important to consume a carbohydrate-rich meal as close as is reasonably possible to the cessation of exercise. The majority of research indicates that there is a 'golden hour' within which cyclists should aim to start the refuelling process, but it is generally regarded that the sooner, the better. The reason behind this recommendation is that metabolic pathways (particularly glycogen resynthesis) are most active in the minutes and early hours following exercise. Evidence suggests that glycogen replenishment is up to around 50 per cent lower if intake is delayed until two hours after exercise. Analysis of a large number of studies suggests that glycogen resynthesis is optimal when carbohydrate intakes of $1.0–1.2$ $g \cdot kg^{-1} \cdot hour^{-1}$ are ingested in the first four hours following exercise.

During this immediate recovery phase, some cyclists may find that the use of supplements is beneficial in fulfilling the need for a quick supply of nutrients. For example, it is common for athletes to report suppression of appetite immediately post-exercise, but most will be able to consume a sports drink or protein shake. In addition, supplements provide a readily available, immediate source of nutrition when access to a more appropriate source is not always possible.

Second, when carbohydrate is co-ingested with protein, research has indicated that the rate of protein synthesis (and, therefore, growth and repair) is significantly higher. The amount of protein required will depend on the nature of the exercise – more intense exercise will cause more muscle damage and so more protein will be required. Nonetheless, it appears that post-exercise protein resynthesis rates peak when a protein intake of $0.3–0.4$ $g \cdot kg^{-1}$ (approximately 20–30 g for most cyclists) is ingested. At present, there is no conclusive research to favour one source of protein over any other. However, there are some indications that dairy, and possibly whey protein, may be most appropriate post-exercise owing to their fast absorption rates into the body.

'Train low, compete high': interesting new research

It has long been established that carbohydrate availability as a fuel is an essential component of performance in both intermittent, short-duration, high-intensity events (sprints, track events, time trials, etc.) and prolonged endurance events (tour stages, classics, etc.) As discussed above, it is generally regarded that a high-carbohydrate diet is the most beneficial for training adaptations and subsequent competition performance.

However, recent research has indicated possible benefits of training with low carbohydrate intakes followed by the replenishment of high carbohydrate stores in the lead-up to competition. This strategy has been termed 'train low, compete high'. It is suggested that the adaptations to training are enhanced when exercise is undertaken with low carbohydrate availability. The proposed mechanism behind this benefit is that there is more expression of genes that are linked to training adaptations and so the training is more effective. While there is mounting evidence that this strategy can promote training adaptations, as yet there is little evidence to suggest that this leads to improved performance. Further research is required before we are able to provide specific guidelines on how cyclists could include a 'train low, compete high' strategy in their own training programme.

It is also important to take into account potential adverse effects that can develop from regularly training with low carbohydrate stores. These adverse effects include increased risk of injury, illness and overtraining. Nonetheless, this may be an interesting area of research in the coming years and some cyclists may wish to test this strategy for themselves when the consequences of any problems are much lower, for example when competition performance is not particularly important or during the off-season.

RESEARCH FOCUS: 'TRAIN LOW, COMPETE HIGH'

Hanson and colleagues undertook a study to investigate whether training with low muscle glycogen content would enhance muscular adaptations. In this study, participants conducted leg-extension training (kicking out) with slightly different protocols for each leg. While the total training load was the same for each leg (5 hours per week), one leg was exercised twice a day, every other day, whereas the other leg was exercised once daily. This design allowed one leg to fully restore muscle glycogen before exercise (the once-a-day leg), while the other leg performed the second session in a glycogen-depleted state. While the results demonstrated similar increases in maximal power for both legs, the time to fatigue was almost twice as long in the leg that had been trained with low muscle glycogen levels. In addition, this performance improvement correlated with an increase in the activity of genes that are associated with training adaptations. The results of this study, and others, suggest that training with low glycogen stores may be more beneficial than when training is undertaken in the high-carbohydrate state.

COMPETITION NUTRITION
How do I ensure that I am fully fuelled for competition?

In the lead-up to a competition, the main aim should be to maximise the carbohydrate stores inside the body as carbohydrate will be the predominant source of fuel during the race. This can be achieved most effectively by increasing the amount of carbohydrate consumed in the diet in the two to three days preceding an event. This practice is termed 'carbohydrate loading'.

Traditionally, carbohydrate loading was suggested to be most effective by following a supercompensatory protocol. With this approach, one week before an event, the cyclist undertakes an exhaustive exercise bout to deplete his glycogen stores. This is then followed by three days of a low-carbohydrate diet and another bout of exhaustive exercise. Only then, three days before competition, does the cyclist start to increase his carbohydrate stores by following a high-carbohydrate diet up until the start of the event.

However, more recently, research has indicated that similar increases in carbohydrate stores can be achieved via more moderate protocols. It is now suggested that a gradual increase in carbohydrate intake accompanied by a gradual tapering of training in the week leading up to competition will result in a similar response.

In the immediate lead-up to competition, scientific research reports significant improvements in performance after consumption of a large meal (ideally high in carbohydrate) approximately 4 hours before the race. For a number of athletes, this would usually be breakfast. This meal is particularly important as some of the body's carbohydrate reserves will have become depleted overnight. Table 12.4 contains two examples of carbohydrate-rich pre-exercise meals that could elicit the observed performance improvements. The time period is also important as it allows sufficient time for gastric emptying and absorption of the carbohydrate, thus minimising the potential for gastrointestinal discomfort during exercise.

Example 1	Example 2
160 g porridge	220 g pasta (cooked weight)
1 banana	45 g tuna
5 g/1 tsp sugar	45 g sweetcorn
2 slices white bread	2 slices malt loaf
30 g fruit jam	10 g fruit jam
250 ml apple juice	250 ml orange juice
Total carbohydrate = 130 g	**Total carbohydrate = 125 g**

TABLE 12.4 Examples of pre-exercise meals

What should I consume during competition?

From a nutritional perspective, during endurance exercise there are two main causes of fatigue: dehydration and depletion of the body's carbohydrate stores. Hydration and fluid replacement strategies are discussed in more depth later in this chapter. This section focuses on the optimal methods of minimising the impact of carbohydrate depletion on cycling performance.

During exercise, the body has two main sources of carbohydrate to use as a fuel for exercise. These sources are referred to as endogenous or exogenous.

- **Endogenous carbohydrate:** carbohydrate that is stored within the body, predominantly in the form of glycogen in the liver and skeletal muscle. The source of carbohydrate will be the principal supply of energy during endurance performance.
- **Exogenous carbohydrate:** carbohydrate that is supplied via an external source, for example consumed in drinks, gels, bars, bananas, scones, paninis and so on. The purpose of this source of energy is to provide a supplementary fuel source to the endogenous carbohydrate as a means of prolonging the point at which it becomes depleted.

It is important to recognise that, while it has long been accepted that carbohydrate ingestion can significantly improve endurance performance, the exact mechanism(s) by which this occurs is (are) not fully understood. Of the various proposed mechanisms, there are three areas on which the majority of scientific literature has focused.

First, it is proposed that consumption of carbohydrate has a 'sparing' effect on the liver and muscle glycogen stores, thus allowing greater capacity to 'dig into' these reserves at a later stage during exercise. However, while some research has shown that this does occur, not all studies have shown that carbohydrate consumption significantly reduces the rate at which glycogen is broken down.

Second, it is suggested that carbohydrate ingestion helps to maintain high blood glucose concentrations and, therefore, high carbohydrate oxidation rates. In other words, for the muscle to use carbohydrate at the optimal rate, the supply of carbohydrate in the blood needs to be high. Consumption of carbohydrate during exercise helps to ensure that the levels of carbohydrate in the blood remain sufficiently high to allow this.

Finally, a relatively recently proposed mechanism has discussed the potential benefits of carbohydrate ingestion on the central nervous system. Perception of effort scores have been shown to significantly improve following the consumption of carbohydrate. Furthermore, positive effects on cognition and performance have been demonstrated when carbohydrate was simply rinsed around the mouth and not ingested. While the exact mechanism is not fully understood, it is suggested that there are carbohydrate receptors within the mouth that, when stimulated, activate areas of the brain that are associated with feelings of pleasure and reward. This causes the cyclist's perception of effort to decrease and thus allows him to exercise at a higher intensity, thereby improving performance. The advantage of this 'mouth-rinsing' procedure as opposed to ingestion of the carbohydrate is that it is common for cyclists to report symptoms of gastrointestinal distress following ingestion. When the carbohydrate solution is rinsed and spat out, these symptoms are significantly reduced.

RESEARCH FOCUS: CARBOHYDRATE 'MOUTH-RINSING'

Chambers and colleagues undertook a study investigating 1-hour time trial performance while cyclists rinsed and spat out either a 6.4 per cent carbohydrate drink or an artificially sweetened placebo solution at regular intervals. During the carbohydrate mouth-rinse trials, cyclists completed the time trial approximately 2 minutes faster than those on the non-carbohydrate placebo trials. In addition, functional magnetic resonance brain imagery revealed greater activation of reward-related regions in response to a carbohydrate stimulus. Figure 12.1 shows increased power output at varying stages of a 1-hour time trial when cyclists rinsed either a glucose (a) or maltodextrin (b) solution in comparison with a placebo. Similar findings have been reported during running performance of similar duration. This research has implications for cycling performance of approximately 1-hour duration and other events where cyclists report gastrointestinal discomfort following carbohydrate ingestion.

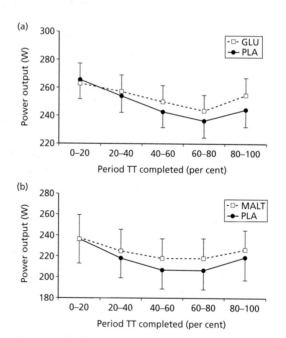

FIG.12.1 The influence of carbohydrate mouth-rinsing on power output during a one-hour time trial (TT) (Adapted with permission from Chambers, E.S., Bridge, M.W., Jones, D.A., 'Carbohydrate sensing in the human mouth: effects on exercise performance and brain activity', *Journal of Physiology*, 587 (2009), pp. 1779–1794)

As mentioned above, to date no single mechanism has been shown to be the underlying cause of carbohydrate-induced enhanced sporting performance. Therefore, it is likely that improvements are the result of a combination of these mechanisms.

Source of 60–70 g carbohydrate

1 l sports drink
2–3 energy gels
1–2 energy bars
3 bananas
75 g boiled sweets

TABLE 12.5 Sources of carbohydrate to meet 60–70 g/hour^{-1}.

During exercise, peak breakdown rates of exogenous carbohydrates are approximately 1.0 g·min^{-1}, and this appears to peak when ingestion rates are around 1.2 g·min^{-1} (72 g·hour^{-1}). Therefore, it is recommended that cyclists aim to consume 60–70 g of carbohydrate per hour if the exercise is likely to persist for periods of 1 hour or longer. If the exercise duration is significantly less than 1 hour, there is little or no benefit of consuming carbohydrate. It is thought that, owing to the limited time available, only a small amount of the ingested carbohydrate can be digested and absorbed to become available to be used as a fuel. Examples of how 60–70 g·hour^{-1} of carbohydrate can be consumed during exercise are presented in table 12.5.

It is important to recognise that there are benefits and disadvantages associated with each of the methods of carbohydrate consumption. For example, both dehydration and fuel depletion can be addressed simultaneously via the consumption of sports drinks. However, a large volume (around 1 L) needs to be consumed in order to achieve this. Some cyclists report feelings of gastrointestinal discomfort following ingestion of large volumes of fluid, so this may not be suitable for those athletes. An alternative could be to consume energy gels or sports bars as the carbohydrate is much more concentrated and therefore only a small volume need be ingested. In addition, gels or bars are much lighter to carry than sports drinks and, in an event where the power-to-weight ratio is crucial, some cyclists feel that the former may be more advantageous. The disadvantages of these bars and gels are that some users find them too sweet to tolerate in the mouth and that fluid would still need to be consumed separately to maintain adequate hydration status. Furthermore, there is evidence to suggest that solid foods may be slower to empty from the stomach than liquids and so the carbohydrate may not become available as quickly.

Clearly, no one source is more advantageous than another. Therefore, individual preference and oral tolerance are the most common factors for differences in carbohydrate choices. Finally, it is important to note that cyclists should always practise their feeding strategies in training first before trying to apply them during competition.

Recovery from competition

We have already discussed in this chapter how best to recover from one training session to the next, and the same basic principles apply following competition:

- Consume something as soon as possible post-exercise
- Ideally, consume something high in carbohydrate ($1.0–1.2$ g·kg⁻¹·hour⁻¹) in the first 4 hours after competition
- A combination of carbohydrate and protein may be more advantageous
- Supplements may be best able to fulfil this role.

FLUID REPLACEMENT
How much fluid do I need to consume during training and competition?

As discussed above, there are two predominant causes of fatigue during prolonged exercise: fuel depletion and dehydration. Earlier in this chapter we focused on strategies to optimise fuel provision and delivery to the muscle. The following sections address the issue of fluid loss during cycling and strategies to minimise the detrimental effects of dehydration on performance.

During exercise, the body temperature rises owing to the inefficiency of muscle contraction; if this is not controlled, exhaustion, heat stroke and even organ failure could occur. In an attempt to keep the temperature under control, sweat is secreted onto the surface of the skin and heat is lost through evaporation. Prolonged sweating will lead to significant loss of fluid and salts from the body, which is termed 'dehydration'.

Fluid requirements will vary considerably according to both the cyclist and the environmental conditions. For example, individual cyclists will have different sweat rates and, therefore, varying water and salt losses. Reported sweat rates in athletes can range from 800 ml·hour⁻¹ to over 3 l·hour⁻¹. These rates may depend on individual characteristics, such as metabolism and bodyweight, and may also change according to the environmental temperature, humidity or even clothing. Therefore, each cyclist will require different amounts of fluid and salts to remain optimally hydrated, so it is recommended that individuals develop their own customised fluid replacement

FIG.12.2 The primary aim of fluid intake during exercise is to ensure that there is no significant loss in body mass from the start to the end

programme. Nonetheless, below are broad recommendations in accordance with the most recent research into this topic.

How much should I drink before cycling?

It is essential that the cyclist is adequately hydrated before training or competition in order to aid optimal performance and decrease the risk of heat stroke and exhaustion. To achieve this, it is good practice to increase fluid intake in the days leading up to competition. A simple estimate of hydration status can be made regularly through observation of urine colour at the start of the day. Generally, a pale light yellow colour is indicative of good hydration status whereas a darker yellow/light brown colour indicates dehydration.

On the day of competition, drink approximately 7 ml·kg⁻¹ bodyweight of fluid (e.g. 490 ml for a 70 kg cyclist) 2–3 hours before exercise to allow adequate time for the fluid to be retained and any excess to be excreted. The addition of a small amount of salt to the fluid or consumption in combination with a salty snack will promote fluid retention and stimulate thirst.

How much should I aim to drink during cycling?

During cycling, the predominant losses of water will be as a result of sweating (with a negligible amount lost through respiration). Sweat loss causes the body to lose not only fluid but also salts. If these salts are not replaced alongside the fluid, retention of the ingested water will be inhibited. The primary aim of fluid intake during exercise is to ensure that there is no significant loss in body mass from the start to the end of the session. Research indicates that a body mass loss of as little as 2 per cent can have a detrimental effect on performance. To ensure that there is no large decrease in body mass, it is essential that the cyclist consumes fluid almost from the outset and continues to do so at regular intervals during exercise. As discussed above, owing to the large variability in individual sweat rates and environmental conditions, it is difficult to provide a 'one size fits all' recommendation for adequate fluid intake. Therefore, it is important that each cyclist routinely assesses his bodyweight losses during exercise in order to develop his own fluid replacement strategy. It is important to recognise that thirst is not a good indicator of hydration status. It is generally accepted that the perception of thirst is not stimulated until an individual has already gone beyond the 2 per cent loss of bodyweight attributable to sweating. So, by the time thirst is sensed, performance will already have been impaired.

How much should I drink to ensure that I optimally rehydrate?

Research suggests that, post-exercise, cyclists should aim to consume 1.5 l of fluid for every 1 l they have lost. It is not enough to simply replace what you have lost, as this does not allow for urine losses in the hours after the liquid has been ingested. As before, fluid consumption in combination with a small amount of salt will promote retention of the ingested fluid and stimulate thirst.

HOW TO ESTIMATE SWEAT RATE

- Record weight before exercise.
- Record any fluid consumed during exercise: weigh the bottle before and after exercise to estimate the amount consumed.
- Record weight post-exercise.
- Total weight loss = (pre-exercise weight – post-exercise weight) + fluid consumed.

Example: Cyclist's pre-exercise weight = 71.4 kg. Cyclist consumed 500 ml in a 1-hour session. Cyclist's post-exercise weight = 70.8 kg.
71.4 kg – 70.8 kg = 0.6 kg
0.6 kg + 500 g (assume 1 ml of fluid = 1 g) = 1.1 kg
Therefore, post-exercise, the cyclist would have to consume 1.5 x 1.1 = 1.65 l to optimally rehydrate.

KEY TAKE-HOME MESSAGES

- Consumption of a high-carbohydrate diet (6–8 $g \cdot kg^{-1} \cdot day^{-1}$; 55–60 per cent total energy intake) will ensure adequate energy provision and aid recovery.
- Sufficient protein intake (1.2–1.8 $g \cdot kg^{-1} \cdot day^{-1}$) will promote optimal adaptations to training.
- In the lead-up to competition, increasing carbohydrate intake to 8–10 $g \cdot kg^{-1} \cdot day^{-1}$ will boost energy stores and may provide advantages for long-duration performance.
- During exercise of 1-hour duration or more, cyclists should aim to consume 60–70 g of carbohydrate per hour.
- Post-exercise, cyclists should aim to consume something within the 'golden hour'. Ideally, this would contain a high amount of carbohydrate and would be ingested as soon as possible after exercise.
- Fluid requirements will vary considerably among cyclists. It is recommended that individual cyclists adopt their own tailored hydration strategy to ensure optimal hydration.
- Cyclists should aim to eat a variety of foods including breads, cereals, fruits and vegetables.

CHAPTER 13

ERGOGENIC AIDS

Kevin Currell

Dietary supplement use is common among both elite and non-elite athletes. Such supplements are commonly referred to as ergogenic aids. Ergogenic aids are supplements or procedures that enhance human performance. However, the information we receive about how to best use supplements and if they even work can be misleading and confusing. The International Olympic Committee statement on sport nutrition states that only four ergogenic aids have been shown to be effective in enhancing performance. These are creatine, caffeine, sodium bicarbonate and beta-alanine. These will be discussed within this chapter, along with others that, although the scientific research is certainly less conclusive, may have a role in enhancing training and performance.

This chapter takes you through supplements that can help to promote adaptation to training, those that help you to cope with training stress and those that can enhance race-day performance.

THE ROLE OF SUPPLEMENTS

Ergogenic aids and dietary supplements can play an important role within both training and racing. However, they should never be seen as a replacement for a good-quality training and racing diet. They should also not be seen as a 'quick fix' or a reason to avoid training. They are the cherry on top of the cake rather than the be all and end all. Taken in conjunction with an appropriate training diet, ergogenic aids can enhance recovery, promote adaptation to training and, come race day, help you to maximise performance.

When deciding whether or not to use a dietary supplement, you should undertake a cost–benefit analysis. In particular, look at whether the supplement has actually been proved to enhance performance or whether it is just marketing hype. Some supplements claim to contain certain products; however, the amounts contained within the supplement are often too small to have an effect on performance or health outcomes. Look at the possible cons of using the supplement, including the financial cost, simplicity of use and whether or not it could contribute to a positive doping test.

THE SAFETY OF SUPPLEMENTS

Many supplements are safe to use and do not confer any negative adverse effects on health and wellbeing. However, the research conducted on ergogenic aids and supplements is limited and is not as thorough or rigorous as the research and legislation applied to pharmaceuticals. Therefore, it is important to use dietary supplements and ergogenic aids with caution.

Where possible, it is best to consult an expert, such as a sport dietician or nutritionist. It is also good practice to discuss the use of any supplement with your general practitioner to ensure that there is no issue with their use and your general health.

It is in the athlete's mindset to believe that more is better. However, this is generally not the case with supplements. Research often shows a dose–response relationship, where continuing to increase the amount taken does not confer any greater performance effects. When using a supplement, stick to the recommended dose.

It is also important to purchase supplements from a reputable source that follows good manufacturing processes. There are reports of between 10 per cent and 30 per cent of available supplements being contaminated with substances such as hormones that are prohibited for use in the sporting environment. Supplements can also contain ingredients not listed on the ingredient list and, where manufacturing processes are poor, there have been reports of impurities such as glass being found within supplements.

THE MAIN SUPPLEMENTS FOR CYCLING PERFORMANCE

It is beyond the scope of this chapter to discuss all of the available supplements; therefore, only the most relevant and effective for cycling performance are discussed below.

Beta-alanine

Carnosine is a naturally occurring protein within the muscle. Carnosine is made up of the amino acids beta-alanine and histidine. Carnosine has an important role to play within muscle as it is one of the most effective buffers of hydrogen ions. Hydrogen ions cause the stinging, burning sensation you feel while working at very high intensities and play a role in causing fatigue at these high intensities.

Beta-alanine is a non-essential amino acid found in many foodstuffs. Particularly high concentrations are found in turkey and prawns. When you supplement with beta-alanine, you can increase the amount of carnosine within the muscle. Four weeks of supplementation with beta-alanine can lead to a 60 per cent increase in

RESEARCH FOCUS: BETA-ALANINE AND SPRINT PERFORMANCE

Van Thienen and colleagues undertook a study investigating eight weeks of beta-alanine supplementation, with 2–4 g·day^{-1} being given compared with a placebo. Before and after the supplementation period, participants cycled for 110 minutes, followed by a 10-minute time trial, a further 5 minutes of rest and, finally, a 30-second all-out sprint. The results showed that beta-alanine supplementation did not affect the 10-minute time trial performance, but sprint performance at the end of the trial was increased by 11.4 per cent. This may have significance for events where a sprint finish is often a deciding factor in the performance outcome.

the amount of carnosine within the muscle. Research has shown that increasing the amount of carnosine within your muscle can enhance high-intensity performance, in particular where repeated bouts of high-intensity exercise are required.

However, supplementing with beta-alanine can lead to the adverse effect of a tingling sensation, termed paraesthesia, in the face and extremities (e.g. fingers). This can be avoided if the dose is split up throughout the day rather than taken in one go.

The optimal dose appears to be 2–5 g beta-alanine taken daily for at least four weeks to maximise muscle carnosine content. Where possible, split the dose up into two to four doses throughout the day and take with food to reduce the chances of suffering from paraesthesia.

Sodium bicarbonate and citrate

Sodium bicarbonate is one of the most research-proven ergogenic aids. It is commonly used in baking processes and as an antacid. However, it has long been used to enhance sporting performance.

One of the causes of fatigue, especially in high-intensity exercise, is a decrease in pH within both the muscle and the blood. This decrease in pH is caused by the production of hydrogen ions during the process of glycolysis. Glycolysis is the process by which the muscle breaks down carbohydrate into energy.

When you ingest sodium bicarbonate, the pH of the blood is elevated by increasing the amount of bicarbonate found within the blood. Bicarbonate is one of the most important extracellular buffers within the body. The increase in blood bicarbonate increases the hydrogen ion gradient between muscle and the blood. This causes the hydrogen ions to leave the muscle cells and enter the bloodstream. This limits the effect of hydrogen ions on the muscle and decreases fatigue.

The most effective dose of sodium bicarbonate appears to be 0.3 g·kg⁻¹ bodyweight taken 90–120 minutes before exercise. This dose does not need to be taken in one go and can be split into smaller doses over a longer period of time.

Sodium bicarbonate ingestion can lead to diarrhoea and bloating. You should therefore test it out in training first. To decrease the risk of these adverse effects, sodium bicarbonate should not be taken on an empty stomach and should be consumed with carbohydrate.

While sodium bicarbonate is effective over short-duration events (40 seconds to 10 minutes), there is little evidence of a performance-enhancing effect over longer timescales. Sodium citrate might provide an effective alternative for long-duration

WHAT IS pH AND ACIDITY?

pH is a measure of the acidity of fluids. When your body becomes more acidic, the pH decreases from a neutral range of around 7.0. When it becomes more alkaline, the pH increases above 7.0. A decrease in pH has been suggested to be a possible cause of fatigue during high-intensity exercise.

events. This supplement can be used before long-duration events to hyperhydrate; essentially, it allows you to start the race with hydration above normal. Consuming 5–10 g of sodium citrate and sodium chloride in a 2:1 ratio together with 500–750 ml of fluid 90 minutes before prolonged exercise in the heat can enhance performance and thermoregulation.

Creatine

Creatine is one of the most popular supplements used today. It is commonly associated with strength and muscle mass gains. Creatine is naturally found within the muscle and is a key component of energy production, particularly over a 5–10-second time period.

Creatine is also found within our daily diet, with 1–2 g per day being consumed by your average meat eater. Supplementing with creatine can increase the concentration of creatine within the muscle by up to 20 per cent. Creatine enhances performance by supporting the training process. When performing repeated bouts of high-intensity exercise, supplementing with creatine allows you to complete more work per training session. This accumulation of increased training load leads to an increase in the adaptation to training. Creatine essentially allows you to train harder.

There is little evidence of a direct influence on performance of creatine supplementation and the greatest gains come through supporting and enhancing training. For the endurance athlete, supplementing with creatine during periods of high-intensity work may be beneficial. However, there doesn't seem to be a direct impact on prolonged exercise performance.

The traditional view of supplementing with creatine is to use a loading dose of 20 g·day^{-1} followed by a maintenance dose of 2–3 g for two to four weeks. However, it appears that if you are looking to increase muscle creatine concentrations over a three- to four-week period, a dose of 2–5 g is more than adequate and you do not need to load with a higher dose.

At present, there are no known or proven detrimental health effects of supplementing with creatine. However, creatine is often associated with weight gain owing to the water retention seen with the increase in muscle creatine concentrations. This effect can be individualistic and therefore needs to be monitored, particularly where bodyweight is a performance factor.

Caffeine

Caffeine is one of the most used ergogenic aids in the world, with some suggestions that 90 per cent of the world's adult population include a source of caffeine in their everyday diet. Caffeine's chemical name is trimethylxanthine and it is found in many common drinks and foods. There are many supplements and sport foods that contain varying amounts of caffeine. Until 2003, caffeine was part of the World Anti-Doping Agency's (WADA's) prohibited substances list, with urine concentrations above 12 mg·l^{-1} resulting in a positive doping test. However, since 2003 athletes have been able to use unlimited amounts of caffeine without fear of a positive doping test.

ENHANCING ADAPTATION TO TRAINING WITH ERGOGENIC AIDS

Training is by far the most effective way in which you can enhance performance. Everything you do around that training session and training block should be focused on improving the adaptation to training. Ergogenic aids provide a method by which you can do this. Consider your desired adaptation to training and work backwards from that to determine which supplement to use.

Increased strength and muscle mass

A variety of supplements have been proposed as being effective at increasing strength and muscle mass. Potentially the most effective is creatine, with beta-alanine and caffeine being of potential benefit too. To maximise strength gains and increase muscle mass, consider the following supplement protocols:

- 2–5 grams of creatine daily, preferably taken with a source of carbohydrate. Taking this as part of your post-exercise recovery meal is the most effective method of ensuring that the creatine you supplement with enters the muscle. Start three to four weeks before you intend to focus on strength gains as it takes this long for the creatine concentrations in the muscle to increase.
- 2–4 grams of beta-alanine daily. Beta-alanine seems to work in synergy with creatine to allow you to train harder. This will allow you to get more out of your training sessions and ultimately to improve performance.
- 1–2 milligrams of caffeine 60–90 minutes before a gym session. Use the caffeine to ensure that you can maximise your training sessions.

High-intensity training sessions

One of the aims of high-intensity training is to increase the buffer capacity of the muscle. Using buffering agents during training may help to enhance this adaptation process. At the very least, they will help the athlete to maximise the intensity attained throughout high-intensity training sessions.

- 2–4 grams of beta-alanine daily. The increase in muscle carnosine concentrations seen with beta-alanine supplementation can help you to train harder.
- Sodium bicarbonate has been shown to enhance adaptation to high-intensity interval training; 90 minutes before you do an interval session, take 0.2–0.3 $g \cdot kg^{-1}$ bodyweight of sodium bicarbonate. Research has shown that this will further enhance adaptations in training such as improved lactate threshold and increased buffer capacity of the muscle and, ultimately, lead to an improvement in performance.

RESEARCH FOCUS: COLOSTRUM AND IMMUNE RESPONSE POST-EXERCISE

Glen Davison and Bethany Diment investigated the effect of supplementing with 20 g·day⁻¹ bovine colostrum for four weeks on the immune response following a 2-hour cycle ride at 64 per cent of maximal oxygen consumption. The immune system is depressed for a period of time after a moderate to hard training session. This research showed that bovine colostrum supplementation prevented the decrease in salivary lysozyme activity and speeded the recovery of neutrophil function post-exercise. These findings show that colostrum supplementation can support the immune system post-exercise.

There is some controversy over colostrum supplementation as it contains the hormone insulin-like growth factor 1 (IGF-1), which is a WADA-prohibited substance. However, IGF-1 does not appear to be absorbed from colostrum and, therefore, the supplement appears to be safe. However, as always, it is taken at one's own risk.

Omega 3 fatty acids

Omega 3 fatty acids are essential fatty acids. Essential fatty acids are those that have to be consumed in the diet as they cannot be produced by the body. The most common supplemental source of omega 3 fatty acids comes in the form of fish oil.

The function of omega 3 is dependent on its ratio with omega 6 fatty acids (also an essential fatty acid) in the body. It is thought that our bodies are designed to work optimally when the ratio of omega 3 to 6 is around 1:1. However, our modern diets generally contain these fatty acids in anything up to a 1:20 ratio. This has led to some suggesting that we have a deficiency of omega 3 fatty acids in our diet or that we consume too much omega 6.

One option to change this ratio is to increase omega 3 intake, particularly through fish oil supplementation. When omega 3 fatty acids are consumed, they replace omega 6 fatty acids in the cell membranes of platelets (important for blood clotting), red blood cells and cells that comprise the immune system. This ultimately leads to changes in the inflammatory signals coming from these cells. This change in the inflammatory signals emerging from cells is important as it can have significant effects on the immune system and the function of the body. Omega 3 supplementation has been shown to improve many health outcomes, including blood pressure, cardiovascular health and glucose homeostasis. The health benefits of omega 3 supplementation are many, with good evidence for their effectiveness.

In athletic populations, the evidence for supplementing with omega 3 is limited, although to date there has been very little research. Research has shown that omega 3 supplementation can reduce the oxygen cost of exercise (although the evidence is very limited for this) and can help to prevent exercise-induced asthma.

Antioxidants

Antioxidant is a term used for many different supplements on the market at present. Antioxidants are agents that help the body to defend itself against oxidative stress. The body itself produces antioxidants and training can lead to an increase in the body's natural antioxidant defence mechanisms. Oxidative stress is a natural process that

USE OF SUPPLEMENTS TO SUPPORT TRAINING STRESS

Training to be an elite athlete can be very stressful on the body. This stress is important as it provides the first stimulus for the adaptation to training. However, there are times when the stress of training overwhelms the body's immune system and an athlete begins to get 'run down', ill and, ultimately, overtrained.

Using ergogenic aids and nutrition can be a useful way of helping the body to cope with the training stress. However, it is important to consider these ergogenic aids in the context of the larger nutritional demands of training. The most effective way to support the immune system is to consume carbohydrate during exercise and as soon as possible after training finishes. When training finishes, including protein together with carbohydrate can also be effective in enhancing recovery. Timing is essential: delaying food intake even for an hour after training can have a detrimental effect on the immune system.

It is also important to make sure that a well-balanced diet is consumed. If nutrients are missing from the diet, this may decrease the body's ability to support training stress. Ensure that the food you eat is of good quality in order to help the body to cope with training stress. Foods such as processed carbohydrate and high-saturated-fat foods can impose a stress on the body, so do your best to remove these from your diet.

When these simple dietary processes have been completed, ergogenic aids can be considered. One of the most common sites of stress on the body is the gastrointestinal system. The intestine in particular is closely linked with the immune system. Two supplements that may be able to support gut health are colostrum and probiotics. Simply consuming two probiotic drinks per day will support the immune system through improving gut health. Colostrum supplementation has been shown to decrease gut permeability, thereby supporting the immune system. Supplementing with 10 g·day^{-1} colostrum will help to support gut health.

Omega 3 fatty acids can also support the immune system during periods of heavy stress. Supplementing with 1–2 g omega 3 fatty acids per day may help the body cope with training stress.

Polyphenols also appear to allow the body to recover more quickly and to cope with a greater training load. However, food sources of polyphenols seem to be more effective than supplementation. Simply looking to include foods containing high amounts of polyphenols such as cherry juice, dark chocolate and cinnamon into your daily diet can improve recovery and support the immune system.

occurs within the body, but can lead to fatigue. In theory, if you can increase the body's antioxidant capacity, you should be able to delay fatigue.

Examples of commonly used antioxidants include vitamins C and E or polyphenols such as those found in green tea or apples. There is good evidence in animal models that supplementing with green tea extract can lead to an improvement in exercise performance and an increase in fat oxidation.

The polyphenol quercetin, which can naturally be found in apples and onions, has been shown to enhance the adaptation to training and ultimately improve performance. Again, this evidence comes primarily from animal models; evidence that has not yet been replicated in humans.

Some food-based supplements such as cherry juice have been shown to decrease muscle soreness and increase the speed at which the muscle can function maximally after exercise such as resistance training or marathon running. Other food-based sources of antioxidants, including cinnamon and dark chocolate, have been shown to improve overall health and to support the immune system.

There has also been some research showing that supplementing with large doses of vitamin C can inhibit the adaptation to training. At present, it is difficult to suggest that antioxidants can help to improve performance. However, from the research available, it seems that antioxidants from a food-based source, such as cherry juice and cinnamon, may be the most effective in supporting training.

Nitrates

One of the most recent and interesting supplement areas to be researched is dietary nitrate. Dietary nitrate has been researched through supplementing with beetroot juice. Beetroot juice is naturally high in nitrates, making it a good vehicle to provide nitrates to athletes.

Dietary nitrates are absorbed in the gut and returned to the saliva, where they are converted to nitrite. The nitrite is then once again swallowed and is converted to nitric oxide within the stomach or is absorbed directly as nitrite and subsequently converted to nitric oxide. This ultimately leads to an increase in circulating nitric oxide. Nitric oxide has many roles within the body, including increasing vasodilation and influencing metabolism of the mitochondria within the muscle.

Research using both beetroot juice (in doses of approximately 0.5 l) and sodium nitrate (a preservative that is generally not allowed in large doses unless for medical reasons) to increase nitric oxide led to an increase in blood flow to the working muscles and, as a consequence, to a decrease in blood pressure. Both have also been shown to decrease the oxygen cost of exercise and lower the amount of adenosine triphosphate needed for a given muscular contraction. Ultimately, this leads to an improvement in performance of a similar magnitude to that seen for carbohydrate ingestion or caffeine use.

An acute dose (2.5 hours before exercise) of beetroot juice of 0.5 l seems to be equally effective in producing these outcomes as does supplementing for 15 consecutive days. This may be important for those who have sensitive stomachs on race day and want to drink beetroot juice for a number of days before competition.

RACE-DAY SUPPLEMENTS

The nutritional and supplementation strategies you use to enhance race-day performance will depend on the distance you are competing at. Some of the supplements will most likely be the same; however, the methods and amounts used will differ. We will consider three different race distances to look at the strategies you may use to enhance race-day performance, starting with the 4 km pursuit on the track, followed by a 40 km road-based time trial and finishing with a 6-hour road race. It should be emphasised that all nutritional strategies should be consumed in training first to ensure that there are no negative effects on performance.

The 4 km pursuit

The 4 km pursuit lasts for approximately 4 minutes 11 seconds through to 5 minutes, depending on your ability (it may take longer). However, the supplementation and nutritional strategies you use will be similar regardless of your finish time. The most important supplements to consider are the buffers beta-alanine and sodium bicarbonate. Three to four weeks before the race, start to supplement with beta-alanine at a dose of 4 g·day^{-1} split into two to four doses throughout the day. This will increase the carnitine content of the muscle, improving the muscle buffer capacity and leading to an improvement in high-intensity performance.

On the day of the race, consume 0.3 g·kg^{-1} bodyweight of sodium bicarbonate 90 minutes before the start of the race. This will increase blood bicarbonate and therefore the blood's buffer capacity. If you find that you have gastrointestinal adverse effects using sodium bicarbonate, ensure that you supplement alongside a source of carbohydrate, and never take sodium bicarbonate on an empty stomach. You can also split the dose into two smaller doses of 0.2 g·kg^{-1} bodyweight taken over a 3-hour period before racing.

The 40 km road-based time trial

For the fastest time triallists, these events will take between 50 minutes and 60 minutes to complete. They are completed at a high intensity, with the nutritional strategies being focused on ensuring that enough energy is available to sustain the high intensity of exercise.

The pre-race meal should be consumed approximately 3 hours before the start of the race and should consist of low-glycaemic-index carbohydrates such as brown rice or porridge. Alongside the pre-race meal, consume 0.5 l beetroot juice to increase nitrate intake, leading to an increase in nitric oxide within the body. This will decrease the oxygen cost of exercise and increase your efficiency.

One hour before the start of the race, supplement with 1–3 mg·kg^{-1} caffeine. For example, if you weigh 70 kg, look to consume 70–210 mg caffeine one hour before the start of the race. This could be one to two cups of espresso coffee. Caffeine has been shown to be most effective over races of approximately 1 hour in duration.

The 6-hour road race

The primary nutritional focus of a long-duration stage race is to ensure that carbohydrate intake is sufficient to ensure that fatigue is delayed and the rider can complete the race. Four ergogenic aids may be of use during this type of cycle race.

Three to four weeks before the race, begin supplementing with 2–4 g beta-alanine per day to increase muscle carnitine content. This has been shown to enhance sprint ability at the end of long-duration exercise. Many long-distance cycle races finish with a sprint finish.

For three to four days before the race, supplement with 0.5 l beetroot juice per day, including on the morning of the race to increase nitrate intake. The decrease in oxygen cost of exercise and increased efficiency will support long-distance performance.

During the race, it may be worth including BCAAs alongside carbohydrate feeding. The evidence is not conclusive; however, this strategy is unlikely to cause harm. Caffeine should be consumed during the race, particularly during the second half of the race. This has been shown to increase carbohydrate absorption at the point at which carbohydrate stores are starting to become decreased.

SUMMARY

In summary, there is a large range of information and a large number of supplements available to cyclists. However, only a limited number are effective in enhancing performance. These should not be used as substitutes for food but, used wisely, supplements can enhance performance.

KEY TAKE-HOME MESSAGES

- Dietary supplement use is common among both elite and non-elite athletes, and are commonly referred to as ergogenic aids due to their performance enhancing potential.
- Taken in conjunction with an appropriate training diet, ergogenic aids can enhance recovery, promote adaptation to training and help you to maximise performance.
- Currently, only four ergogenic aids have been shown to be effective in enhancing performance: creatine, caffeine, sodium bicarbonate and beta-alanine.
- Many supplements are safe to use and do not confer any negative side effects on health and wellbeing. However, often rigorous research and legislation is lacking. Therefore, it is important to use dietary supplements and erogenic aids with caution.
- When deciding whether to use a dietary supplement, you should undertake a cost–benefit analysis.

SECTION G
HOW SHOULD I RACE?

Cycle sport is characterised by a range of events, each varying in duration, type and the terrain over which the race is run. The duration of these events might last from 30 seconds for a 1 km track time trial to in excess of 100 hours over multiple days for a Grand Tour. Consequently, the physiological demands of these events are extremely different and, as a result, the approaches that need to be taken during such races differ dramatically.

The aim of the cyclist racing a track time trial is to complete the distance in the fastest possible time, the winner being the quickest rider. These types of event are often characterised by pacing strategies in which the cyclist produces as fast a start as possible before then attempting to limit the fatigue-related decline in speed until they have crossed the finishing line. This pacing strategy is complicated if several cyclists compete at the same time, as in a team pursuit, where drafting comes into play. However, not all cycling events take place on a smooth surface inside a velodrome. For example, the optimal pacing strategy needs to be quite different for mass-start races over hundreds of kilometres where finishing time is relatively unimportant. Road or mountain bike races are characterised by varying terrains and weather conditions. Therefore, the optimal pacing strategy will need to be adapted according to the individual race route. Chapter 14 discusses these issues and asks if we can learn or train how to optimally pace an event.

By the end of this section you should have an understanding of how your approach to racing needs to vary according to the duration of the race, type of event and environmental conditions.

PACING STRATEGIES FOR CYCLING

Florentina Hettinga

This chapter focuses on optimal pacing in cycling. Most research on this topic has focused on time trials, where no direct competitors are involved and pacing is completely dependent on the energy production and distribution of the individual athlete. For all-out exercise lasting less than 2 minutes, a fast start strategy is crucial. For longer-duration events, a fast first 10 seconds is important, followed by an evenly paced strategy, as will be explained and illustrated using both modelling and experimental studies. The influence of external circumstances such as wind, hilly terrain and high temperatures is discussed, as well as how to adapt to these varying circumstances. Subsequently, underlying mechanisms of pacing are discussed, particularly in the context of learning: can we learn how to optimally distribute the available energy? Lastly, recent knowledge of pacing in other sports is evaluated and applied to time trial cycling and other cycling disciplines, such as multiday events like the Tour de France or Vuelta a España. The concluding remarks focus on the practical implications: what is the optimal strategy in the different circumstances that have been discussed, and how can we optimally train to pace optimally?

THE IMPORTANCE OF PACING

The Tortoise and the Hare, by Aesop (620–560 BC)
   The hare was once boasting of his speed before the other animals. 'I have never yet been beaten,' he said, 'when I put forth my full speed. I challenge anyone here to race with me.' The tortoise said quietly: 'I accept your challenge.' 'That is a good joke,' said the hare. 'I could dance around you all the way!' 'Keep your boasting until you've beaten me,' answered the tortoise. 'Shall we race?' So a course was fixed and a start was made. The hare darted almost out of sight at once, but soon stopped and, to show his contempt for the tortoise, lay down to have a nap. The tortoise plodded on and plodded on, and when the hare awoke from his nap, he saw the tortoise nearing the finish line and he could not catch up in time to save the race. (Source: Joseph Jacobs, The Fables of Aesop *London, 1894, no. 68.)*

   This fable shows that pacing strategy was of interest 2500 years ago, when this story was written by the Greek storyteller Aesop. Nowadays, pacing is still an issue, in sport performance in particular: it is not only about being stronger than the opponent but also about being smarter. How can you use your energy resources better than your opponent can use his?

Contribution of the different energy systems

First, it is important to understand the contributions of the different energy systems (aerobic and anaerobic) and how they are affected by different pacing strategies. In exercise lasting 1–2 minutes, the contribution of both energy systems is equally large; however, depending on the time trial distance that needs to be covered, the contribution from both the anaerobic and aerobic energy systems varies. Shorter race distances require a larger relative contribution of the anaerobic system, while longer race distances depend largely on the aerobic system.

The aerobic energy system

The aerobic energy system, referring to the combustion of carbohydrates and fats, is most important for longer distances such as the 4000 m pursuit in track cycling or time trials in road cycling. The aerobic system needs some time to reach its maximal contribution, but as long as the cyclist keeps on breathing, there is oxygen available and the aerobic energy system is responsible for energy production. A fast start (first 10 seconds) speeds up this aerobic system. This means that, with a fast start, more energy can be generated during a time trial from aerobic sources.

TIME TRIAL TACTICS

Many athletes increase their speed when they get near the finish line: the end spurt. Does a fast start negatively impact on this end spurt? Research by Bailey and colleague has shown that for exercise durations of about 3 minutes, a fast start does not impair the end spurt and results in a better overall performance. For longer exercise durations (e.g. 6 minutes), no results were found in terms of performance but the same trends were seen. One of my studies has shown trends suggesting that too slow a start can impair performance: the lower contribution of the aerobic energy system cannot be compensated in the second half and, thus, the aerobic energy system is not optimally used.

The anaerobic energy system

In the 4000 m pursuit (see figure 14.1), where more than 80 per cent of the required energy is delivered aerobically, the anaerobic system is also important. Variations in pacing strategy (speed fluctuations) are mainly caused by variations in the anaerobic energy system. The anaerobic system, referring to the processes involved in the splitting of the stored phosphagens, adenosine triphosphate (ATP) and phosphocreatine (PCr), and the non-aerobic breakdown of carbohydrate to lactic acid through glycolysis, is even more important for short events of less than 2 minutes. In a 1000 m event, about 50–60 per cent of energy is delivered anaerobically. In contrast to the aerobic energy, anaerobic energy stores are limited. Therefore, it is important to make full use of the anaerobic energy stores in an attempt to fully deplete them as the finish line is reached.

FIG.14.1 Pacing strategy has to be carefully considered in short duration track cycling events

Total mechanical power output

Only about 20–25 per cent of the metabolic energy that is generated by both the anaerobic and aerobic systems is turned into mechanical power output to propel the bicycle. The remaining 75–80 per cent is lost as heat. To monitor mechanical power output and pacing strategies, it is now possible to analyse profiles of mechanical power output and the resulting velocity profiles. Many power meter systems (*see* chapter 5) can now be used to directly measure mechanical power output. Such devices are being used by several national and trade teams to evaluate training, performance and pacing strategies.

RESEARCH FOCUS

In a study by Stefan Vogt and colleagues, nine stages of the Giro d'Italia were monitored in one professional cyclist. His mean power output was 132 W for the flat and 235 W for mountain stages. Mountain stages showed higher maximal mean power (367 W) for longer durations (30 mins) then flat stages (239 W). Regarding pacing, it was found that flat stages were characterised by large variability in power output: bursts of high power output were accompanied by long periods of reduced intensity. Mountain stages, on the other hand, required sub-maximal constant power over longer periods. In agreement with these data, Tammie Ebert and colleagues identified mean power outputs of 192 W (flat) and 169 W (hilly) during women's World Cup races, with, again, higher variability in the flat trials. This shows that pacing strategies in mountain stages were relatively constant, whereas in the flat trials pacing was more variable over the race.

TAKE-HOME MESSAGES

- A fast start speeds up the aerobic system.
- With too slow a start, the aerobic system reaches its maximum too late in the race, which negatively influences performance during both short- and middle-distance performances.
- Total mechanical power output, the mechanical equivalent of the power delivered by the aerobic and anaerobic energy systems, can be monitored during competition or training in order to make pacing profiles visible.

MODELLING PERFORMANCE

Testing different pacing strategies by modelling performance is an appealing way to study pacing strategy. Various patterns of energy expenditure and their effect on performance can be simulated while environmental conditions are held constant. For example, performance can be described with the use of an energy flow model (*see* below) based on power equations describing mechanical power production (power that is generated by the athlete) on the one side and mechanical power losses (power used to overcome frictional forces) and changes in kinetic energy (power involved in acceleration or deceleration of the centre of mass) on the other side.

Performance can be optimised by maximising the mechanical power that can be produced (P_{tot}), but also by distributing energy in such a way that the available resources are used in the most efficient way and a high mean velocity over the race is achieved. This provides the optimal pacing strategy.

THE ENERGY FLOW MODEL

The energy flow model was first introduced in endurance sports in 1990 by Gerrit Jan van Ingen Schenau:

$$P_{tot} = P_{lost} + dE_{kin}/dt$$

Where P_{tot} is the mechanical power output generated by the athlete, P_{lost} is the mechanical power used to overcome frictional forces and dE_{kin}/dt is the change in kinetic energy ($\frac{1}{2} \cdot m \cdot v^2$, where m is body mass and v is velocity) of the centre of mass of the athlete over time.

How to model optimal pacing?

To find the optimal pacing strategy, ideally, an athlete has to experiment with multiple pacing strategies under controlled conditions to see which one is optimal. This is usually carried out in the early career of an athlete by trial and error. Using energy flow models we can simulate many different pacing strategies under the same environmental and internal conditions. If velocity is the only unknown variable in the equation, velocity can be calculated numerically. For each step in the simulation, this differential equation is integrated. The anaerobic power distribution, and therewith the velocity profile, can be systematically changed, keeping anaerobic capacity constant.

The first study that simulated different pacing strategies numerically using the energy flow model was performed in the 1990s. A 'time to constant power' was introduced to find the point in time from which it is beneficial to start distributing energy equally over the remaining part of the race. In other words, the 'time to constant power' indicates the time at which an athlete has to change from following the traditional 'all-out' anaerobic profile to performing an 'even-paced' strategy and distributing the remaining anaerobic energy equally over the rest of the race. It was shown that for shorter distances (e.g. 1000 m cycling ≈ 1 minute), all-out performance was optimal. It is very important to have spent as much energy as possible before the finish line is reached to optimally make use of the available energy. For the longer distances (4000 m ≈ 5–6 minutes), energy could best be distributed equally over the race after a fast start of 10–15 seconds. The non-linear relation between power used to overcome air friction forces and velocity is very important here: cycling 2 km·h⁻¹ faster requires more extra power output than is saved when cycling 2 km·h⁻¹ slower and, thus, velocity fluctuations should be minimised. For longer distances, the optimal pacing strategy is an even-paced strategy.

Recent modelling results: what is optimal?

For shorter distances, it is important to use the available energy before the finish line is reached, whereas for longer distances, the aerodynamic benefits of an even-paced velocity profile are more important. Although this clearly shows that the distance to be covered is an important issue in pacing strategy, this rather global way of varying pacing patterns must be refined to study pacing strategy per individual athlete for middle-distance events. This has been done in cycling. By manipulating the variables that define the distribution of anaerobic power (such as the maximum aerobic power, the anaerobic time constant and the asymptotic end value of the anaerobic power curve) and keeping the total anaerobic energy contribution constant, different pacing strategies could be simulated more accurately. The results of such work show that, during 2 minutes of cycling, better performances are associated with faster starts (in both the modelled and the actual performances). Such modelling work has also suggested that many experienced cyclists are already close to their theoretical optimal pacing profile.

How about the tortoise and the hare?

As for the tortoise and the hare story, it can be concluded that, when both hare and tortoise follow their optimal pacing pattern, it is impossible for the tortoise to win. Mean power output is the determining variable in performance. However, the hare misjudges his pacing strategy severely and, although it seemed impossible, the tortoise wins. Being strong is not enough; you also have to be smart to win. Mistakes can have large consequences. In the athletic world, differences are very small and sometimes only 0.01 seconds can be the difference between winning and losing. With such small margins, what counts is how smartly the available energy is distributed. Of two equally strong athletes, the smarter will win by choosing a better pacing strategy. Experienced athletes possess a pretty accurate and rather robust system to determine their pacing strategies based on earlier experience. The interplay among P_{tot}, P_{lost} and DE_{kin}/dt seems to be incorporated in this pre-determined exercise template.

TAKE-HOME MESSAGES

- A fast start is optimal for shorter distances such as 1000 m, where an all-out strategy is optimal. For the 4000 m, a fast start (12 seconds) is advised, followed by the maintenance of an even pace.
- For longer time trials (i.e. 4000 m and above), an even-paced strategy is advised.
- Cyclists seem to be close to their optimal strategy: best performances are associated with a faster start.

HOW TO ADAPT PACING STRATEGY TO VARYING CIRCUMSTANCES

So far, this chapter has focused primarily on track cycling and indoor circumstances. However, the role of environmental circumstances such as a hilly environment, windy conditions or high temperatures – all of which are relevant for cycling time trials in the Tour de France, Vuelta a España or Giro d'Italia – must also be considered. In the previous section on energy systems, it was shown that pacing strategies on flat terrain show more variability. Modelling performance might again be helpful here.

Wind and hills

By using a modelling approach, it has been predicted that varying power output in parallel with changes in gradient and wind speed was the optimal pacing strategy under these environmental circumstances (i.e. wind and hills). The data presented from the women's World Cup and Giro d'Italia stages show that athletes do not use a variable power output during mountain stages. There might therefore be room for improvement in achieving optimal pacing.

RESEARCH FOCUS

Researchers have modelled optimal pacing strategy in hilly and windy conditions. The largest time savings are found for the cyclists with the lowest mean power outputs (in a range between 100 W and 600 W), who could vary power to the greatest extent. Alejandro Lucia has shown that elite cyclists can maintain exercise intensities above 90 per cent of maximal oxygen consumption (VO_{2max}) for up to 1 hour. The suggested 15 per cent increase in power that was predicted for optimal performance in wind and hills is, therefore, hard to sustain. Fortunately, a 5 per cent variation already leads to meaningful differences and reduces overall perceived exertion. It is therefore advised to vary power in parallel with hill gradient and wind direction to minimise differences in speed over the race.

Temperature

Besides wind and hills, there is another environmental factor that is very important for performance and pacing: temperature. In particular, performance in the heat has been investigated, since fatigue at exhaustion has been related to factors associated with thermoregulation and hyperthermia. Time trial performance can frequently be reduced by as much as 6.5 per cent in hot conditions compared with thermoneutral circumstances. A large part of the deterioration in performance is caused by a reduced gross efficiency in the heat. The proposed mechanisms for this reduction are associated with elevated body temperature. Anticipatory changes in pacing strategy are made based on subjective ratings of perceived exertion to ensure the prevention of overheating. In other words, based on how they feel, athletes cycle at lower power outputs early in the race to prevent becoming too hot in the last stages. By pre-cooling, the reduction in self-paced performance can be prevented.

TAKE-HOME MESSAGES

- Power output should be varied in parallel with environmental changes in hills and wind direction.
- In the heat, an anticipatory reduction in power output occurs to prevent hyperthermia. Pre-cooling can help to optimise performance and pacing.

CAN I LEARN OR TRAIN HOW TO PACE OPTIMALLY?

Elite athletes are thought to develop appropriate pacing strategies by developing an exercise template. Learning such a template apparently occurs relatively quickly, with fit non-athletes developing a stable template within six repeated trials. The initial pace is set in a feed-forward manner (e.g. a cognitive motor programme), but is continuously adjusted during exercise based on both internal and external feedback. Because it takes time to interpret the received feedback, the athlete is continuously a little bit too late to adjust his pacing strategy, resulting in a fluctuating power output. As the athlete becomes more experienced, the template is refined such that there is less need for this regulatory fluctuation in power output. Based on how the athlete rates his perceived exertion during the race and how he expects he should feel based on earlier experience, he can regulate his strategy. To train the pacing template, and to accurately interpret signals from the body and the environment, it is advised to practise with different pacing strategies: try to start faster or slower than normal in a training competition regularly.

TAKE-HOME MESSAGE

To be able to judge possibilities accurately, it is advisable for athletes to experiment and keep experimenting with different pacing strategies together with their coaches. In this way they can obtain a well-documented, up-to-date exercise template based on prior experience.

ARE THERE POSSIBLE APPLICATIONS TO DISCIPLINES OTHER THAN TIME TRIAL CYCLING?

So far, we have discussed pacing strategies within one event only, with no other direct competitors in the race. How about pacing in the Grand Tours such as the Giro d'Italia, Vuelta a España and Tour de France, where many consecutive daily races are performed and where other competitors are cycling at the same time? What about pacing a team pursuit?

Pacing in multiday events: the Grand Tours

In cycling events lasting up to three weeks, winning is based on the optimal performance over all stages summed. In this context, another issue becomes of importance for optimal pacing. For very long trials, the possible negative consequences of too fast a start are larger than those of too slow a start in terms of premature fatigue. Performance in the upcoming stages of the multiday event must be 'protected' as well. There is a distribution in physiological load that is dependent on the length of the tour: the longer the tour, the lower the relative intensity (*see* box on page 200). Also, differences in the role of the cyclist (contending/non-contending) influence the chosen pacing profiles in a Grand Tour.

THE AIS SKILL COMPETENCY CHECKLIST

Riding two abreast	Riding single file
Riding in a bunch	Bunch awareness (peripheral vision)
Descending	Fast braking
Cornering at speed	Cornering in wet conditions
Downhill cornering	180-degree U-turn
Riding with no hands	Using a track stand
Riding rollers	Riding rollers no hands
Riding one-handed on top bar/drops	Riding one-handed looking behind
Obstacle avoidance	Wheel touching
Shoulder to shoulder	Holding the wheel
Leading out riders	Paceline/echelons
Access clothes/pockets	Laying off wheels
Look behind/ride straight	Look behind under armpits
Stretch while riding (on-bike stretching)	Pick up bidon off ground
Bidon feed	Mussette feed
Control on time trial bars	Seated climbing
Out of saddle climbing	Appropriate gearing changing
Appropriate gear selection/cadence	Distance/pace judgement

Over time, it is important to master all of these skills to help ensure your safety and the safety of those you ride with.

a training programme is the menstrual cycle, the use of oral contraceptives and the impact these have.

Structuring training around the menstrual cycle

Taking the time to plan training around one's menstrual cycle may have some benefits in terms of performance. Currently, the available data are mixed on the impact of the menstrual cycle on athletic performance, as there are many variables to consider when interpreting the results. We should ask: Does the rider have a normal menstrual cycle? Is she trained or untrained? Is she using an oral contraceptive and, if so, what type, e.g. monophasic or triphasic? Finally, when was performance measured during the cycle?

During a normal menstrual cycle, the levels of oestrogen, progesterone and testosterone vary in your body. Oestrogen and progesterone play a role in regulating substrate metabolism during exercise, with oestrogen reducing carbohydrate oxidation but increasing fat use and progesterone reducing lipolytic activity. A 'normal' menstrual cycle (i.e. no oral contraceptive usage) progresses through the following phases over approximately 28 days: follicular, ovulation and luteal. During these phases there is a significant change in basal body temperature, which is highest in the luteal phase and lowest just before ovulation. When taking an oral contraceptive, you experience a 21-day phase of oestrogen and progesterone consumption (oral contraceptive consumption phase) followed by a withdrawal phase of seven days in which a placebo is consumed. The result is the inhibition of ovulation that would otherwise occur during a normal menstrual cycle.

Judy Daly and Wendy Ey provide a summary of the possible training modifications that can be made for athletes experiencing a normal menstrual cycle based on the impact of oestrogen and progesterone. During the early follicular phase (days one to five) and the late luteal phase (days 25–28), levels of oestrogen, progesterone and testosterone are low. This results in mood changes, poor perception of effort, increased reaction time and immune suppression. During these times there should be a reduction in stress and training volume and a focus away from skill-based activities. A focus on high-intensity, low-volume work that is power and strength based is best conducted during the mid-follicular (days six to eight, oestrogen rising) and early luteal (days 15–20, progesterone rising) phases owing to increased carbohydrate use and glycogen stores, which can fuel high-intensity efforts. Conversely, low-intensity, high-volume aerobic activity should be the focus of the late follicular (days 9–13) and mid-luteal (days 21–24) phases when oestrogen and progesterone are peaking, as there is an increased fat use. Testosterone is highest on day 14 (ovulation); here, and into days 15–20, strength training can be the focus. However, it is important to note that the scientific jury is still out on the impact of the 'normal' menstrual cycle on actual athletic performance.

The prevalence of the use of oral contraceptives among female athletes is rising and in some cases oral contraceptives are used to manipulate the menstrual cycle or to reduce the symptoms/discomfort often experienced. Unpublished observations by Rechichi and colleagues at the Western Australian Institute of Sport show that 55 per cent of athletes from 11 different sports were using oral contraceptives, with the majority using monophasic types. They also provide a comprehensive summary of the research pertaining to the impact of oral contraceptives on athletic performance. Although the evidence is not totally clear on the impact of oral contraceptives on athletic performance, the researchers did note the following from the available research:

- A possible reduction of 5–15 per cent in VO_{2max} with oral contraceptive use.
- Higher ventilation for a given workload during the oral contraceptive consumption phase in comparison with the withdrawal phase.
- Possible improvement in anaerobic capacity during the oral contraceptive withdrawal phase as a result of low progesterone levels, which may positively impact buffering capacity.
- Inconclusive impact of oral contraceptives on strength despite a possible impact during a regular/normal menstrual cycle.

There are some benefits to using oral contraceptives that may indirectly assist performance. These include:

- a possible decrease in iron-deficiency anaemia owing to reduced blood loss when on oral contraceptives;
- control of pre-menstrual symptoms; and
- protection of bone mineral density by maintaining hormone levels.

Taking the time to know your body and plan training appropriately may help to improve your performance and maximise the adaptations from training.

MONITORING TRAINING

Everyone wants to know if they have improved and, although you can often tell if you have improved just by how you feel on the bike, it is also good to quantify your improvement. Chapters 3 and 5 provide a number of options. In Australia, we use a test called the power profile. The aim of this test is to look at both aerobic and anaerobic (sprint) improvements. The test is as follows: 5-second sprint, 1 minute 55 seconds recovery, 15-second sprint, 3 minutes 45 seconds recovery, 30-second sprint, 5 minutes 30 seconds recovery, 1 minute effort, 8 minutes recovery, 4 minutes effort, 10 minutes recovery, 10 minutes effort. Average power, also referred to as the maximal mean power, is then calculated for each effort, with the aim of improving these values over time. The benefits of the power profile are that it is possible to look at improvements made for different phases of training. If in a low-intensity, high-volume phase, an improvement should be made in 4- and 10-minute efforts. When focusing on short interval work, improvements should be seen in 5–30-second efforts. Table 15.3 outlines some data from elite females to provide a guide.

NUTRITION

Getting the right food and fluid on board as a cyclist is of vital importance to maximise training adaptations and race successfully. Section F of this book outlines the major areas of importance for a cyclist with regard to nutrition. The information below outlines research conducted specifically on female cyclists.

At the AIS, we investigated what elite female riders actually eat and drink during competition; in this instance, a multiday stage race. We followed the Australian national women's team during a 10-day tour covering 788.5 km in order to see what they ate and drank. Riders were weighed before and after each stage to get an indication of hydration status and were asked to recall food and fluid intake. We also recorded their placings to see if there was any impact of food and fluid intake on finishing position.

For the long stages of the tour (over 100 km), the riders consumed between 16 and 27 $g \cdot h^{-1}$ of carbohydrate. This is below the American College of Sports Medicine (ACSM) recommendation of 0.5–1.0 $g \cdot kg^{-1} \cdot hour^{-1}$. Their carbohydrate intake was achieved by

Variable	Unit	Females		
		Mean ± SD	Min	Max
Body mass	kg	60.8 ± 5.5	48	74
VO$_{2peak}$ (4 min)	l·min^{-1}	3.6 ± 0.3	2.96	4.41
VO$_{2peak}$ (4 min)	ml·kg^{-1}·min^{-1}	59.3 ± 4.6	47.7	68.4
VO$_{2peak}$ (10 min)	l·min^{-1}	3.55 ± 0.3	3.08	4.15
VO$_{2peak}$ (10 min)	ml·kg^{-1}·min^{-1}	60.0 ± 4.8	48.05	65.4
MMP 5 sec	W	792 ± 100	534	1077
MMPM 5 sec	W·kg^{-1}	13.0 ± 1.1	9.3	15.8
Ave cad 5 sec	rpm	116 ± 11	84	142
MMP 15 sec	W	638 ± 83	479	885
MMPM 15 sec	W·kg^{-1}	10.5 ± 0.9	8.6	12.7
Ave cad 15 sec	rpm	116 ± 10	91	143
MMP 30 sec	W	500 ± 58	340	690
MMPM 30 sec	W·kg^{-1}	8.2 ± 0.7	6.2	9.7
Ave cad 30 sec	rpm	115 ± 9	89	149
MMP 60 sec	W	392 ± 44	301	496
MMPM 60 sec	W·kg-1	6.5 ± 0.6	4.8	7.9
Ave cad 60 sec	rpm	110 ± 8	88	138
MMP 4 min	W	279 ± 32	218	357
MMPM 4 min	W·kg^{-1}	4.6 ± 0.3	3.6	5.6
Ave cad 4 min	rpm	101 ± 6	87	114
MMP 10 min	W	248 ± 23	195	320
MMPM 10 min	W·kg^{-1}	4.0 ± 0.6	3.2	5
Ave cad 10 min	rpm	98 ± 7	80	117

Ave cad = average cadence; MMP = maximal mean power output (average power for the effort); MMPM = maximal mean power output divided by body mass; SD = standard deviation. Data from approximately 100 tests over three years (some athletes have contributed multiple tests over those years).

TABLE 15.3 Power output and cadence for elite female cyclists undertaking the power profile test

eating foodstuffs such as sports bars, sports gels and small cakes. The riders experienced an average change in body weight of −2.2 per cent, or about a 1.3 kg loss, at the end of a stage. They sweated nearly 1.0 l·hour^{-1} despite the conditions being quite mild (approximately 20°C ambient temperature). The female riders consumed between 0.2 and 0.7 l·hour^{-1}, or 0.3–2.5 l per stage. According to the ACSM fluid consumption recommendations, athletes should be consuming 0.6–1.2 l·hour^{-1}. This recommendation should be treated with caution, as some researchers indicate that too few controlled, randomised studies have been conducted to truly provide a universal guideline for fluid intake. In our observations, only 16 per cent of the time did the female riders consume volumes at the level of the ACSM recommendations (*see* figure 15.3).

TAKE-HOME MESSAGE

Given the smaller muscle masses used by handcyclists, they may be more prone to repetitive strain injuries. This should be considered when planning training and recovery. Care must be taken to consider the capabilities of the rider, ensuring that training volume and intensity are individually determined to provide the optimal training effect.

of heart-rate monitors to control training intensity. The coach/scientist will look for improvements in the threshold markers as well as the maximum aerobic power. The smaller muscle mass used will ultimately dictate the power production, but the efficiency of movement can be improved through specific training. Although the values that handcyclists can achieve may be lower than those of able-bodied individuals, the principles of training are similar.

Characteristics of an elite cerebral palsy paracyclist

An incremental test was carried out with a 25 W increment every 3 minutes with capillary blood and heart rate sampled every 3 minutes. Figure 16.7 shows data from the test. Notice that the first breakpoint in the lactate curve occurs at 225 W, with the second at 275 W. The data collected from the laboratory physiological assessment can be used to set training intensities as well as the typical amount of time to be spent at each intensity (as shown in figure 16.7). The intensities have been defined here as:

- moderate: sustainable for over 1 hour;
- heavy: sustainable from 20 minutes to 1 hour; and
- severe: interval work or 3–4 km pursuit efforts.

Heart rate can be used as a gauge for exercising in the field, but adjustments may need to be made if laboratory testing was conducted on a stationary cycle ergometer.

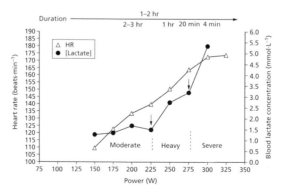

FIG.16.7 Data from an incremental protocol to determine lactate threshold; training domains and typical time durations are also shown

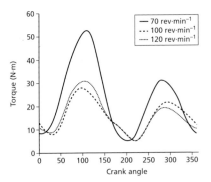

FIG.16.8 Torque curves produced during one revolution from an elite cerebral palsy cyclist at different cadences. (Adapted with permission from Brickley, G., Gregson, H., 'A case study of a paralympic cerebral palsy cyclist using torque analysis', *International Journal of Sports Science and Coaching*, 6 (2011), pp. 269–272)

Torque analysis: an important issue for cerebral palsy cyclists

To examine imbalances in pedalling action, torque analysis can be carried out using an SRM or a Wattbike cycle ergometer. These ergometers measure torque throughout each revolution of the crank. Figure 16.9 shows the average torque curves from a rider with cerebral palsy exercising at 300 W using three different cadences. There are clear differences between the torque on the right and left side, an effect that is amplified at the lowest tested cadence of 70 rev·min⁻¹.

Torque analysis may be used to determine differences, but may also be used as part of rehabilitation for injured athletes who should try to ensure similarities in torque production from both legs. Based on the data presented in figure 16.8, the rider decided to fit an elliptical chain ring that was positioned to ensure maximal force production throughout the pedal revolution (the chain ring appeared to have performance benefits for this individual). As a result of this type of torque analysis, the rider may focus on their pedalling action at lower cadences.

When dealing with the disabled cyclist, the muscle mass that can be activated on each side of the body should also be considered. For example, if there is severe muscle wastage on one side of the body, this may explain observations from the torque analysis profile. Subsequently, technique could be adjusted to improve pedalling action and to compensate for this imbalance.

TRAINING FOR THE PARACYCLIST

Typical training zones for the rider with cerebral palsy (discussed above) are shown in table 16.1. In a rider who may have poor balance (e.g. as a result of cerebral palsy), heart rate could be elevated at very low intensities of effort as he may have to try to compensate for his poor balance with increased muscle activity or by having a greater sympathetic (adrenaline release) response. This should be considered in the planning of training zones for this population.

Intensity	Heart-rate range	Time range	Purpose
Recovery	Below <121 bpm	Up to 1 hour recovery	Short rides (non-training) for recovery
Zone 1	122 bpm to 131 bpm	Up to 6 hours	Development of economy and efficiency with very high-volume, low-stress work. Very long sessions improve the combustion and storage of fats. Combine with zone 2 for practical unstructured low-stress rides.
Zone 2	132 bpm to 152 bpm	Up to 4 hours	Development of economy and efficiency with high-volume, moderate-stress work. An important intensity for establishing a firm base for all riders. Combine with zone 1 for practical unstructured low-stress rides.
Zone 3	153 bpm to 166 bpm	Up to 2 hours	Development of aerobic capacity and endurance with moderate volume work at a controlled intensity. Should be done alone or in a small group in order to stay in zone. Possible (but boring) on a turbo trainer for up to 1 hour in bad weather. 'Modules' can be incorporated into zone 1 or 2 rides to increase intensity while maintaining volume.
Zone 4	167 bpm to 178 bpm	Up to 1 hour	Typical 'mean' intensity of most road races. Useful for tapering and as preparation to simulate race pace rather than as training. Sessions should be ended when the effort starts to tell.
Zone 5	179 bpm to 188 bpm	Up to 40 min	Raising of anaerobic threshold, improvement of lactate clearance and adaptation to race speed. Should be done alone and: • as a specific road or turbo session; or • for controlled periods within a shortened zone 1 or 2 session; or • in a 10 or 25 mile time trial.

Intensity	Heart-rate range	Time range	Purpose
Zone 6	Above 188 bpm	Up to 20 min (dependent upon intensity and rest/ recovery periods)	High-intensity interval training to increase maximum power and improve lactate production or clearance. Probably best done on hills or a turbo trainer. Note 1: Should be done only when completely recovered from previous work. Note 2: Heart rates are not the best guide for this type of training. Intensity should be such that the effort can just be held to the end of the interval. Ride on feel and use heart rate for feedback.

TABLE 16.1 Training zones for a cerebral palsy cyclist with a maximum heart rate of 202 beats·min[-1]

Paracyclists may have come from a different sporting background before taking up cycling. In other cases, the rider may be an ex-cyclist who has been injured and hence acquired a disability condition. In other situations, the rider may come from a different sport and adopt cycling as an alternative method of training. Therefore, the previous volume and intensity of training should be considered before setting up a training programme for the paracyclist.

NUTRITIONAL AND ENVIRONMENTAL CONCERNS FOR DISABLED ATHLETES

All athletes have different responses to exercising in the heat. This may be influenced by a number of factors including prior acclimatisation, number of active sweat glands, typical sweat content, responses in different humidity, clothing worn and body surface area in contact with air. Therefore, strategies that relate to effective heat loss in hot and humid conditions are of primary concern for the paracycling athlete. Consider the handcyclist in figure 16.4; note that the total surface area in contact with the air is very small. The handcyclist has a limited area to dissipate heat losses. In this position the abdomen is fixed in position with Velcro to prevent slipping in the seat, but this also means that the skin cannot release its heat effectively. This leads to a rapid rise in body core temperature. The seat is often foam-padded, which will further accelerate the sweat response, often leading to the cyclist sitting in a pool of water. This is in direct contrast to an able-bodied cyclist, who would have a greater area for airflow to pass over their body, aiding heat loss via evaporation.

CHAPTER 17

THE AGEING CYCLIST

Richard Davison

The exact underlying mechanism of biological ageing is unknown. It is certainly multifactorial and involves declines in virtually all body structures and functions. While there is a large body of evidence which confirms that individuals who exercise regularly tend to live longer, this is not attributable to exercise slowing the ageing process. Regular exercisers live longer by minimising health risk factors that are associated with inactivity, such as high blood pressure, obesity and high cholesterol, all of which tend to lead to ill health and thus shorten life spans. There are no longevity data specifically on cyclists, but research on long-distance runners and cross-country skiers suggests that they live on average three to six years longer than the general population. While different parts of the body age at different rates, impacting on physical performance in different ways, the overall outcome is a pattern of declining physical performance as we age. This chapter describes the changes in cycling performance seen with ageing, explains why this might happen and suggests how training might be modified to minimise the declines in performance.

SUCCESSFUL AGEING?

Master elite athletes who continue to train and compete at a high level represent a unique population demonstrating remarkable physiological characteristics that could be considered 'exceptionally successful ageing'. However, they still exhibit the typical characteristics of ageing with the associated decline in physiological function and performance.

THE EFFECTS OF AGEING ON PERFORMANCE
Methods used to study ageing

When studying the effects of ageing on performance or physiological function, the most common technique is to use cross-sectional analysis by measuring a large population of athletes of different ages. An example of such data is shown in figure 17.1. This figure clearly shows the age-related decline in time trial performance for a group of cyclists aged 40–91 years.

It is also possible to look at the age of competitors who have won Olympic medals or, as in figure 17.2, those cyclists who have won the Tour de France. This shows a very clear peak in the age distribution of the winners of the Tour de France and suggests that it is rare and thus extremely difficult to win the Tour if you are over the age of 35.

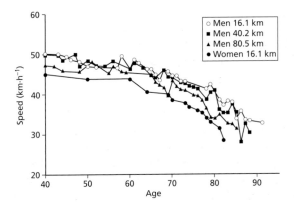

FIG.17.1 Speed (km·h) for UK age group records for 10-, 25- and 50-mile time trials for men and 10-mile time trial for women (data obtained from the Road Time-Trials Council)

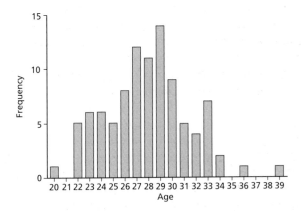

FIG.17.2 Distribution of the age of Tour de France winners (1903–2010)

An alternative, more difficult method of evaluating age-related changes is to monitor the changes in performance and physiological function of a group of athletes over time; that is, longitudinally. The major problems with this approach, apart from the time it takes to collect the data, are retaining a large enough sample of individuals willing to be tested and maintaining the same measurement methods over an extended period of time. Interestingly, studies that have compared both approaches suggest that the rate of age-related decline is perhaps twice as high according to the longitudinal design. Thus, cross-sectional studies may underestimate the true effect of ageing. It has also been suggested that a longitudinal research design is more accurate than a cross-sectional approach. When using a cross-sectional design, samples can be biased by sample selection methods and can exclude longitudinal changes in lifestyle and training habits. All cyclists know that they have periods in their life where they do not train/compete as much and this does affect the age-related decline in performance.

The decline in performance

Overall, there seems to be a fairly consistent pattern of decline in athletic performance as we age (*see* figure 17.1, page 233). This can be described according to three phases: a relatively slow linear decline from peak performance up to age 50, after which there is some acceleration in decline, probably still linear, followed by a much steeper exponential decline from the age of 70. Despite the evident decline in these record performances, we still see remarkable performances such as the sub-30-minute 16.1 km time trial achieved by a 91-year-old. This general trend would seem to be consistent across cycling, running and swimming. However, there are reported differences in the rate of decline between these sports, with cycling being at the lower end compared with running and both running and swimming in triathletes. Certainly, compared with running, this may be attributable to the fact that there is an increase in running injuries with age, which would prevent the maintenance of the same intensity and volume of training compared with when younger.

There also seems to be a gender-based effect, with greater declines seen in women. The reason for this is unknown. However, this difference needs to be viewed with some caution, as the numbers of older women competing is significantly lower than the number of competitive older men. This in turn reduces the level of competition, potentially preventing the true rate of decline in performance being evident in the data.

Figure 17.1 (*see* page 233) clearly shows the typical decline in time trial performance that occurs as a result of ageing. The main physiological factors that have been investigated to explain these declines in performance are changes in maximal oxygen consumption (VO_{2max}), economy, strength and maximal aerobic power. Although these are the headline variables reported in the literature, it is important to appreciate that there are a number of underlying physiological factors that interact to give this outcome. For example, economy can be influenced by age-related changes in muscle fibres as well as changes in central cardiovascular performance (heart and lungs). The typical decline in maximal aerobic power and average power for a 16.1 km time trial can be seen in figure 17.3. It would seem that the declines in both are equivalent at

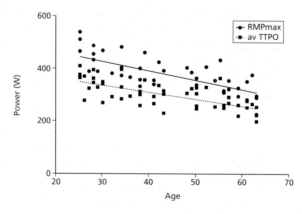

FIG.17.3 Decline in maximal aerobic power and average power for a 16.1 km time trial in a group of 40 cyclists aged 25–63 years

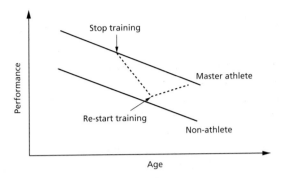

FIG. 17.4 Hypothetical model describing the changes in performance with age for master athletes and non-athletes

about 7 per cent per decade. This equates to a 30 W per decade decline in maximal aerobic power and a 24 W per decade decline in average time trial power. The strong relationship between maximal aerobic power and time trial power is extremely useful for the sport scientist and coach as a laboratory maximum test can then be used as a guide for a pacing strategy for road-based time trials. Available data also suggest that this relationship between maximal aerobic power and average time trial power is unaffected by age; therefore, this test can be used as a guide to potential time trial performance regardless of age.

Interestingly, a recent 10-year longitudinal follow-up of the same riders tested for the data in figure 17.3 suggested a much steeper decline, equivalent to 17 per cent for maximal aerobic power and 15 per cent for average time trial power. The most likely explanation for this difference is the fact that not all of the cyclists maintained the same level of training for all of the 10 years. What is not known is, if these riders did revert to their previous training levels, would the decline in performance match the slower decline found in cross-sectional data?

The model presented in figure 17.4 illustrates the decline in performance with age for master athletes and non-exercisers, with the rate of decline being similar in both. However, as mentioned above, as long as master athletes maintain appropriate training, they have performance and physiological measures that are superior to non-exercisers at all ages. However, if they stop or even reduce their training, there is an additional decline, indicated by the dotted line in figure 17.4.

The research literature does not tell us if a master athlete stops training, how fast performance will decline or whether it at some point reaches that of the non-exerciser;

TAKE-HOME MESSAGE

The decline in laboratory and time trial performance is in the region of 7–17 per cent per decade depending on the level of continued training load.

> ## TAKE-HOME MESSAGE
>
> Reducing or stopping training increases the overall age-related decline in performance. However, resumption of appropriate training should restore most, if not all, of that accelerated decline in performance.

presumably, it eventually does. Equally, we have no research evidence on how 'recoverable' performance levels are after a period of no or reduced training. Yes, training always makes us better, but is it possible to claw our way back from the hypothetical decline in performance seen for the master athlete in figure 17.4?

There is a commonly held view that we have better endurance capacity as we get older and the research on cyclists would seem to back this up, with endurance performance declining slightly more slowly than track sprint performance. Figure 17.1 (*see* page 233) also does not seem to show any difference in the decline across time trial events ranging from 20 minutes to 2 hours. However, there are data showing a greater age-related decline in the cycling performance at age 55 years and over in the Ironman compared with the Olympic triathlon. It is possible that age-related declines in fuel storage and use have a greater impact on these ultra-endurance events that last between 5 and 7.5 hours, which could account for the contradictory findings.

THE PHYSIOLOGICAL EFFECTS OF AGEING
Changes in muscle

One of the well-documented reasons for declines in physical performance with age is the decrease in muscle mass as we get older. This is technically called 'sarcopenia' and most simply can be seen as a reduction in the cross-sectional area of muscle. This loss of muscle tissue starts around the age of 50 years, but more dramatic declines occur after 60 years of age. The exact reason for this is unknown and there is some debate as to whether there is an equal loss of muscle tissue across different muscle fibre types. Certainly, there seems to be a significant reduction in the volume (known as atrophy) of fast-twitch type II fibres. This leads to a reduction in the maximal force produced by that muscle and an associated reduction in the ability to generate higher power outputs. However, most of the research in this area has used muscle from untrained individuals and it is somewhat unclear if there are similar trends with master athletes. Cross-sectional studies suggest that the rate of decline of strength with age is similar between trained and untrained groups. In cycling terms, this is likely to manifest itself in a greater reduction in performance in those cycling events requiring higher power outputs or bursts of higher intensity. More detailed analysis of the molecular structure of the muscle protein also suggests that there is an age-related shift of fast type II muscle fibres to slightly slower versions (towards type I slow-twitch muscle fibres). In addition, it has been shown that, at the molecular level, changes in skeletal

> **TAKE-HOME MESSAGE**
>
> Muscle strength declines with age owing to a reduction in muscle volume. Older muscle may not adapt to training as well as younger muscle.

muscle protein occur at a much slower rate in response to endurance training. This suggests that older muscle would require a greater training stimulus to achieve the same muscle protein adaptation as younger muscle.

Changes in VO_{2max}

One of the most measured physiological variables is VO_{2max}. Research data show a clear decline from the age of 25 years at a rate of about 10 per cent per decade, although some researchers have reported that the rate of decline seems to be related to the intensity of continued training. In runners, the change in VO_{2max} is correlated to age and intensity of training, particularly in the 60+ age range.

The decline in VO_{2max} is considered as being primarily responsible for reductions in endurance performance. One obvious factor that accounts for some of the decline in maximal aerobic power is the age-related reduction in maximal heart rate, reducing the volume of blood that the heart can pump. Interestingly, one longitudinal study that followed five individuals over a period of 30 years found that the heart adapted to the reduced maximal heart rate by increasing its stroke volume. This study suggested that the reduction in VO_{2max} was as a consequence of a reduction in the ability of the muscle to extract oxygen. This could be the result of a number of reasons, including inappropriate redistribution of blood, reduced capillarisation and reduced diffusion of oxygen into the muscle. These factors would also influence the rate at which a cyclist could increase oxygen consumption at the start of exercise (this relates to the area of science known as VO_2 kinetics). Several studies have shown that, in the general population, oxygen uptake kinetics are slowed by ageing. Therefore, the rate of change in oxygen consumption is compromised, suggesting that older athletes cope less well with changes in exercise intensity. Consequently, they may experience more 'oxygen debt' as there is a greater mismatch between oxygen demand and supply. However, endurance-trained master athletes seem to experience a much reduced rate of decline in VO_2 kinetics compared with both sprint-trained athletes and sedentary counterparts. This suggests that appropriate training is an important factor in maintaining fast VO_2 kinetics. It is thought that the specific adaptations leading to these improvements are intramuscular changes and not related to oxygen delivery.

Adequately ventilating the lungs is important in ensuring enough oxygen is transferred to the blood, thus ventilation is an important factor for achieving VO_{2max}. At higher exercise intensities, we need to be able to push large volumes of air in and out of our lungs using our respiratory muscles. Like the other muscles in our body, respiratory muscle performance declines in terms of strength and endurance with age, making it more difficult to ventilate the lungs to the required level. On top of this decline, there is a significant increase in the stiffness and a loss of elasticity in the tissues of the lungs and chest, making each breath much harder and requiring more energy. Experience of testing many master cyclists in the laboratory confirms that these cyclists complain more often about breathlessness. Like all other muscles in the body, our respiratory muscles can be trained to improve performance and there are a number of respiratory muscle training devices specifically designed for this purpose. These normally require you to breathe through a device that restricts airflow by a specific amount. Some studies have even shown significant performance gains from this type of training for younger cyclists and there is certainly a strong case for including it in the training programme of a master cyclist.

Changes in maximal heart rate

Unlike changes in maximal aerobic power and performance, maximal heart rate declines across the lifespan in a linear manner. Regular exercise does not seem to have any impact on this decline. Therefore, there are a number of predictive equations that are used to calculate maximal heart rate based on age. The most common of these is '220 – age'; this therefore assumes a 10 beat per decade decline in maximal heart rate. However, research on trained cyclists has shown that the decline is 6.6 beats per decade and thus a more accurate equation to use for cyclists would be '210 – [0.66 x age]'. This has practical implications for riders and coaches when they are trying to calculate training zones as a percentage of maximal heart rate, in that they should use this modified equation to estimate maximal heart rate.

Changes in cycling economy/efficiency

Strictly speaking, economy and efficiency are different measurements but, for cycling, they basically relate to the same functional ability, which is a key determinant of cycling performance (*see* chapter 1 for further discussion). Cycling economy is a measure of how much oxygen is required for a set exercise intensity, whereas efficiency is the ratio of energy in (from nutrients) and energy out (power). There is clear evidence that economy acutely declines immediately after training or competition. It has also been shown that it is possible for a younger rider to increase cycling economy over a period of time with high-level training and competition. Lance Armstrong was reported to be particularly efficient, and this has been used to explain his superior performances. Better economy is associated with higher proportions of the more efficient type I muscle fibres. As suggested above, there is an ageing-related decline in type II fibres and more reliance on type I. Therefore, it might be assumed that older riders would have better economy. However, despite the literature clearly showing declines in many of the physiological systems associated with economy, there is no direct evidence that cycling economy changes with ageing.

Changes in power-to-weight ratio

Many older riders complain of a reduced performance in hill-climbing ability. This is the result of a decline in the power-to-weight ratio. Figure 17.5 shows the typical decline in maximal aerobic power:weight with age for trained cyclists. The average decline here is about 0.4 $W \cdot kg^{-1} \cdot decade^{-1}$. There are two reasons for this: a reduction in power production, mostly attributable to a reduction in muscle mass, and a rise in total body mass as a result of age-related increases in body fat. Although the increases in body fat reported for cyclists are much less than those found in the general population, they are still evident even with continued vigorous training. The reduction in muscle mass (in particular fast-twitch muscle fibres) and the subsequent decrease in anaerobic performance will result in a reduced ability to 'power' over the shorter climbs. This suggests that older riders need to ensure that they carefully control their weight and include high-intensity intervals within their training to maximise the anaerobic potential of the reduced volume of fast-twitch muscle fibres.

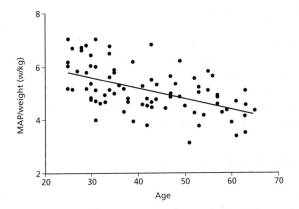

FIG.17.5 Ratio of maximal aerobic power to weight for 83 trained cyclists aged 25–65

The effects of ageing on muscle fatigue and recovery

While we can all relate to the concept of muscle fatigue, in terms of exercise physiology it is extremely complex and difficult to define. The key question is: how does age affect the fatigability of muscle? Many older riders complain of fatigue and taking longer to recover from training. A recent review of this area suggests that for isometric contractions, older non-sporting individuals exhibit less fatigue, whereas for dynamic contractions the reverse is true. So, although there is no evidence that exercise can slow the decline in absolute strength, it would seem that there might be some adaptation to improve fatigability. However, in athletic populations there are similar declines in maximal voluntary contraction after fatiguing exercise between old and young populations. The research specifically on cyclists has also shown no age effect when comparing the performance of old and young well-trained cyclists over three

30-minute time trials on three consecutive days. This would suggest a similar rate of aerobic recovery for young and old riders between trials.

Most cycling events, unlike many other sports, involves only shortening (concentric) muscle contractions and thus does not experience as high a level of muscle damage as, for example, running. This is advantageous in that higher volumes of training can be completed using older (more fragile) muscle, and also that recovery does not involve major remodelling of damaged muscle fibres, presumably increasing the rate of recovery compared with other sports. As would be expected, events of longer duration tend to result in greater reductions in maximal strength.

The effect of ageing on cadence

It has been observed that older cyclists tend to pedal at a slower rate. The exact reason for this is unknown, but it could be linked to a reduced proportion of fast-twitch muscle fibres. However, contraction speeds used during normal cycling are not actually that high and are well within the range for slow-twitch fibres. Declines in the function of the neuromuscular system may explain these changes but, unfortunately, most of the research studies looking at this decline with age have used untrained individuals. It is, therefore, difficult to tease out the effect of ageing from the effects of a decline in use. Anecdotal evidence suggests that older riders with a continued track racing background are able to maintain similar cadences to their younger counterparts. This may be attributable to the repeated high cadences required for track racing providing an ideal stimulus to retain this neuromuscular function. Thus, it would seem that older cyclists should incorporate some high-cadence work in their training programme to retain this functionality.

TRAINING

Research shows that there is a tendency for older cyclists to complete the same volume of training as their younger counterparts, but they do so at a lower intensity and cut out the really high-intensity sessions. In theory, if ageing has the effect of reducing muscle volume, particularly type II muscle, it might be important to include high-force and high-intensity activities in training. This would make sure that these muscle fibres were activated and stressed regularly to help retain their function. This might also suggest that weight training would be more beneficial to master cyclists. In addition, it is well documented that cyclists have lower bone density than equivalent aged runners or even non-exercisers. So, despite the large volumes of exercise, the fact

TAKE-HOME MESSAGE

Additional weight training may help to minimise the effects of the decline in muscle mass with age.

that the bike supports a cyclist's bodyweight leads to weaker, less dense bones. This is an additional reason for older riders to include weight training in their training programme.

SUMMARY

Cycling is much kinder to the body than many sporting activities, enabling continued high-level competition into old age. Despite the remarkable performances of master cyclists, the ageing process cannot be halted and there is an inevitable decline in physiological function. This is not a constant linear decline but one that starts slowly from the age of 40 to 60 years, with more rapid declines in later life. The overall rate of decline in maximal aerobic power is in the region of 7–17 per cent per decade. These changes are linked to declines in muscle mass, VO_{2max}, power-to-weight ratio and maximal heart rate. Lack of continued training will increase the rate of decline towards the upper end of this range. It may be possible to alter training to include more high-intensity and weight training to better maintain performance capabilities.

KEY TAKE-HOME MESSAGES

- The decline in cycling performance with age is not linear but tends to start slowly from the age of about 35 years, speeds up a little after 40 years of age and becomes particularly rapid after 60 years of age.
- Maximal aerobic power declines by 7–17 per cent per decade.
- Maximal heart rate declines by about seven beats per decade.
- There is no evidence that a large volume of exercise training slows the rate of decline in physiological function associated with ageing.
- There is no direct evidence that older muscle fatigues faster or recovers more slowly with cycling exercise.
- Cycling economy does not seem to change with age.
- More research is required to understand the potential benefits of maintaining the amount of high-intensity training into old age.

HOW DO I GET THE MOST OUT OF COACHING? THE COACH–ATHLETE RELATIONSHIP

Coaching is at the heart of successful cycling performance. This is true when teaching basic bike handling skills to the novice, right through to when discussing the intricacies of programme planning with an Olympic athlete.

Modern coaches need to be more like applied scientists who keep up to date with the latest research and are able to apply this multidisciplinary understanding to their practice. The earlier chapters of this book have examined the areas of cycling physiology, training, biomechanics, nutrition and psychology as well as their application to special populations. It is anticipated that, having read these sections, the cycling coach will have furthered their knowledge in at least some of these areas. This section considers the coaching process and provides a framework for shaping the role of the coach. The coaching philosophy and coach–athlete relationship are also discussed.

By the end of this section you will have considered the importance of coaching philosophy and its impact on the coach–athlete relationship. As a coach, you should have the knowledge to develop a coaching framework that can guide your work with athletes. As an athlete, it is hoped that you will have gained a deeper appreciation of what to look for in a coach and considered how you would want to be coached.

CHAPTER 18

COACH–ATHLETE RELATIONSHIPS

Helen Carter

Entering a coach–athlete relationship is an effective way of managing sport performance, with attention being given to fitness, nutrition, preparation for competition and the mental/emotional aspects of cycling. However, this does not guarantee
success; the coach and athlete must work as a team in order to maximise the chances
of optimal performance. In this chapter, while the coaching science literature is drawn
upon, it is important to stress that the content is based on direct experience. There
is no single way to coach, nor is there a 'perfect' coach–athlete relationship. Coaches
each have their own coaching style; likewise, athletes are individuals. However, all
good working relationships share similarities, including the commitment to share the
responsibility for performance improvement.

THE IMPORTANCE OF THE COACH

The progress of sport science and technology is changing the nature of coaching. With
downloadable cycle computers, power measurement and global positioning systems
(GPS), it is possible for the coach to 'live' each session with the athlete. There are no
longer geographical restrictions for the athlete setting up a relationship with a coach,
as much of the daily coach–athlete interaction can take place online. However, this is
still a relationship between two people. Indeed, the one-to-one interaction is often the
main reason people enter into coaching – to share the experience with someone else
and gain emotional support for what can be a very challenging environment.

Why should I have a coach?

There are many ways in which a coach can aid an athlete. However, it is important
to start with what coaching is not: having a training plan written for you is only one
aspect of working with a coach. Following a training plan does not mean you are being
coached. Coaching is a two-way process involving planning, feedback and refinement.
When asked what characteristics a coach should have, athletes typically list a few key
criteria: someone who is an 'expert' (in sport science and training theory), who has
some experience as a competitor and, finally, who is a good communicator. Possessing
this combination, the coach can help the athlete to make the most of the training
time available, which is equally important to the professional full-time athlete and to
the 'weekend warrior'. Knowledge of how to create and implement optimal training
is very important and, indeed, there is a growth in sport scientists being recruited as
coaches. However, without the ability to communicate this knowledge, the athlete will
not benefit.

When selecting a coach, the athlete must start with the question of what attributes are most important to them. The roles of the coach are many: advisor, data analyst, teacher, trainer, motivator, disciplinarian, friend and mentor, organiser and manager, press secretary and fund raiser, to name a few. Which skills will you need to tap? There is not one perfect coach for each athlete; rather, it is the *interaction* between coach and athlete that holds the key to success. An athlete may be given recommendations of a 'great coach' but then find he doesn't connect with that coach. There are many different coaching styles, personalities and needs of the athlete to consider.

The preparation of an athlete for a key event is very similar to project management. While the nature of the management might vary by coach, the athlete and the time that they have been working together (*see* later in this chapter), it is typical for the athlete to bring the goal and for the coach to organise how to approach the goal.

A COACHING PHILOSOPHY

When a coach and an athlete start working together, much gravitas is associated with the 'coaching philosophy', yet very few coaches publish what that means to the athlete. Usually, a philosophy will draw upon certain values the coach brings to his work. Possessing a defined and explicit philosophy helps to provide the framework within which the coach and athlete can work; this might simply be seen as 'boundaries' or conditions. This can help the athlete to appraise how the coach is performing against a list of criteria. As mentioned previously, different athletes need different things: one size does not fit all in coaching. An official statement regarding values and working practices helps the athlete to decide what is best for him when selecting a coach.

As with all human relationships, knowing where you stand is critical to maintaining a healthy interaction. Values and beliefs determine our behaviour and our expectations of others. If the values of the coach and athlete match up, the chances of a successful partnership are magnified. Critical to the practical operation of the coaching philosophy, therefore, is how the coach plans to live by his values: what processes do they put in place? An example philosophy in practice is given in table 18.1, which also shows how the coach and athlete can work within the framework.

FIG.18.1 Whether riding with a pro team or competing as a weekend warrior, all cyclists can benefit from working with a coach.

Value	Impact on coach–athlete relationship	Examples of actions to ensure that value is met
Trust	• Trust that the athlete is committing fully to the coaching process and training delivered • Trust that the coach is buying into the performance project to the same extent as the athlete	• The coach ensures that the athlete understands the 'why' of each training session so that the athlete understands the importance of its position within the training plan • Feedback on training is given in the spirit of helping the athlete to move forward and improve, not against any pre-judged expectation • The coach delivers the training plan based on the best estimation of required training stress at that time; there is no such thing as a 'perfect plan' and what appears in the diary is negotiable and refined based on how both parties feel that goals/targets are being met
Knowledge	• The coach keeps abreast of the latest developments in sport science and performance innovation • The athlete commits to learning and being his own best self-expert; being aware of how his body is reacting, what has worked in the past and what might be worth trying; getting engaged with the physiology of performance and training	• The coach commits to updating his knowledge across sport science, research physiology, coaching theory and coaching processes; attendance at conferences in applied sport science • Development of resources to help educate the athlete; delivering material in an accessible manner (at events such as workshops and training camps)

TABLE 18.1 An example of a coaching philosophy, giving a list of values held by the coach and how they intend to put those into actions; the table also suggests how the athlete can contribute to the relationship

Value	Impact on coach–athlete relationship	Examples of actions to ensure that value is met
Team	• The athlete brings the goal, ensuring that he feeds back to the coach on how he feels the process is going • The coach buys into the goal, bringing his expertise as physiologist and his experience of principles that are known to work in training, performance, recovery and nutrition • Developing a shared project	• The athlete maintains his training diary on a daily basis; the coach spends time each day analysing the training data • The coach and athlete ensure that the goal-setting process is up to date and relevant; the same for the race diary/plans
Motivation/ enthusiasm	• The coach is reliable, being there for the athlete to share in the success and the failures • The athlete understands that within the training process there is always choice; there is no 'have to' or 'should do'. At the same time, the athlete has to appreciate that with each choice there is a consequence – acceptance of the 'choice/consequence' is essential when weighing up priorities and thus how you approach training, performance and nutrition	• The coach will try to be present at races, especially at key events • The coach loves to hear about race performances, even if he can't promise to be at the race or to be in a position to respond to texts, emails or phone calls on the day • The coach will help the athlete to think of appropriate benchmarks/ criteria by which to rate performance(s)

Value	Impact on coach–athlete relationship	Examples of actions to ensure that value is met
Honesty	• The coach knows the limits of his expertise and is not afraid to admit that he doesn't have all the answers • The athlete needs to share what is truly going on with him in and around his training/racing life	• Regular phone conversations allow the coach and athlete to share their views on the coaching process • Mid- and post-season reviews are fundamental to building the coach–athlete relationship • The coach truly wants feedback on how training is going – the athlete is encouraged to be open with comments and to know he is not being judged at any point
Professionalism/respect	• The coach keeps the athlete's information confidential and applies best practice in moving the athlete's development forward • The athlete recognises that the coach is sharing the goal and can be relied upon, is committed and is applying a solid work ethic	• The coach keeps laboratory test data, race data or athlete goals to himself unless the athlete specifically agrees to sharing this information with others • The coach is always open to feedback on how the athlete feels about the relationship, the methods being used and the progress made • Both the coach and athlete are entitled to considerate action and language in the relationship; the coach in particular promises that anything said about the athlete in his absence is only what the coach would be happy to share in the athlete's presence

Coaching in action: the underpinning factors

Taking the project management analogy, the coach is seen as the manager of the timeline: preparing the training and feeding back to the athlete how he is progressing along the timeline. But first, the athlete presents the coach with the project goal. The coach can certainly help the athlete with the goal setting, but the goal itself must come from the athlete (by contrast, in professional cycling the goals are mainly team directed). Without that, the athlete will not be passionate about attaining the goal. This is critical at times when the training is hard and the athlete struggles to hit the training or race targets. The exact nature of the relationship between coach and athlete may change year on year. In my own work I have noticed how the interaction moves from being coach-driven in the infant stages of the work together, to being co-pilots in the middle stages, and eventually evolving to being athlete-led in the latter stages.

For example, the approach taken and role that I play is different with the novice riders compared with the professional athletes with whom I work. With the novice cyclist, my coaching style might be more 'autocratic': essentially directing the athlete as to what he should do. Plans are explicit and little flexibility is granted in each training session. By contrast, with professional riders I work more as a consultant. At this level, the cyclists know their bodies better than I possibly can; they tell me how a session felt, while I guide and advise based on what I see in their power files.

CASE STUDY 1:

THE PROFESSIONAL RIDER

'Riding within a pro team can bring challenges: especially balancing my own aspirations with the goals of the team. Having Helen to help me with those demands is priceless. In the two years of working with her, it feels like we are learning together. We are beginning to understand how we can peak for my race goals even when I am having to race most weekends from February to September.'

CASE STUDY 2:

FULL-TIME WORKER

'As a "weekend warrior", it is hard to fit 15 hours of training into my week. Having a coach gives me confidence that each of those hours is the most effective use of my time. I totally trust Helen's expertise. In return she has asked me to be open and honest as to how I am coping not only with the training but also with family, work and other commitments. I am totally sold on her view of "total stress": you can't make the overall tolerance of stress any bigger, it's about learning to juggle the components within to stay on top and healthy.'

The evolving nature of the coach–athlete relationship means that it is important to start the partnership with a working agreement. This can take the form of an oral agreement, but is probably best stored as a written document so each party knows the expectations and roles. One of the dilemmas can be 'who is boss, who is client?' in the relationship. Consider the following: coaching a child athlete where the coaching fee is paid by the parent versus working with an athlete who has a scholarship from a governing body. The question of 'boss' is most often posed when a coach is 'employed' by the amateur athlete: here the coach is trying to be 'project manager' to the person paying the bills. It helps to state all these things up front. How does the athlete wish to be coached? Should the coach adopt a democratic or autocratic style? Does the coach have permission to chase athletes for training files and feedback? Obviously, these aspects of the coach–athlete agreement should be renegotiated regularly; the end of each season is a good time for this.

Coaching in action: the practicalities

What follows is more detail on the day-to-day workings of the coach–athlete relationship. While planning is fundamental, just as much attention should be paid to the *fluidity* of the plan. No plan is perfect; it should simply be a template. There must be constant monitoring, with adjustments being made when necessary across the key components of athlete preparation: training, nutrition, recovery and competition. The coach brings his expertise in these areas, while the athlete brings self-awareness and information on how he is coping with the 'total stress' in his environment (i.e. the additional stresses of lifestyle, environment, work, etc.)

Defining the goal

Perhaps the most important role of the coach is to help the athlete with goal setting. In the majority of relationships, the athlete comes to coaching because he has a challenge he wishes to approach and has decided to do this through a structured, organised method. The athlete comes with the idea and the coach helps transform that idea into a goal; or, ideally, into a series of goals over the short, medium and long term. Movement through those stages puts the coach in an overseeing role built upon experience of the process and knowledge of the physiology of training.

Establish current position and profiling

Once the goal and the timeline are in place, the first task is to assess where the athlete is relative to the goal. The process is very much like a 'gap analysis':

- Where are you now?
- Where do you want to be? (And when?)
- How do we get there?

It need not be just about the physiology. Assessment of the skill set required to complete the goal is important: what is the need for psychological, nutritional and tactical/technical strategies and methodologies?

A useful framework to consider at this stage is that of long-term athlete development (LTAD), presented by scientists working at the National Coaching Institute of Canada. LTAD involves taking athletes through stages of development, ensuring that progress is incremental and takes into account all of the skill sets required. While originally developed in youth sport, the LTAD concept can be applied to athletes of all ages. Indeed, in my experience, athletes coming to cycling later in life often rush in to the race environment without considering the need for developing the basic skills first. For example, I had one novice who could not remove the bottle from his bike while moving – what would be the point of him participating in a road race without that skill? Other examples include developing a sound warm-up method or having practised opening an energy gel while on the move.

The coach should perform an audit across all the relevant sub-components of performance (physiological, psychological, nutritional, technical, tactical and competitive) and help assign the athlete to a phase: training to train, training to compete or training to win. There should be no embarrassment in starting at the very beginning; indeed, if an athlete comes with a long-term goal (three to five years), this can feel spacious and exciting, giving time to develop everything thoroughly before moving on to the next phase. The phase the athlete sits in will dictate the amount of competition in a season and even the number of 'peaks' in the more advanced stages of 'training to compete' and 'training to win'. The reader is directed to the literature in LTAD to explore this further.

Process monitoring

As with any project, there need to be mechanisms to assess progress towards the goal. One of the advantages of working with a coach who has sport science training is that laboratory testing can be performed at regular intervals over the course of the season. At the first laboratory test, this allows the strengths and weaknesses of the athlete relative to the goal event's demands to be assessed. Subsequent time periods for re-testing are planned to track progress, helping not only to keep training load optimal but also to understand whether the current training is working or needs to be adapted. From a motivational point of view, frequent testing can also help the athlete see that the 'gap' is being closed.

I am often asked what laboratory testing brings to the training process above field testing or keeping a log of race performances. Completing work over set time durations and estimating race performance (so called 'power profiling') is useful. However, used alone, these tests just tell us if performance is 'good' or 'could be improved'. A physiologist can use performance alongside the measurements from tests such as maximal oxygen consumption (VO_{2max}) or lactate threshold to understand the 'why' of performance: what is the physiology currently limiting performance, and what can we do to shift the physiology to remove the limitation? A classic example is being able to measure efficiency using oxygen uptake measurement. Two athletes might develop the same power over a 20-minute block of work. By measuring their efficiency, we might detect that one uses a lot more oxygen than normal at that power. This can inform what to do in the training plan to improve efficiency and thereby 'spare' oxygen available for a higher performance power.

Typically, the following testing regimen is very effective:

- Lactate threshold, VO_{2max} and efficiency testing should be undertaken approximately three times per year: the first in the autumn (pre-base training); the second in the spring (to assess the effectiveness of the base training); and the third during the season (to determine if race performances can be further refined). The exact timings of the tests depend on the timing of the goal events and the cycling discipline (track, cyclo-cross, road or time trial).
- In between tests, power profiling should be performed to allow training zones to be kept up to date. These might be included every second training block (e.g. every eight weeks).
- The third form of 'test' found to be useful is the Lamberts sub-maximal cycling test (LSCT) (*see* chapter 3, page 49). This test helps the coach to assess how well the athlete is coping with the training load. A short test, it is easily incorporated within the athlete's training once per week as a warm-up to a main training session.

It is critical that the athlete understands the purpose of each of these testing occasions. This allows coach and athlete to work scientifically under 'controlled' conditions, such as treating the physiological tests like race days or ensuring the LSCT is performed at the same time of day each week.

The communication processes employed on a day-to-day level are discussed in more detail below; at an 'umbrella level', it is important to have assigned reviews at pre-determined points in the yearly cycle. For example:

- **Yearly planning meeting:** Normally held within the off-season break, this meeting establishes the main objectives for the next season. Based on laboratory testing, this is the time to develop the first draft of the year's periodisation schedule.
- **Pre-season planning:** This meeting takes place approximately 12–14 weeks after the yearly planning meeting and sets up the racing programme to assist the major goals. From this point, changes need to be minimised, allowing the coach to flesh out the periodisation over the season and to ensure that all aspects of race preparation are covered sequentially and comprehensively. The second half of the year can be left as 'draft' (to be reviewed at the mid-season review).
- **Mid-season review:** Athletes should be encouraged to take a minimum two-week period mid-season with non-structured riding and no racing: this gives them a chance to re-energise physically and mentally and also the space to reflect on the year so far. In the meeting, the coach and athlete can debrief: assessing what did and did not work in the first half of the year. It is suggested that the coach develop a questionnaire to which the athlete responds. This helps give a structure to the discussion as well as forming notes to refer back to at the end of the year. The meeting allows refinement of the second half of the season, particularly relating to goals and periodisation.
- **End of season review:** This is the time to review not only performance but also training, nutrition and recovery and to feed back on how the coach–athlete relationship has worked. The discussion will allow a re-negotiation of the coach–athlete

agreement, ultimately leading to a decision as to whether or not the relationship will continue into the following year. Sometimes, the difficult decision to end the relationship might have to be made. If not, the discussion here will feed into the yearly planning meeting, and the cycle begins again.

Managing the project through regular communication

As well as the formalised meetings over the yearly cycle, regular contact between rider and coach is needed, the exact nature of which should be negotiated by the partnership. I have different arrangements with each individual that I coach. Some clients hate the telephone and my main contact is via email. Others prefer meeting up with me face to face. As a coach, I must be open to what the athlete prefers and be prepared to work with that.

In partnership, daily, weekly and training cycle communication expectations are set. If these are not overt, problems can occur because one assumes things from a personal position. My athletes know that I expect daily updates of their training diaries and, in return, my athletes receive regular training data analysis. By working together in this way, I can feed back information while it is still relevant, leading to refinement of the training plan. As mentioned above, this enables fluidity, which is critical to an effective training plan. If an athlete fails to update after a session on Monday (where they felt tired and unable to hit the targets set), how am I to intervene if their data suggest imminent illness? Catching issues quickly helps long-term consistency in training load.

An important aspect of the coach's job is to ensure logging of information. Although this administration can be mundane, recording progress is critical in recognising patterns. Alongside daily communication, the main bulk of my work is recording information such as performing analysis of laboratory test and power profiling data and interpreting the scores based on event demands; analysis of the training data to ensure adequate training progression and updates to training zones; monitoring the outcomes of the weekly LSCT, which helps me to assess the state of 'restfulness'; and, finally, logging race performances.

In my formative years of coaching, I soon learned the importance of educating the athlete and my role in helping athletes to develop self-awareness. Initially, I thought the important aspect of my role was delivering scientifically sound training and subsequently analysing the data. However, I soon realised that, more often than not, the training was not being completed as I intended. Life often gets in the way! Just as the 'perfect plan' does not exist, the likelihood of the athlete having the 'perfect conditions' to perform the plan is rare. The coach and athlete pairing makes a lot more progress by agreeing to learn together. My role has therefore expanded to teaching the athlete how to adapt the plan when necessary (when to train versus when to rest, how to re-organise the week, etc.) None of this could be possible without discussion of each training block, cycle and/or phase. It is down to the coach to set and communicate the objectives of each block and of each training session: what increments are being looked for? How do we monitor this? The coach and athlete, working together, also ensure that objectives cover nutrition and recovery, such as the fourth week (or similar) being a restitution week. Asking 'what's important now?' has become useful for me, bringing awareness to the athlete as to what action will help take them closer to (not further away from) their goal.

Racing season

The racing season is the time when the coach and athlete finally see the rewards of the effort invested. However, as excitement builds, so does expectation and, inevitably, disappointments take place. The coach is responsible for managing this period. Arguably, communication becomes its most critical with parameters changing in a short space of time (fitness, form, fatigue), akin to an 'emotional rollercoaster', for coach as well as athlete. The primary role of the coach is to be an anchor, keeping the question of 'what's important now?' at the forefront of the athlete's mind.

Frequent reviewing of performance is essential throughout the race season. Don't overlook the importance of debriefing the good as well as the poor performances. It is a good habit to review all races, whether preparatory/training races or the 'real deal' key events, as follows:

- Establish the criteria for 'success'
- Ensure there is a clear purpose: is this a training race? Is there a particular performance outcome desired or is the emphasis on within-race 'process' goals?
- Follow-up with a review: were the criteria for 'success' attained?

In my experience, many athletes find it very hard to let go of performance outcomes. Bravery is required in approaching racing. Without focus at times on process goals, the athlete will fall into the trap of making every race an important race. The coach needs to find ways of selling the development of particular abilities rather than always looking at achieving peak performance.

WHEN THINGS CHANGE: ALL GOOD THINGS COME TO AN END

Not all relationships are successful, and none last forever. One of the hardest positions to be in is when one or both parties knows that a split is the most beneficial answer: an example might be a junior athlete requiring a coach with a deeper knowledge of sport science than his club coach can provide. At the same time, the developing athlete must weigh up whether the change in coach will suit them: many juniors making the transition feel bereft at losing the coach they started the sport with and find it hard to be on the receiving end of a very different relationship.

Even when a relationship works well, there may come a time when the athlete outgrows the coach, or performance might become 'stale'. Acknowledging that things have come to an end is difficult, particularly if this is only felt on one side. The key to an amicable ending is to stay open at all times; hopefully this will prevent things sliding in the first place, but at the very least it will enable a frank and honest conversation when terminating the agreement. In practice, if the coach and athlete adopt a season-by-season approach, the nature of the relationship can be re-negotiated at the end of the yearly cycle.

SUMMARY

This chapter has provided an overview of the coach–athlete relationship. Much of the material presented here is by no means written in stone. There is much that can only be learned 'on the job' even if the coach has a secure grounding in sports or coaching science. The athlete needs to bring a commitment to increasing his self-awareness and also to sharing responsibility for the success of the project. The coach–athlete

A PHILOSOPHY OF COACHING, BY ANDREW KIRKLAND

The role of an effective coach is to support a rider in a manner that allows the rider to adapt physiologically and psychologically at a rate that is appropriate for his stage of development and individual needs. A scientific approach to coaching is important insofar as prescribed training or coaching interventions should be logical, justifiable and underpinned by sound rationale. However, coaching also requires that the coach adapts his approach based on the requirements and feedback of his riders.

Long-term athlete development models can be useful to ensure that the type of coaching provided is appropriate for the rider's level of maturation, physical ability and stage of learning. Riders should learn fundamental movement patterns early in their development as they provide the foundations upon which more complex race-specific skills, techniques and strategies are based. If fundamental skills and techniques are not learned early on, the chance of success is substantially reduced. For example, a rider may have an excellent physiological capacity to perform; however, performance may be compromised if he is unable to ride in a bunch or negotiate a corner at very high speed, regardless of the power he is able to deliver.

Coaches may not always have the opportunity to work with riders from an early age when technical, tactical and psychological components of performance are most effectively developed. Nevertheless, these components must be integrated with physiological components in every training programme. Coaches should understand the process of physiological adaptation in which the body responds to the demands of the environment to which it is exposed. Similarly, it is important to be aware that there is a very large variation in the rate and size of inter-individual adaptation. For this reason, generic training programme prescription is probably appropriate only at the beginning of the coach–athlete relationship, before the coach has formed an understanding of the rider.

There are many factors, including family environment, sociological factors, financial constraints and training location, that will assist or be a barrier to the rider reaching his long-term performance goals. A successful coach, therefore, needs an adaptable and holistic approach that also takes into account a rider's personality, volition to train and physiological abilities in order to help him reach his potential. For these reasons, prescribing specific training sessions may form a only small part of the overall coaching process.

relationship is not a static one; with time, you will notice how the relationship evolves. Be prepared to see the athlete's role change from a degree of dependency on the coach, moving to becoming more independent, through to the athlete taking over the driving seat of the project and racing goals. At a highly evolved level, a subtle shift takes place again and a strong *inter*-dependence is created, with the coach and athlete working as a team in the very deepest of methods and communication.

KEY TAKE-HOME MESSAGES

To maximise the chances of success, the following seven factors are chosen for suggested focus (presented in no particular order):

- Know the stage of development that the athlete occupies according to the LTAD concept.
- Plan the goal events and then understand the importance of minimising deviation from the initial plan in order to prevent being underprepared at key times in the year.
- Know objectives for each training cycle and how to monitor those objectives using laboratory testing and power profiling.
- Use objectives for each training block to address how to keep on top of training load, such as the importance of monitoring recovery as well as other factors.
- Keep the training diary up to date ... daily.
- Remember that, while daily and weekly communication is excellent, specific communication at the end of a training cycle allows a step back to review how training is going: 'seeing the wood *and* the trees'.
- Avoid going through the motions in races by deciding in advance if the event has a performance (e.g. time, ranking) or a process outcome (e.g. racing at a set cadence). Debrief after the event.

SECTION J

WHAT ARE THE MEDICAL CONSIDERATIONS IN CYCLING?

Section J is divided into two chapters. Chapter 19 focuses on cycling injuries, their treatment and their prevention. The increasing participation levels in all forms of cycling necessitate that greater attention be paid to the traumatic and overuse injuries experienced by cyclists. However, within the scope of this book, the main focus of chapter 19 is overuse conditions as their potential for self-management is much greater than that of traumatic injuries. Owing to the length of time that cyclists spend in the saddle during training and racing, it is highly likely overuse injuries will occur. These may occur as a result of errors in training load, improper bike fit or unsuitable bike component use, to name but a few. Chapter 19 also provides some guidelines on the prevention of overuse injuries.

Chapter 20 discusses the use of drugs in cycle sport. Unfortunately, professional cycle sport is repeatedly blighted by drug scandals. The Union Cycliste Internationale and the World Anti-Doping Authority are working hard to develop a system that will eventually eliminate drug use, or at least provide a significant deterrent. Chapter 20 provides a review of the main drugs that have been found in blood or urine samples taken from cyclists and indicates what effect (both performance enhancing and health related) they have on the body. The chapter then outlines what the anti-doping authorities are doing to combat drug use in cycling by implementation of a 'biological passport'. Finally, the chapter discusses how it is not just the cyclist who is intentionally taking performance-enhancing drugs to gain a performance advantage that might get caught at a doping test. Over the last few years, a number of high-profile positive doping tests have been the result of contamination of food, supplements or via unlisted ingredients in common over-the-counter medicines.

CHAPTER 19

CYCLING INJURIES, PREVENTION AND MANAGEMENT

Roger Palfreeman

Injuries to cyclists fall into two general categories: traumatic and overuse. This chapter will deal mainly with overuse injuries as the potential for prevention and self-management of such injuries is far greater.

OVERUSE INJURIES

Cycling is an activity where the biomechanics (and potential for injury) are largely determined by how the bike is set up and the way in which the rider interacts with the bike. As such, many injuries can be explained by an understanding of these issues and, thereby, prevented and treated. Certain injuries will require the involvement of suitably qualified professionals, such as a doctor, podiatrist or physiotherapist/sport therapist.

There are a number of factors that influence the loading of vulnerable tissues (joints, tendons, muscles, nerves, blood vessels) and increase the likelihood of injury. These fall into several categories, as follows:

- Bike positioning:
  - seat height;
  - saddle set back;
  - handlebar height and reach; and
  - joint orientation as a result of bike set-up.
- Equipment choices:
  - pedals, shoes and cleats;
  - cranks, saddle, frame design and bar tape; and
  - mitts and shorts.
- Shoe–pedal interface:
  - foot position – inwards/outwards, forwards/backwards;
  - foot angulation – use of cleat wedges;
  - pedal float; and
  - foot mechanics.
- Cycling activity:
  - seated climbing;
  - unseated climbing; and
  - gearing.

- Intrinsic/individual factors:
  - leg length differences; and
  - other anatomical variations.

It is important to try to identify the aetiology (or cause) of overuse injuries. The above classification can be simplified so that injuries can be considered under one or more of the following headings. These will be referred to at various points throughout the chapter and are:

- activity related;
- equipment related; and
- intrinsic factors.

For purposes of simplification, the various overuse injuries will be organised into different body regions, with the more common lower limb injuries considered first.

LOWER LIMB INJURIES
Knee pain

The knee is a complex joint and pain can arise from a number of structures within it. However, in practice, knee pain in cyclists most often originates from the patel-lofemoral joint (between the kneecap [patella] and thigh bone [femur]) and related soft-tissue structures.

Typical symptoms

Anterior knee pain is felt around the front of the joint, often behind the kneecap. It is usually worse when using big gears and is predominantly felt during the downstroke of the pedal cycle. When not riding, there may be discomfort when descending stairs, squatting down, kneeling or sitting for long periods. It is unusual for the knee to swell. If swelling occurs, it is important to consider other diagnoses.

If there has been a heavy blow to the kneecap during a crash, the condition some-times occurs as a traumatic injury. Non-traumatic causes include an inappropriately low saddle (which increases pressure between the patella and femur). Another predis-posing factor is if the cyclist is riding with a relative 'heels-out' foot position where he is unable to drop his heels in to the extent he would wish. A clue that an excessive 'heels-out' position is being used is to see significant wear to the surface of the crank as a result of the ankle brushing against it during the pedalling action (see figure 19.1). However, this does not always apply, as some individuals may adjust the cleats to prevent the ankles touching.

An inability to adopt an adequate 'heels-in' posture can be attributable to errors in cleat positioning, an inappropriate choice of pedal system, use of cranks with a straight (rather than a curved) profile, shoes with a bulky tightening system on the inside of the upper or thick neoprene overshoes; indeed, anything that prevents the

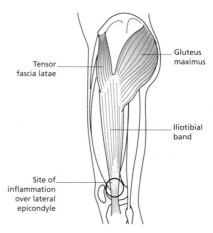

FIG.19.2 The anatomical structure of the leg showing the iliotibial band and the common site of inflammation owing to fat pad inflammation

beneath it, close to the point where it passes over the outside of the femoral epicondyle (the bony prominence on the outer side of the knee). This fat pad is vulnerable to compression when the ITB comes under increased tension while riding. In some circumstances, the fat pad can then become inflamed, causing pain.

Typical symptoms

The typical symptom is pain during the downstroke felt over the outside of the knee. There is often a well-localised area of tenderness just above the lateral epicondyle. It can be associated with pain in the outer part of the quadriceps or the upper leg, just below the front of the pelvis. A sensation of tightness on the outer part of the thigh is quite common.

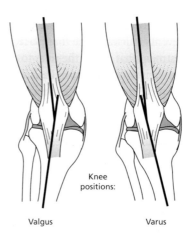

FIG.19.3 Illustration showing valgus and varus loads being applied to the right knee; varus means the lower part of the leg below the knee is bent *inward*, resulting in a bowlegged appearance, while valgus means the lower part of the leg is bent *outward*, resulting in a knock-kneed appearance

CAUSES OF ITB SYNDROME

- Equipment related:
  - pedal system – short functional spindle length;
  - shoe design – bulky fastenings on inside of shoe;
  - errors in cleat positioning (foot too close to crank/not allowing natural foot position to be adopted);
  - excessively low/high saddle height;
  - inappropriate use of varus wedges under cleats; and
  - excessively highly arched footbeds (can act like a varus wedge).
- Intrinsic causes:
  - foot biomechanics; and
  - rotational lower limb profile – out-turned foot posture. Can be difficult to accommodate the natural foot position owing to ankle-contact.

The cause of ITB syndrome is still not fully explained, although it appears that excessive varus bending loads (*see* figure 19.3) and inward twisting forces acting at the knee may be involved. Additionally, there may be increased activity and tightness in some of the muscles associated with the ITB. Collectively, these act to raise the compressive forces on the underlying fat pad. The influence of saddle height is not clear, although marked deviations from recommended measurements could theoretically be implicated.

An important consideration is the need to adopt a natural foot position on the pedal, in particular being able to place the foot sufficiently far away from the crank and let the heels drop in. This is largely a function of pedal choice and cleat adjustment, as discussed in the section on anterior knee pain. Failure to do this can generate the type of unwanted knee loads that predispose to ITB syndrome.

Treatment and prevention

Treatment and prevention are primarily aimed at addressing the biomechanical issues that predispose to the condition. ITB stretching programmes don't actually stretch the ITB itself (which is a rigid structure) but do help to reduce tone in its associated muscles (such as the tensor fascia latae at the top of the thigh; *see* figure 19.2, page 262). The resultant muscle lengthening will act to decrease tension in the ITB. Temporary use of a valgus wedge (thick part towards the outside of the shoe) placed beneath the cleat will reduce varus knee loads by moving the knee towards the top tube. This will shift the position of the knee to be more in line with the direction of the pedal downstroke. Corticosteroid injections into the inflamed fat pad will often provide relief in persistent cases but are unlikely to provide a cure if the underlying biomechanical errors are ignored.

LOWER LIMB TENDON INJURIES (TENDINOSIS)

The most commonly affected areas are the Achilles, patellar and biceps femoris tendons. Occasionally, the tendon grouping on the inside of the knee (the pes anserine insertion) can also become painful. In contrast to activities such as running, tendon injuries tend to be less common and less severe in cyclists. This is probably a result of lower forces and much smaller eccentric muscle contractions.

Achilles tendinosis

The Achilles tendon connects the large calf muscles to the heel bone (calcaneus), transmitting the pull of these muscles to plantarflex the ankle into a 'toes down' position (i.e. pointing your toes) (see figure 19.4).

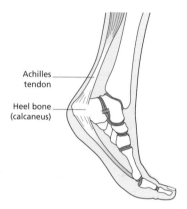

Achilles tendon

Heel bone (calcaneus)

FIG.19.4 Anatomical structure of the lower leg

Typical symptoms

The typical symptom is heel pain located over the Achilles tendon. The pain is often worse after activity, although it usually also causes discomfort while riding, especially in the early part of a ride. During longer rides, however, the pain will sometimes diminish, only to return later after rest. When not riding, pain while climbing stairs is common, as is pain during any activity involving raising the heels off the ground. If the tissues surrounding the tendon are inflamed, a creaking sensation with ankle movement is common (a condition called paratendonitis). There is usually tenderness at a specific point on the tendon.

Achilles tendinosis can be caused by unaccustomed seated climbing, such as occurs when riding on Alpine-style climbs (if you are not used to it). When riding uphill in the saddle, the true top dead centre of the crank is shifted to an earlier point in the pedalling cycle, with the result that the ankle/calf muscles have to overcome an additional gravitational force. This increases loading of the calf muscles and Achilles

CAUSES OF ACHILLES TENDINOSIS

- Activity related: unaccustomed seated climbing, sudden increases in training volume.
- Equipment related: forward positioning of cleat.
- Intrinsic: tight, inflexible calf muscles.

tendon, predisposing to injury. Sudden increases in training volume during the early phases of a training season are another common trigger for Achilles tendinosis. Using a forward cleat setting on the sole of the shoe increases the work performed by the calf muscles. Therefore, changes in the cleat position can cause calf muscle and Achilles pain. This is most likely to occur when changing to a new pair of shoes or when replacing a worn cleat.

Treatment

Treatment involves reducing activity levels while addressing any underlying factors. The cleat can be temporarily moved further backwards in order to reduce calf muscle work. A heel raise in everyday walking shoes may also help. If the symptoms don't settle, a programme of eccentric heel drops, ideally supervised by a suitably qualified therapist, may be needed.

Patellar tendinosis

The patellar tendon connects the patella to the front of the tibia, forming the lower-end quadriceps muscle group attachment. The quadriceps muscle group acts to extend (straighten) the knee joint.

Typical symptoms

Pain is located just below the kneecap, often with point tenderness over the patellar tendon itself. The pain pattern is often very similar to that with anterior knee pain, although it is sometimes worse following, rather than during, activity.

Treatment

Treatment involves reducing activity levels as needed. Attend to any underlying issues. If the condition fails to improve, a supervised programme of eccentric decline squats will often help to improve matters.

CAUSES OF PATELLAR TENDONITIS

- Saddle is set too low.
- Saddle is set too far behind the bottom bracket.
- *See* also 'causes of anterior knee pain' page 261

CAUSES OF PLANTAR DIGITAL NERVE COMPRESSION

- Activity related: long rides, especially those without periods of unseated climbing.
- Equipment related:
  - inadequate, thin footbed;
  - footbed/shoe with insufficient medial arch support;
  - shoes with intrinsic varus wedge have the potential to contribute to symptoms in some riders; and
  - errors in cleat placement/pedal choice can create supinatory forces on the foot and increase lateral foot pressure.
- Intrinsic factor: extreme foot types.

Typical symptoms

A numbness, burning pain or pins and needles sensation is felt on the sole while riding. The pain is often centred on the ball of the foot or toes. Most often it affects the big toe, but can involve the outer aspect of the foot. If mild, the symptoms are transient and present only when riding. More severely affected individuals may find they have persistent numbness or burning pain at other times.

The condition is related to sustained high pressure on the sole of the foot, which may be an indication of an underlying issue with foot posture. Those with excessive pronation (flat arches) characteristically suffer from high pressures towards the medial (inner) aspect of the foot. Conversely, those with supinated foot types (high arches) are most likely to experience symptoms laterally, on the outside. Cycling shoes with poor medial arch support fail to redistribute pressure adequately, while those with inbuilt varus wedging are likely to increase medial foot pressures. Some footbeds are too thin and fail to provide sufficient cushioning, given that the underlying sole is often manufactured from rigid materials such as carbon composites. Excessive tightening of the shoe can add to the compression.

A key point is the use of a footbed with an appropriately sized medial arch support together with adequate cushioning of the front part of the foot. Further modifications to this arrangement can then be made as necessary. In some cases, the addition of a forefoot varus/valgus wedge underneath the footbed will help, but this is usually best performed under the guidance of a podiatrist.

Treatment

If consideration of the points listed in the box above does not alleviate symptoms, the opinion of a podiatrist with experience of dealing with cyclists is recommended. Some riders may benefit from a custom-made orthotic device formed by making an impression of the rider's feet.

LOWER LIMB MUSCLE INJURIES

Muscle injuries in cyclists, unless caused by trauma, tend to lie towards the milder end of the spectrum. Typically, they are of gradual onset, where the affected muscle becomes uncomfortable when used. Additionally, the muscle may develop one or more area of exquisite tenderness to palpation, often referred to as trigger points. Trigger points develop as a result of overuse rather than a sudden, excessive overload.

The most commonly affected muscles are those primarily concerned with generating torque as opposed to those regulating joint moments. Muscles commonly involved include the gluteus maximus (large buttock muscle) and the quadriceps (anterior thigh muscles). Within the quadriceps group, the vastus medialis, on the inner aspect, and vastus lateralis, on the outer side, are most frequently involved. On occasions, the calf muscles can also be a source of muscle pain, the causes being similar to those for Achilles tendinosis (*see* page 265).

Deep to the main buttock muscle lie a number of smaller muscles whose role is essentially a stabilising one, preventing unwanted movements at the hip during the cycling action. These too can become problematic and their management is occasionally complex as there are a number of reasons why this particular group of muscles might become overloaded.

Gluteal (buttock) muscle pain

Gluteal muscle pain can arise from the gluteus maximus muscle itself or from the deeper hip-stabilising muscles. Gluteal pain that is associated with a more deeply located tenderness suggests an origin from a muscle with a hip-stabilising role, in which case the underlying cause may be more complex than discussed here.

Typical symptoms

The main symptom is discomfort in the buttock when riding, although the sensation might also be felt at other times, such as when sitting on firm surfaces. Discrete areas within the muscle may feel very tender to slight pressure.

CAUSES OF GLUTEAL MUSCLE PAIN

The gluteal muscles tend to increase their activity as the rider moves further back behind the bottom bracket. This may be as a result either of the saddle position or of the rider intentionally pushing himself further backward on the saddle while riding. The latter situation sometimes occurs when climbing in a seated position to compensate for being slightly overgeared. Adopting an aerodynamic position often results in smaller hip angles, which promotes an increase in gluteal muscle activity at the expense of muscles at the front of the pelvis (hip flexors), which tend to show changes in the opposite direction.

Treatment and prevention

Treatment and prevention is aimed at avoidance or modification of the above factors. Tender trigger points often respond well to needling (acupuncture), administered by a suitably qualified therapist. A programme of specific stretching may also be beneficial.

Quadriceps muscle pain

The quadriceps is comprised of four separate muscles (*see* figure 19.7), whose main function is to extend the knee during the early part of the downstroke. However, two of its component parts, the vastus medialis and vastus lateralis, also have a potential role in resisting unwanted twisting (internal/external) and bending (valgus/varus) loads at the knee. Consequently, they can become overworked as part of an anterior knee pain syndrome or in isolation.

Typical symptoms

Symptoms include muscle pain felt during the early to mid-section of the pedal downstroke. One or more tender trigger points are frequently present and are easily localised by palpation. Finger pressure applied at these points usually reproduces the pain experienced while cycling. Most of the associated factors to consider are covered by the section on anterior knee pain (*see* page 259).

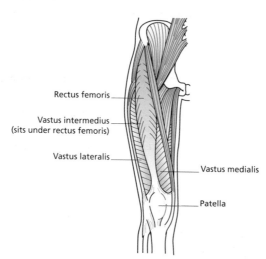

Rectus femoris

Vastus intermedius
(sits under rectus femoris)

Vastus lateralis

Vastus medialis

Patella

FIG.19.7 Quadriceps muscle group

CAUSES OF QUADRICEPS MUSCLE PAIN

- An excessively forward saddle position, as this increases quadriceps muscle activity.
- A marked deviation from the recommendations on saddle height.

Treatment and prevention

Pay attention to possible contributory factors. Stretching and physiotherapy, including needling, usually provide relief.

LOWER LIMB VASCULAR INJURIES

The iliac arteries are the main source of blood supply to the working leg muscles (*see* figure 19.8). There are a number of conditions, relatively rare in other sports, that can affect this arterial supply and, hence, blood flow to the muscles during exercise, thereby compromising performance.

The body position during seated cycling places the hip in a significant degree of flexion (bending) as the foot approaches the top of the pedal stroke. This can result in kinking or compression of the iliac artery, especially when it is combined with one or more recently recognised risk factors. These risk factors include excessive iliac artery length, tethering of the artery by side artery branches to the underlying psoas muscle (the main hip flexor) and psoas muscle hypertrophy.

In addition to arterial kinking/compression, the artery can develop an intrinsic narrowing, termed endofibrosis. It is thought this may develop as a result of long-term mechanical stress to the vessel wall, possibly as a result of untreated arterial kinking or compression. It is likely that the high rates of arterial blood flow generated during competitive cycling also contribute to wall stress and play an additional role in the condition.

Typical symptoms

Often, there are no symptoms at rest, or sometimes even during sub-maximal exercise. As the exercise intensity increases, complaints of muscle pain, cramps, leg weakness or numbness are likely to develop. Sometimes an unexplained deterioration in performance is the only indication. Symptoms are usually experienced in a single leg, although bilateral involvement is seen clinically in around 15 per cent of cases.

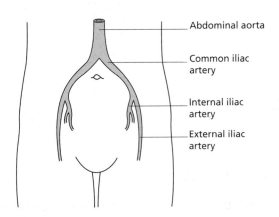

FIG.19.8 Anatomical structure of the iliac arteries

CAUSES OF ILIAC ARTERY INSUFFICIENCY

- Activity related:
  - aerodynamic riding position, with increased hip flexion;
  - high mileage; and
  - years of riding.
- Intrinsic factors:
  - vascular anomalies, such as excessive blood vessel length, which predispose to arterial kinking; and
  - psoas hypertrophy.

The development of iliac artery insufficiency is probably a result of possessing one or more of the arterial anomalies combined with the repetitive hip flexion that occurs while cycling. Adoption of extreme aerodynamic positions and a high volume of riding will further increase the risk of acquiring the condition.

Treatment and prevention

It is essential to have any symptoms suggestive of iliac artery insufficiency fully investigated. Diagnosis relies on a combination of the rider's symptoms, examination findings and the results of a variety of tests. These typically include simultaneous measurement of arm and leg blood pressure while riding and imaging of the blood vessels using magnetic resonance angiography. Analysis of pedal forces during an incremental exercise test often shows a characteristic picture, with the affected leg being the dominant one during low-intensity exercise and the unaffected leg gradually taking over as the workload progressively increases.

Management involves the modification of risk factors, such as adopting a less extreme riding position. The more upright posture of mountain biking may help to alleviate symptoms. A permanent reduction in the amount of riding undertaken may be advised. However, as many of those affected are keen competitive cyclists, such measures might not be acceptable. If this is the case, a variety of surgical procedures could be considered. The exact operation performed depends largely on the nature of the underlying vascular problem and, ideally, should be performed only in specialist centres experienced in dealing with the condition. If endofibrosis has developed, or there is excessive vessel length, the surgery is likely to be more complex.

SADDLE INJURIES

There are a number of injuries caused by contact between the rider's perineum ('saddle area') and the saddle. These include damage to the skin and soft tissues, infections, nerve and blood vessel damage and urethral trauma. They occur as a result of combined compressive and shear forces applied to the skin surface. Male and female injuries are considered separately.

Male saddle injuries

Repeated friction (shear stress) between the skin and the shorts insert can result in skin abrasions. If there is also a significant element of compression, subcutaneous nodules can result, caused by damage to the underlying tissues. A break in the skin surface will allow bacteria to gain access, which may result in a localised infection, termed an abscess. Excessive or sustained compressive forces in the midline of the perineum can affect the function of adjacent penile nerves and blood vessels, as well as traumatise the urethra, resulting in urinary symptoms. The aetiology of erectile dysfunction is multifactorial and can be caused by prolonged or repeated disruption to penile blood flow and nerve compression.

Typical symptoms

Skin abrasions are apparent as areas of sore, reddened skin. Subcutaneous nodules and abscesses are both felt as lumps. Abscesses are always tender and the overlying skin may also be red and inflamed. However, the only reliable way to distinguish between the two is to decompress the lump using a sterile needle after first thoroughly cleansing the skin surface. Abscesses will release pus, whereas subcutaneous nodules will often produce blood or clear fluid. It is recommended that a suitably qualified practitioner perform this procedure.

Compression of the dorsal penile nerve will produce penile numbness, which usually resolves rapidly once the rider changes position on the saddle or adopts a standing posture. Persistent numbness, which is still present at other times, needs to be taken seriously, as it is often a marker of the development of erectile dysfunction. Erectile dysfunction can develop very rapidly. Permanent impairment can occasionally occur after only days of experiencing severe symptoms while riding.

Urethral trauma usually manifests as burning or stinging when passing urine shortly after a ride. In severe cases, the urine may be discoloured by the presence of blood.

Causes

The most common reasons for incurring such problems are related to errors in equipment choice and adjustment. Failure to apply skin emollient or chamois cream to the perineum before a ride will increase skin friction. Such preparations also help hydrate the skin, preventing skin cracking, which promotes access of bacteria and infection. It is important to use good-quality shorts with a well-designed insert to reduce perineal compression.

There are a number of extremely light saddles on the market, but the low weight is sometimes achieved at the expense of comfort. In a typical riding position, the highest saddle pressures are often towards the front of the saddle, which also corresponds to the more vulnerable areas of the perineum where important anatomical structures are located. Unfortunately, this is often the least well-padded area on lightweight

CAUSES OF MALE SADDLE INJURIES

- Activity related:
  - riding in an extreme aerodynamic position; and
  - track riding.
- Equipment related:
  - poor saddle choice;
  - excessive backward saddle tilt;
  - saddle not aligned with top tube;
  - saddle too high;
  - poor shorts insert; and
  - failure to use emollient/chamois cream.
- Intrinsic factors:
  - leg length inequality;
  - spinal asymmetry; and
  - other causes of asymmetrical position.

saddles. Irrespective of the saddle design, it is essential that the saddle be correctly adjusted. A common fault is excessive backward tilt of the saddle nose as this increases perineal compression, particularly when the rider adopts a more aerodynamic posture. Excessive saddle height will have a similar effect, whereas failure to align the long axis of the saddle with the top tube may lead to recurrent unilateral problems.

Certain cycling disciplines are especially problematic. Those demanding an extreme aerodynamic posture, such as time trialling, are usually implicated, as the vulnerable anterior perineum is in contact with the saddle as the pelvis rotates forward. Track riding may also be particularly problematic owing to the significant increases in saddle pressure that occur on the banking as a result of centripetal forces.

Intrinsic factors also need to be considered in those who have regular injuries, especially if they are on only one side of the body. Leg length inequalities can cause the rider to adopt an asymmetrical riding position, as can other anatomical anomalies, such as a scoliosis (a type of spinal curvature).

Treatment and prevention

Treatment and prevention is mostly concerned with a modification of any potential risk factors. A good saddle choice is one with sufficient padding in the critical front area. A number of models with a longitudinal groove (not cut out) are now available. These may help offload critical midline structures such as penile blood vessels and nerves, without creating excessive pressure elsewhere in the perineum. Saddles with a cut-out create pressure 'hot spots' around their edge and, while this effectively offloads midline tissues, it can cause the development of discomfort in adjacent areas. Another important aspect of saddle choice is the width, which should be appropriate for the pelvic dimensions of the rider. Several manufacturers now offer the same model in different sizes to accommodate individual variation in the width between the ischial tuberosities (your 'seat bones').

Use of an emollient or chamois cream helps to hydrate and reduce skin friction, thereby reducing the chance of infection. Set the front of the saddle so that any backward tilt does not exceed four degrees and check saddle height and alignment with the top tube. A computed tomography scan can check for any significant bony leg length inequality but doesn't take account of any soft-tissue adaptations, so is an indicator of the degree of asymmetry only. Large discrepancies can be partially corrected by the use of shims placed under the cleats, although corrections in the length of the tibia and femur are often achieved by slightly different means. It is worth remembering that an asymmetrical riding position can be the result of a saddle injury (e.g. in an attempt to reduce discomfort).

Skin abrasions and sterile nodules can be treated with a corticosteroid cream providing the skin surface is intact, while abscesses often require antibiotics. In severe or protracted infections, surgical drainage may be required, hence the importance of early recognition and diagnosis. Erectile dysfunction and any persistent penile numbness require specialist referral.

Female saddle injuries

In addition to the skin injuries suffered by male riders, women riders are quite commonly affected by repetitive microtrauma to the tissues of the outer labia. If this is not promptly treated, it often results in the development of a chronic inflammatory condition characterised by labial swelling, which eventually will fail to resolve. The enlarged labium is consequently even more vulnerable to compressive injury, with the result that a vicious cycle often ensues. Secondary injuries to the spine or knees may follow as the rider adopts an asymmetrical saddle position in an attempt to relieve the discomfort.

The inner labia can also be affected, particularly if they are quite prominent, which is a normal anatomical variation. In contrast to the outer labia, the inner labia do not usually become significantly enlarged. Urethral trauma is more common owing to the relatively exposed position of the urethral opening.

CAUSES OF LABIAL INJURIES

- Labial injuries can occur with most of the predisposing factors outlined for male riders.
- In addition, the use of saddles with a central cut-out can exacerbate the situation for those with outer labial swelling. This is because these saddles redistribute pressure away from the midline, towards the area where the outer labia is in contact with the saddle surface.
- Women with isolated inner labial problems are less likely to suffer discomfort with cut-out saddles as they effectively offload the midline structures.

a fracture of the wrist bones in close location to the nerve. Rare anatomical variations within the hand can also predispose an individual to injury.

Treatment and prevention

Treatment and prevention involve addressing the underlying cause. Gel pads placed underneath padded bar tape can be used to provide additional cushioning. For mountain bike riders, specific grips that anatomically adjust the hand position on the handlebar can be used. A variety of cycling mitts with ulnar nerve protection are also available. Persistent symptoms should be referred to a hand specialist for confirmation of the diagnosis and further investigations to determine the exact cause.

Median nerve injury

The median nerve supplies a number of muscles acting on the thumb. Skin sensation over the front and base of the thumb, the index and middle fingers and often half of the adjacent ring finger also depends on the median nerve. The median nerve is less commonly affected than the ulnar nerve.

Typical symptoms

Symptoms depend on the site of compression but can involve thumb weakness, altered sensation in the areas specified above or both. The causes are similar to those described for the ulnar nerve, as is the prevention and management.

LOW-BACK PAIN

Low-back pain is common among cyclists, although it is rarely of sufficient severity to prevent riding. It usually occurs as a consequence of sustained posture and has a significant muscular component.

CAUSES OF LOWER-BACK PAIN

- Activity related:
  - sudden increases in training load; and
  - use of relatively big gears.
- Equipment related:
  - saddle too high; and
  - inappropriate drop or reach.
- Intrinsic factors:
  - poor flexibility;
  - leg length inequality;
  - saddle injury; and
  - poor core stability.

Typical symptoms

Discomfort is felt in the lower back, which can either be centrally located or predominantly on one side. Arching the back or riding out of the saddle often transiently relieves it. Pain is frequently worse when using relatively large gear ratios. Symptoms usually improve rapidly after the ride.

Pain that persists when not riding, that radiates down the leg or that is associated with altered sensation or weakness in the lower limbs, needs further medical assessment. Back pain that is accompanied by sensory disturbance in the saddle region or altered bladder/bowel function can indicate a rare medical emergency and urgent medical attention should be sought.

Causes

Errors in bike positioning are frequently responsible for the most common pattern of back pain in cyclists. A high saddle will cause the rider to rock to either side as he pedals, greatly increasing the load on the soft-tissue structures in the lower-back region. Similarly, a riding position with extreme amounts of drop or reach creates additional postural demands, particularly when coupled with poor hamstring flexibility. Recurrent unilateral symptoms raise the possibility of a leg length difference. Saddle injuries can also cause back pain as the rider attempts to reduce his discomfort by adopting an asymmetrical riding position.

Treatment and prevention

Treatment and prevention rely on addressing potential causes of the pain. This may involve having an assessment of riding position. A physiotherapist/sport therapist can assist with poor core stability. A useful check to identify whether or not poor core stability is an issue is the inability to maintain a stable trunk region while pedalling, such as temporarily riding no-handed or putting on a cycling cape without stopping.

TRAUMATIC INJURIES

While cycling is generally considered to be a very healthy pursuit, it does carry with it the potential for significant traumatic injury. In the majority of cases, these injuries are not life threatening but do cause a great deal of discomfort and might necessitate a prolonged period of recovery before the individual is able to begin riding again. Clearly, there are many different injuries which could occur, but several warrant consideration here owing to the frequency with which they occur and inconsistencies in their management.

that corticosteroids exert a direct influence on the central nervous system, reducing the perception of fatigue. As these products also have a legitimate use in treating certain sporting injuries and allergies, it can sometimes be difficult to distinguish 'legal' from 'illegal' doping practices. This is partly a result of the fact that only certain routes of administration (such as intramuscular or oral) are proscribed, whereas others, including injections into joints, are not.

DOPING CONTROL AND DOPING DETECTION

With the appearance of new doping substances over the decades, the doping controls have continuously had to adapt. Previously, in-competition urine controls represented the main deterrent to doping. At every UCI race, the winner and a certain number of random riders would be required to provide a urine sample for subsequent laboratory analysis. These were soon complemented by out-of-competition tests to limit the use of forbidden substances in training. As many substances were not detectable in conventional doping tests, biological markers in blood began to be monitored, as these had the potential to indicate the use of doping substances. This so called 'indirect doping detection' was pioneered by the introduction of thresholds for certain markers such as haematocrit or haemoglobin concentration. Haemoglobin concentration is a marker of red blood cell mass, which is enhanced after EPO use or blood transfusion. Athletes above a certain limit were banned from competition for 14 days, officially for 'health reasons'. In recent years, this indirect approach to fighting doping has developed into the new and more sophisticated concept of the 'biological passport'.

The biological passport

Based on experiences from the earlier forms of blood testing, UCI soon recognised that indirect detection of doping substances was likely to be the more successful approach in the long term. Many newly developed pharmaceuticals are unlikely to be detectable by conventional tests and thus can be discovered only through their effects on the body. For this reason, the so-called biological passport, a longitudinal monitoring system for blood values, was introduced for all professional cyclists. In contrast to the previous system, where a fixed limit for certain values was used (e.g. haematocrit 50 per cent or haemoglobin concentration 17 $g \cdot dl^{-1}$), the biological passport calculates individual reference values for each rider for several variables using an elaborate software system based on Bayesian statistics. These reference ranges are based on each athlete's previous results, thereby setting individual thresholds for each of the blood test parameters. After its introduction in 2008, 10,603 controls for the biological passport were conducted during the following year.

If an athlete is found to have blood values beyond his calculated reference range (as shown in figure 20.2, page 287), they are invited to offer an explanation for the finding and, if this proves unsatisfactory, a sanctioning procedure for anti-doping rule violations can be initiated. Several athletes were sanctioned based on their blood values in 2011, the first of which was Franco Pellizotti (*see* figure 20.3).

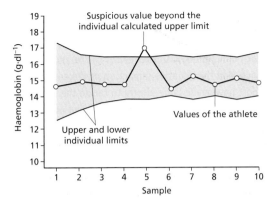

FIG.20.2 Graphical representation of the individually calculated upper and lower limits for haemoglobin (plain lines) and the values obtained in blood tests from an athlete (line with markers) in the 'athlete's biological passport'; this athlete has one suspicious value that falls beyond his individual reference range

FIG.20.3 In 2011, the former 'King of the Mountains' of the Tour de France, Franco Pellizotti, was one of the first athletes to be convicted of blood manipulation based only on blood values from his biological passport

THE LIST OF PROHIBITED SUBSTANCES

The WADA publishes annually a list of prohibited substances and methods, which is adopted by the UCI and most other international sporting governing bodies. The detailed list can be downloaded at www.wada-ama.org/en/World-Anti-Doping-Program/Sports-and-Anti-Doping-Organizations/International-Standards/Prohibited-List/. A summary of the different classifications is given below.

Substances and methods prohibited at all times (in competition and out of competition)

- **S0 – non-approved substances:** This is a new classification introduced to account for the use of experimental drugs not currently in medical use.
- **S1 – anabolic agents:** This category includes anabolic androgenic steroids as well as testosterone. Clenbutarol, which is an asthma medication purported to have anabolic effects, is also found here.
- **S2 – peptide hormones and growth factors:** EPO and modified forms of EPO, such as continuous erythropoiesis receptor activator (CERA), fall into this category. Growth hormone is also included here, as are other growth factors.
- **S3 – beta-2 agonists:** These are medicines commonly used to treat asthma. Some are prohibited only if excessively high levels, which are not consistent with therapeutic use, are found in the urine. However, other beta-2 agonists are prohibited at all levels and a TUE will need to be applied for prior to their use.
- **S4 – hormone antagonists and modulators:** These aim to increase the amount of oestrogen in the body or to block oestrogen receptors. They are not thought to be widely used in cycling.
- **S5 – diuretics and other masking agents:** Of particular note in this category are plasma expanders, such as albumin solution and hydroxyethyl starch, which are used to add fluid to the circulation, thereby reducing the concentration of red blood cells and haemoglobin. This is usually done in an attempt to hide recent EPO use or transfusions.
- **M1 – enhancement of oxygen transfer:** Blood transfusions and the use of modified haemoglobin products (e.g. Hemopure) are listed here.
- **M2 – chemical and physical manipulation:** This covers a range of techniques and substances used to prevent detection of prohibited substances. The substitution of someone else's urine would be an illustration of physical manipulation of the sample. Proteases are an example of chemical manipulation; proteases are enzymes that are introduced into urine samples, often at the time the specimen is being produced, to degrade the remaining fragments of peptide hormones (such as EPO), preventing their detection. They are now included in the testing procedure.
- **M3 – gene doping:** Gene doping refers to a variety of mainly experimental procedures that could be used to change the genetic profile of an athlete. Also listed are several experimental drugs that are known to influence the genetic pathways involved in the adaptation to endurance training (GW1516 and AICAR).

Substances prohibited in competition only

- **S6 – stimulants:** Substances in this category are quite frequently implicated in positive dope tests. In some instances there is clear intent to artificially enhance performance, while in others it is quite possible that the product has been inadvertently ingested, often in the form of a cold remedy (ephedrine, pseudoephedrine) or as a contaminant in a nutritional supplement (methylhexaneamine, for example). Some of the listed products are only proscribed above a certain threshold level, particularly for substances more likely to be contained in non-prescription medicines.
- **S7 – narcotics:** These are strong painkillers, similar to, and including, morphine. Weaker analgesics such as codeine aren't prohibited. They would typically be used in the period following a surgical procedure and are likely to be completely eliminated from the body within several days of the last dose. As it is uncommon for athletes to be competing so soon following surgical procedures, samples positive for narcotics are unusual. However, this situation does occur occasionally, in which case it is essential to get a list of all medications given during a hospital stay, including those drugs given during and immediately following an operation.
- **S8 – cannabinoids:** These include naturally occurring (cannabis) and synthetic cannabinoids as well as a number of related substances found in recreational drugs. Some of these are slow to clear from the body and can be detected a number of days later.
- **S9 – glucocorticosteroids:** These are prohibited in competition only via certain routes of administration: orally, intravenously, intramuscularly and rectally. Use of corticosteroid inhalers for asthma, nasal sprays for hay fever or creams containing corticosteroids for treating skin conditions are not banned at any time. Corticosteroids taken via a proscribed route but outside of competition pose a particular problem, as they can be detectable for a long period of time afterwards, during which the rider may well begin competing again. In such cases, it is sensible to contact the national anti-doping organisation for advice on the requirement for a TUE.

Therapeutic use exemptions (TUEs)

In circumstances when a rider subject to anti-doping regulations needs to use a prohibited substance, it is necessary to apply for a TUE. The submission of a TUE requires full medical documentation of the medical condition that is to be treated.

The TUE is forwarded to a TUE committee, which comprises a number of doctors with experience of working in elite sport. The TUE committee considers the application with respect to a number of criteria, including the medical justification for using the proscribed medication as well as the option to use alternative drugs that aren't prohibited. If a TUE is granted, a certificate is provided to the rider giving him permission to use the proscribed substance for a specified period of time together

Chapter 20

Pottgiesser, T., Sottas, P.E., Echteler, T., Robinson, N., Umhau, M., Schumacher, Y.O., 'Detection of autologous blood doping with adaptively evaluated biomarkers of doping: a longitudinal blinded study', *Transfusion*, in press.

Sottas, P.E., Robinson, N., Saugy, M., Rabin, O., 'The athlete biological passport', *Clinical Chemistry*, in press

Thieme, D., Hemmersbach, P., *Doping in Sports: Biochemical Principles, Effects and Analysis. Handbook of Experimental Pharmacology* (Springer Verlag, 2010).

Zorzoli, M., Rossi, F., 'Implementation of the biological passport: the experience of the International Cycling Union', *Drug Testing and Analysis*, 2 (2010), pp. 542–547.

GLOSSARY

Acceleration: The process of increasing work rate, cadence or velocity. Measured by the rate of change in velocity per unit of time.

Aerobic: Conditions or processes occurring in the presence of or requiring oxygen.

Amino acids: The basic building blocks of proteins.

Anaerobic: Conditions or processes not requiring oxygen; in the absence of oxygen.

Anaerobic work capacity: The maximum amount of work that can be produced by the anaerobic energy systems.

Antioxidants: Molecules capable of inhibiting the oxidation of other molecules. Oxidation is a chemical reaction that transfers electrons from a substance to an oxidising agent, which produces free radicals. These free radicals are capable of causing cell damage or even cell death.

ATP (adenosine triphosphate): A high-energy compound found in every cell in the body. It is the only form of energy that can be used directly by a cell for its activities. The breakdown of ATP is accompanied by the release of energy which is used to drive energy-demanding metabolic activities.

BMX: Bicycle motorcross.

Body composition: A method used to describe the ratio of body fat, bone and muscle tissue.

Cadence: The rate of crank revolution (rev·min⁻¹) at which the cyclist pedals.

Caffeine: An alkaloid that is found in tea and coffee and is a stimulant of the central nervous system.

Colostrum: Milk taken from a cow one to two days after the birth of a calf.

Creatine: An amino acid that is naturally found within the muscle and is a key component of energy production, particularly energy production over a 5–10-second time period.

Critical power: The slope of the work–time relationship, representing a power that can be sustained for a very long time without fatigue.

Detraining: The effects seen when a cyclist stops training, including a loss of training-induced adaptations.

Drag: The resistance of air to the forward movement of the cyclist and his bike.

Economy: The energy required to sustain a given power output or velocity.

Efficiency: The relationship between the amount of work done and the energy expended in doing the work. It is usually expressed as a percentage of work done to energy expended: efficiency = (work done/energy expended) x 100 per cent.

Enzyme: A specialised protein that acts as a catalyst to bring about a specific chemical reaction.

Ergogenic aids: Any factor that enhances physical or mental performance.

Fatigue: Exhaustion of muscle resulting from prolonged exhaustion or overstimulation.

Force: The effect one object has on another, such as a push or pull, which causes a change in motion. Force is measured in Newtons and is the product of the mass of an object and its linear acceleration.

Frequency: The regularity of training, for example how many times a rider trains per week.

Goal setting: A motivational technique used in sport that involves the assigning and choosing of specific, objective targets or goals which an athlete strives to achieve.

Heart-rate training zones: A range of heart rates indicating an intensity of effort that should be undertaken if training is to be beneficial.

Heart-rate variability: A measure of the variation in time interval between heartbeats.

Hypoxia: A condition in which there is an inadequate supply of oxygen to respiring tissue.

Intensity: The quantitative indication of total training work rate or training effort.

Lactate: A dissociation product of lactic acid that occurs in the blood. Resting levels are usually 1–2 mmol·l^{-1} and increase with increasing exercise intensity, especially when there is a high reliance on anaerobic metabolism.

Lactate threshold: The exercise intensity at which the release of lactate into the blood first begins to exceed its rate of removal, such that blood lactate levels begin to rise.

Lactic acid: A product of anaerobic glycolysis. Most of this dissociates quickly into hydrogen ions and lactate.

Macrocycle: A term often used to describe an entire training programme. The term macrocycle is used to describe a training cycle that typically lasts for a year.

Macronutrient: An essential nutrient required in relatively large amounts, such as carbohydrates, fats, proteins or water; sometimes certain minerals are included, such as calcium, chloride or sodium.

Maximal aerobic power (MAP): The highest power held for one minute in a ramp test.

Maximal lactate steady state: The highest exercise intensity at which blood lactate levels remain essentially constant over time.

Mesocycle: A period of training generally two to six weeks long.

Metabolic rate: The energy expended by a person, usually expressed in units of energy per unit body mass, per unit time.

Metabolism: The sum total of all of the chemical reactions that occur in the body necessary to sustain life.

Microcycle: A period of training of approximately one week.

Mitochondria: A structure within the cell that is mainly concerned with aerobic energy metabolism. Mitchondria are often referred to as the 'powerhouses' of the cell because they are the sites where the majority of ATP is generated.

Muscular endurance: The ability of the muscle or muscle group to perform repeated contractions over a long period of time, thus avoiding fatigue.

Nitrates: An inorganic compound that is composed of one atom of nitrogen and three of oxygen. Dietary nitrates are absorbed in the gut and returned to the saliva where they are converted to nitrite. Nitrite is then once again swallowed and is converted to nitric oxide within the stomach or is absorbed directly as nitrite and subsequently converted to nitric oxide. This ultimately leads to an increase in circulating nitric oxide. Nitric oxide has many roles within the body, including increasing vasodilation and influencing metabolism of the mitochondria within the muscle.

Normalised power: An estimate of the power that you could have maintained for the same 'physiological cost' if your power had been perfectly constant (e.g. cycling on a turbo trainer or cycle ergometer at a fixed resistance), instead of variable.

Overreaching: A temporary decrease in performance following a period of intensive training without adequate rest. A two-week recovery period allows for restoration of performance level.

Overtraining: Training at levels that are beyond the physical tolerance limits of the body so that extreme mental and physical fatigue are incurred. Even after two weeks of recovery, the body fails to adapt and return to expected performance levels.

Peaking: The process of achieving an optimal performance on a specific occasion.

Peak power output: The highest 1-second power output achieved during a sprint test. This often occurs within the first 5 seconds of the sprint test and is an indication of the maximal rate of anaerobic energy metabolism.

Periodisation: A planned training programme in which the year is divided into periods or cycles often of different duration. Each period has a different purpose or focus, for example a preparation period, a pre-competition period, a competition period and a transition period.

Polarised training: The practice of conducting low-intensity training and very high-intensity sessions within a week, often in an 80:20 split. The aim is to limit the amount of time spent around lactate threshold as it has been suggested that too much training at this intensity tends to reduce the quality of higher intensity workouts and ultimately leads to training monotony and overtraining.

Power: The rate of doing work, where work is equal to force x distance.

Probiotics: A micro-organism introduced into the body for its beneficial properties in promoting intestinal microbial balance.

Rating of perceived exertion (RPE): An individual's subjective evaluation of how intense or strenuous a particular exercise intensity feels. Typically, this is rated on a linear 20-point scale developed by Gunnar Borg.

Recovery: The physiological process that takes place following a bout of exercise. Within this period the body replenishes muscle glycogen and phosphate stores, replaces and repairs muscle protein, and removes lactic acid and other metabolic byproducts.

Repetition: The number of work intervals within a set. For example, an interval training programme of 4 x 4 minutes at 300 W would comprise of one set of four repetitions at 300 W, each lasting 4 minutes.

Repetition maximum (RM): The maximum load that a muscle or muscle group can overcome for a given number of repetitions (e.g. 1RM or 10RM) before fatigue prevents further muscle action.

Resistance training: Training aimed at developing power or strength using either static or dynamic actions, including weight training, plyometrics and all other forms of training that involve working against greater resistance than normally experienced during everyday life.

Dr. Thomas Korff is a biomechanist who works as a senior lecturer at Brunel University. In 2000, he received the equivalent of an MSc in sport sciences and mathematics from the University of Münster, Germany. In 2005, he was awarded his PhD in biomechanics from the University of Texas at Austin. During his PhD, he used cycling as a tool to investigate developmental changes in movement mechanics in children. Thomas has been working in the Centre for Sports Medicine and Human Performance at Brunel University since 2004. There, he conducts biomechanical research relating to both child development and cycling performance. His work has been published in prestigious journals such as *Medicine and Science in Sport and Exercise*, the *Journal of Applied Physiology* and the *Journal of Biomechanics*. Thomas is a recreational triathlete/cyclist, which inspires him to put some of the cycling-related myths to the test.

Professor Paul Laursen is lead performance physiologist for the New Zealand Academy of Sport, where he oversees physiological support for the national sporting organisations of priority in New Zealand. His primary role is to work with various national sporting organisations in New Zealand, including the New Zealand Bike programme, on ways of optimising performance using sport science. He is jointly an adjunct professor of exercise physiology at AUT University in Auckland. This combined role sees him supervising a number of postgraduate students directly involved with the sporting organisations, whose projects aim to solve coach-driven research questions. His specific areas of interest include training programme design and optimisation, pacing and fatigue, thermoregulation, recovery and heart-rate variability. He has published over 80 refereed manuscripts in moderate- to high-impact exercise and sports science journals, and this work has been cited more than 700 times. In a former life he was a category A cyclist, but now simply enjoys weekend rides with friends, and remembering the good ol' days.

Mr. Nigel Mitchell qualified as a registered dietician in 1991, and has worked in a variety of clinical roles and sporting roles. Since 1999 he has worked more or less full time in sports nutrition and is currently head of nutritional services for British Cycling and the British Professional Cycling Team 'Sky'. He also leads the British Cycling nutrition innovation and research strategy. In addition to cycling, Nigel has worked with a wide variety of sports/athletes, including winter Olympic athletes. Nigel has a special interest in elite athletes with post-viral syndrome, critical weight management and supporting athletes to manage training stress. His other research areas include fluid dynamics of elite cyclists and current dietary practices of elite athletes. Nigel believes an athlete's nutritional needs should be provided through the diet and specialises in performance-focused diets to help athletes train and compete better.

Dr. Iñigo Mujika earned PhDs in biology of muscular exercise (University of Saint-Etienne, France) and physical activity and sport sciences (University of the Basque Country). He is a Level III swimming and triathlon coach and coaches world-class triathletes. His main research interests in applied sports science include training methods and recovery, tapering, detraining and overtraining. He has performed extensive research on the physiological aspects associated with sports performance in various sports, including professional cycling. He has published over 80 articles in peer-reviewed journals, two books and 13 book chapters, and has given over 160 lectures and communications in international conferences and meetings. Iñigo has been senior physiologist at the Australian Institute of Sport, physiologist and trainer for Euskaltel Euskadi professional cycling team, and head of research and development at Athletic Club Bilbao professional football club. He is now director of physiology and training at USP Araba Sport Clinic, physiology consultant for the Spanish Swimming Federation, associate editor of the *International Journal of Sports Physiology and Performance* and associate professor at the University of the Basque Country.

Dr. Roger Palfreeman began work as team doctor to the British Cycling Team shortly after graduating from Sheffield Medical School in 1997. He initially combined this work with training in general practice (with a specialist interest in sports medicine). He fulfilled his team doctor role until 2010, being privileged to be part of the highly successful Great Britain cycling team at three Olympic Games as well as numerous World Championships. He now combines musculoskeletal clinic sessions with cycling-specific sports medicine, based at the Claremont Hospital in Sheffield. He also works as a research physician for UK Sport/English Institute of Sport and is consultant to UK Anti-Doping, where he chairs the blood passport panel. He is a very keen cyclist, regularly competing in long-distance cyclosportives.

Professor Louis Passfield is Head of the Centre for Sports Studies at the University of Kent. He lectures and researches in sports science. Louis has published over 20 scientific papers, most of which are related to cycling performance. Louis is also an applied sports scientist and has worked with British Cycling in various capacities since 1990, helping British riders and coaches prepare for major competitions such as World Championships and Olympic Games. Most recently, he was part of Great Britain's highly successful 2008 Beijing Olympic cycling team. Consequently, he has worked with most of Britain's most successful cyclists in recent years. Louis is also an experienced cycling coach and has coached world and Olympic medallists. Currently, he is working with a mountain bike rider who is preparing for his fourth Olympic Games at London 2012.

Dr. Bent R. Rønnestad received his PhD in exercise physiology from the Norwegian School of Sport Sciences, where he studied the effect of strength training on cycling performance. He is a lecturer at Lillehammer University College in Norway, where he teaches exercise physiology. The major research interests of his group include training for strength and power, optimising strength training for sports performance and the effect of strength training in endurance sports such as cycling, running and cross-country skiing.

Professor Yorck Olaf Schumacher specialised in internal medicine and sports medicine and was for many years chief medical officer of the German Cycling Federation. He has worked in the field of cycling for more than 10 years. He is currently focusing his work on anti-doping research and is a member of the Medical Commission of the

Union Cycliste Intrnationale (UCI) and the expert panels for the Athlete's Biological Passport of the World Anti-Doping Agency, UK Anti Doping and the UCI.

Mr. Mark Walker is the Deputy Head of the School of Sport, Equine and Animal Science at Writtle College in England, where he teaches exercise physiology and nutrition. He received his BSc (Hons) in biotechnology from the University of Reading, a postgraduate certificate in education from the University of Leicester, and his MSc in sports science from the University of Essex. Mark has worked with road and cyclo-cross riders of all abilities, from novice to professional, and currently sits on the Eastern Cyclo-cross Association athlete development committee. His research interests are in pacing, tactics and power distribution during cycle racing, and he is undertaking a PhD at the University of Essex in the modelling of cyclo-cross performance. Mark competes in cyclo-cross when time allows.

INDEX